D1044690

THE WIT AND WISDOM OF CONGRESS

By the Same Author

BEEFSTEAK RAID
GHOST SHIP OF THE CONFEDERACY
SEA DEVIL OF THE CONFEDERACY

THE WIT AND WISDOM OF CONGRESS

★

A Treasury of Anecdotes & Epigrams, Quips & Puns, Nuggets of Historical Debate & Gems of Eloquence—All Handpicked from the Annals of Congress . . . 1789 to the Present

EDITED BY

EDWARD BOYKIN

FUNK & WAGNALLS COMPANY

NEW YORK

LIBRARY OF CONGRESS CATALOG CARD NUMBER 61-14852

PRINTED IN THE UNITED STATES OF AMERICA

1

FOREWORD

The Editor has often wondered why a book such as this has not appeared long before now. Perhaps there are ample reasons, one of these being the massive research involved. Just to wade into—not through—the mountainous wordage of eighty-six Congresses is exhausting; to plunge beneath the surface, as was done for this book, is a formidable exercise.

Consider the fact: a single bound volume of the *Congressional Record* of the Eighty-sixth Congress (1959–1961) contains 1,439 pages measuring eight and a half by eleven inches. The Editor does not mean to say that he read every word on every page of this or any other volume of the annals of Congress, but he did devise a homely method of scanning a volume and tapping what was best in it. This was, of course, followed by much sifting and elimination.

But there are two further probable reasons why no similar book has ventured into the field. The first is the unfortunate, but apparently prevailing, idea that the *Congressional Record* and its predecessors are chock-full of stuff and nonsense seasoned with much or little lawmaking; the second is that the average American takes his Congress too much for granted, though it all but patterns his way of life (within limits), and even that of generations to come after him.

Actually, Congress is a mill whose grist is the problems of the nation and whose product is the laws of the nation. It is the mill's by-products, however, that are the subject of this book:

the humor, witty repartee, puns, yarns, parliamentary maneuvers, lively debates, and the heavier stuff of wisdom and horse sense.

Were it not for the flashes of levity that so often relieve the solemnity and dignity of its proceedings, the records of Congress might well make pretty heavy reading. Wit, humor, and the ability to illustrate a point with an amusing anecdote are among the happiest gifts the gods can bestow on any man, particularly a politician, and the gods seem to have been specially generous in this respect to many of those who have occupied the seats of the mighty in the Houses of Congress. Such talents give wings to argument, enliven debate, relieve tension, and often explode taut situations into gales of laughter.

The basic sources of every word in this book (except the editorial comments) are *The Congressional Record* (1873 to date), *The Congressional Globe* (1837–1873), *The Register of Debates* (1824–1837), and *The Annals of Congress* (1789–1834). These are the verbatim transcripts of the proceedings of the Senate and House of Representatives from their beginning to the present. "Extended Remarks," that subterfuge by which a statesman can insert in the *Record* what he *wished* he had said rather than what he *did* say on the floor, have been soft-pedaled in this book. This "doctoring" of a member's supposed eloquence or skill in debate is not a new device. It has been a handy, reputable make-believe ever since Congress opened shop in 1789, though it should be remembered that in the old days statesmen spoke mostly "off the cuff," aided perhaps by a few notes. Stenography was in its infancy; a Congressman was often his own stenographer. It was not uncommon in bygone eras for a lawmaker to harangue his colleagues for two or three hours at a stretch. In his Reply to Hayne in 1830 Webster spoke for over two hours, with notes to which he gave hardly a glance.

For guidance in searching the records, the Editor consulted upwards of a hundred biographies of outstanding figures in the background of Congress. These, of course, pointed up highlights in the legislative careers of these men, but finding instances of their wit, wisdom, and passion for debate called for hardpan digging—research with a vengeance. Try it sometime.

Even a casual skimming of the records gives the impression that there is no subject on earth on which Congress has never turned its spotlight. One thing is certain: Congress never lacks for variety. The lawmakers opened their show in 1789 with the Great American Infant—the tariff—which is still with us, as a Fourth of July orator, echoing Shakespeare, once said, "muling and puking in its nurse's arms." Between then and now, the statesmen on Capitol Hill have aired something of everything in our national life, from draw poker (once so popular with the gentlemen on the hill) to potlikker (immortalized by Senator Huey Long in 1935).

Henry Clay, Daniel Webster, and John C. Calhoun, the Great Triumvirate who sat supreme on Capitol Hill during the "cold war" which preceded the holocaust of the Sixties, cut little figure in this book. Oratory as such, in which these three greats excelled, has passed into limbo. There is not too much of it between these covers. The play goes chiefly to lesser lights.

Personal encounters between statesmen have left their mark on the records too. American politics has always been a hot-blooded, partisan business. Time was when heated debates not settled in the halls of Congress were frequently adjourned to the field of honor, a secluded glade near Bladensburg where statesmen, with pistols at a few paces, could shoot out their feelings—and sometimes their lives. Political "insults" dot the records of Congress, and some of them make good reading. Back in 1894 Representative Champ Clark of Missouri, later Speaker of the House, compared the Republican side of the lower chamber to Hell itself. Had Clark drawn this comparison in an earlier era—say, half a century before—he would certainly have been "called out" by a gentleman on the other side of the political fence who resented such a libel.

For a quarter-century after settling their differences at Appomattox in 1865, the Blues and the Grays kept up the fight in Congress—with words instead of gunpowder, but that many a word is as hot as a passage at arms is well demonstrated in these pages. The verbal war began the moment the Southern States resumed their seats in the national legislature, and reached its high point in 1887, when Senator John Sherman of Ohio labeled the Democratic Party "the left wing of the new Confederate army."

Politics is always on tap in Congress. Like the Hatfields and the McCoys, opposing parties seldom neglect an opening to take potshots at each other. This order of things began long before the Grand Old Party and the Sons of Wild Jackasses divided up the House and Senate between them to the exclusion of all others. Most of the talk about legislating on a nonpartisan basis usually boils down to mostly talk, and the records prove it. Cutting down the other party is an ancient, accredited Congressional custom. In their day the Whigs were industrious hatchet men and the Federalists, who ran things for the first ten years of our constitutional existence, were certainly no laggards at political throat-cutting. Nor were Jefferson's original henchmen far behind in the skilled use of the political ax. The records of Congress are full of this sort of thing, and this book carries a fair sampling of the art.

The famed Kentucky humorist, Irvin S. Cobb, once observed, "Congress is the chief assembling plant of coagulating dullness," which makes it clear that the Sage of Paducah never flipped through the records of Congress to see what was there other than what he complained about. Had he done so he might not have made this error in judgment. He needed only to have looked into the career of a fellow Kentuckian, Representative James Proctor Knott (later Governor), who brightened the House for twelve years with his genius as a humorist.

Knott's maiden speech, a delicious diatribe on a bill for "Paving Pennsylvania Avenue," still ranks as an all-time classic.

In 1920 Champ Clark listed the six first-order humorists of the House. Abraham Lincoln headed the procession, though Lincoln's brief service in the House contributed little to this aspect of his reputation. Clark's All-House of Representatives selections, in addition to Lincoln, were Thomas Corwin of Ohio, Samuel Sullivan "Sunset" Cox of Ohio and New York, James Proctor Knott of Kentucky, "Private" John Mills Allen of Mississippi, and Francis Wellington Cushman of Washington. Just why Clark omitted Thomas B. Reed of Maine from his selections is not clear; no man was ever dowered with a greater supply of wit and humor than Reed.

Clark failed to pick an All-Senate team, but he did list Chauncey Depew of New York, William Maxwell Evarts of New York, George G. Vest of Missouri, Robert L. Taylor of Tennessee, Zebulon Vance of North Carolina, and John P. Hale of New Hampshire. From Hale, incidentally, came the wisecrack, "I did not say that all Democrats were rascals; only that all rascals were Democrats"; the comment was matched by Vance, who likened himself to the man who killed snakes [Republicans] wherever he found them.

Humor still flourishes in Congress, though you have to look deeper and longer for it than in the comparatively slender records of a quarter-century ago. Lyndon Johnson of Texas and Everett Dirksen of Illinois left a fairly wide trail of smiles through the Eighty-sixth Congress. Both men seem well endowed with this much-to-be-desired talent. The really legendary storyteller of our own time is the late Senator Alben Barkley of Kentucky, whose wit glowed like a light throughout his long service in Congress. In a class with Barkley (the Editor believes, though some may differ) was a man whose trail can be picked up in the records of the early Nineties. He was W. Jasper Talbert of South Carolina and he served in the House from 1893 to 1903. It's doubtful if Talbert's name rings a bell with one American in ten thousand, but he possessed an apparently inexhaustible store of droll stories which he trotted out, to the amusement of the House, to illustrate almost every point he tried to make in debate.

Congress has always had, and no doubt always will have, its wise men and its wits. In the recent round-the-clock Civil Rights debate, this editor counted a score of amusing stories and quips that certainly helped to relieve a bit the tension engendered by the subject. A few of these will be found herein.

The Editor is much indebted to the Alderman Library of the University of Virginia for many favors. This splendid institution possesses among its magnificent collections complete editions of *The Annals of Congress*, *The Register of Debates*, *The Congressional Globe*, and *The Congressional Record*. To Miss Frances Smith, head of the Public Documents Room, the Editor is most grateful for many courtesies during the assembling and editing of these "takes" from Congress. And his thanks go also to Mrs. Marjorie Wolfrey of Charlottesville, Virginia, his most efficient typist.

EDWARD BOYKIN

Charlottesville, Va.
July 1, 1961

CONTENTS

SPICED WITH WIT

BY THEIR FRUITS YE SHALL KNOW THEM

In a speech in the Senate in 1894 Jacob H. Gallinger of New Hampshire quoted these words of a country parson taking leave of his congregation:

Brothers and sisters: I come to say good-by. I don't believe God loves this church, because none of you ever die. I don't think you love each other, because I never marry any of you. I don't think you love me, because you have not paid my salary. Your donations are moldy fruit and wormy apples, and "by their fruits ye shall know them." Brothers, I am going away to a better place. I have been called to be chaplain of a penitentiary. Where I go ye cannot now come, but I go to prepare a place for you, and may the Lord have mercy on your souls. Good-by.

* * *

May 8, 1879, and the House was hotly debating the Eight Hour Law. Up rose Samuel "Sunset" Cox of New York to deliver his celebrated Spit Speech.

Mr. Speaker, let any member of the House go through the government departments and look in the open doors; and, except for the women who work faithfully, he will find a good many clerks, when not engaged in reading newspapers, talking politics and spitting tobacco juice. There is no man in all the world like a government clerk for splendid spitting. There never were clerks or persons who could excel them in the flux of their salivary glands! No country, sir, rejoices in such great prairies, wonderful rivers, high mountains, and such a great people as in our own beloved land; but in one thing, sir, we surpass the world and ourselves. Our government clerks can spit higher, spit farther and spit more than any people on the face of the earth—and get more pay for the performance! I still except the ladies from this salivary achievement.

* * *

I am like the preacher who sometimes made mistakes. He was asked by a young lawyer if he always corrected them. The preacher said, no, not always; sometimes he did and sometimes he did not. For instance, he said, when he was preaching once he intended to say that Og was the king of Bashan, but by a slip of the tongue he said that "hog was the king of bacon," but he did not correct it because it was true. So, in another case, when he intended to say that the devil was the father of all liars, he happened to say that "the devil was the father of all lawyers," but he let that stand also, because it was correct in a sense.

Representative W. Jasper Talbert
of South Carolina, 1897

* * *

[Susan B. Anthony] did indeed have a quick wit. She was one of the few persons, whether male or female, ever to silence, however temporarily, the sharp-tongued Horace Greeley. At a meeting just after the close of that period which some refer to as "the recent unpleasantness," Susan Anthony was found speaking out for equal votes for women. Greeley remarked that the ballot went with the bullet and inquired of Miss Anthony whether she would be willing to have this right. She replied, "Yes, Mr. Greeley, just as you fought in the late war, at the end of a goosequill."

Representative Katharine St. George of New York, on the 189th anniversary of the birth of Susan B. Anthony, pioneer for women's rights, 1959

* * *

About once a year the great Senator Zebulon Vance of North Carolina used to regale the Senate with the story of an old preacher who traveled his state dispensing the gospel and depending on voluntary contributions of his congregations for his support. One night he stopped at a small town and preached earnestly, saving sinners by the score. Before closing his act he circulated his hat among the packed benches for a contribution. No one was overlooked, and when the hat was passed back up to the pulpit the preacher gazed into it, but there was not even a copper penny in it. Raising his hands, with much pious fervor, he said, "Brethren, let us thank God that this hat got back safely out of this crowd."

* * *

There was a young lawyer in a small town in my district who made a specialty of personal injury cases. He won two or three cases and got a snug contingent fee in each, and he concluded that he would go after a larger clientage, so he moved down to the "blue grass" and opened up a rather pretentious office in the city of Lexington. After he had been there a month a friend of his met him on the street and asked him how he was getting along. "Well," he said, "business is not as good down here as I had expected to find it. I am going to try it a little while longer, but if business does not pick up pretty soon I'll be damned if I don't intend to take my witnesses and move to Chicago."

Representative John W. Langley of Kentucky, 1909

* * *

Mr. Speaker, we can't afford to repeal these laws in order to strengthen the already too strong hand of Tammany. Tammany is swallowing up the Democratic party. It reminds me of a story that fits the case exactly. An Englishman had gone game hunting in the wilds of India and the news came that he had been killed and that his body was on the way home. His friends went to meet the steamer that brought the remains back. They took the coffin out of the vessel when it reached Liverpool, but upon opening it they could find nothing but the embalmed body of a tiger with a bullet hole in it. They immediately telegraphed Calcutta, "Where is George? There is nothing in the coffin but a tiger." Back came the answer, "George inside tiger."

Representative John F. Lacey of Iowa, during an election law debate, 1893

* * *

Down in Mississippi a wicked sheriff was suddenly taken ill and was about to die. He sent for the preacher, who got out of his bed and hurried to the sheriff's bedside where he prayed and prayed with the sheriff, who got more distressed the more the preacher prayed and sang to him. But the preacher couldn't get the sheriff to do anything but bewail and bemoan his dying condition. Presently the preacher got worn out with this sort of thing. It was long after midnight. Finally he said, "My dear man, I cannot save you. I can do nothing but show you the way to salvation. You must have confidence in Christ and in God." Replied the dying sheriff,

"I've got lots of confidence in Christ and God and all the saints up there, but the trouble is they haven't got any in me."

Representative Thomas R. Stockdale of Mississippi, 1890

* * *

The Attorney General has a criminal statute which he can use. He has a civil statute which he can use. Yet he comes to Congress to ask us to give him a third statute. The Attorney General reminds me of the fellow who went "a-courtin'." John was "a-courtin' " Mary, and John said to Mary, "Mary, if you wasn't what you is, what would you like to be?" Mary said, "I would like to be an American beauty rose." And then she inquired of John, "John, if you wasn't what you is, what would you like to be?" And John said, "Mary, if I wasn't what I is, I would like to be an octopus." Mary said, "John, what is an octopus?" John said, "An octopus is sort of a fish that has got a thousand arms." Mary said to John, "Well, now, John, if you was an octopus, what would you do with those thousand arms?"

And John said, "Mary, I would put every last one of them around you." Mary said to John, "Go on away from here, John; you ain't usin' the two arms you've already got." (Laughter.)

The Attorney General of the United States already has two arms. I assure Senators that either one of them is sufficient to put around any person anywhere in the South who is willfully denying to any qualified person of any color or race the right to register or to vote or to have his vote counted, as cast.

Senator Samuel J. Ervin, Jr., of North Carolina, during the civil rights debate, 1959

* * *

Once in a while you run across a man who does not know which side he is on. There used to be a very smart man in the county in which I now live who was a great wag. He was summoned to serve on a jury. He swore that he had not formed or expressed an opinion about the case. The prosecutor took him in hand. "My friend, you say you have formed no opinion in this case."

"No, I have formed no opinion."

"Have you talked with anybody who pretended to know the facts of this case?"

"Yes, both the plaintiff and the defendant told me all about it."

"How does it happen, then, that you have not formed any opinion?"

"Because they are both such infernal liars that I would not believe either of them on oath."

Representative Champ Clark of Missouri, 1919

* * *

SENATOR ALBEN BARKLEY TOLD THIS STORY

It was a good one, too, and Senator Richard B. Russell of Georgia retold it apropos of the proposed civil rights legislation in 1960. Said he: The 1957 bill was as sweeping as anyone could conceive of. What need for more? Senator Russell B. Long of Louisiana cut in with a suggestion that inspired Senator Russell to repeat this story, a legacy from that legendary storyteller, Alben W. Barkley of Kentucky.

Mr. LONG. It seems to me that somebody wants to get in on the act. Someone who was not here when the 1957 act was passed is saying to Congress, "Pass another one, so that I can say I had something to do with this."

Mr. RUSSELL. Is the Senator from Louisiana familiar with

the story told by the late, lamented Alben Barkley, who said that a farmer had told him that the Senator had not done anything for him lately?

Mr. LONG. I understand that Senator Barkley told such a story.

Mr. RUSSELL. Yes. The man had had his whole family on the WPA. Senator Barkley had his brother appointed postmaster. He had got his son home from the army. He had the man made a foreman on the WPA. Still, Senator Barkley heard that the man was going to vote against him, so he went to see him. He said to him, "Think of what I have done for you." He recounted all that he had done and asked, "Didn't I do all that for you?"

The man replied, "Yes."

Senator Barkley asked him, "Did I do all of those things for you?"

The man replied, "Yes."

The Senator then asked, "And do you mean you are still going to vote against me?"

The fellow looked at him and said, "You haven't done nothing for me lately."

So it is in this instance. Congress has not passed a bill on this subject since 1957. This happens to be a presidential year. Presidential candidates are about a dime a dozen in the Senate.

* * *

During his ten years in the House, W. Jasper Talbert of South Carolina tossed off enough jokes and smart sayings to fill a book. Champ Clark called him the "best anecdote-teller" in Congress. Talbert adorned the annals of the House with more laughs and stump stories than any other member of Congress in the last seventy-five years. Here's a sample:

Now, my friends, the way that some of our Republican friends treat the colored man is very amusing to me and reminds me of an old Republican who had died and gone to Heaven, or started up that way. He knocked at the door and one of the saints came and opened the door and said to the applicant for admission, "Are you riding?"

"No, I'm walking," replied the good old Republican.

"Well," said the saint, "you cannot come in here."

So the poor old Republican went away, sorrow-stricken, down the hill. At the bottom of the hill he met old black Uncle Sambo. He said to him, "Where are you going?"

"I'm going to Heaven," replied Uncle Sambo.

"Well," said the old Republican, "you can't get in unless you ride in."

"Well, what are we to do?" asked Uncle Sambo.

"I will tell you, Uncle. Just let me get up on your back, and you carry me up to the gate. I will knock and they will ask me if I am riding. I will say 'yes,' and then they will open the door, and I will just ride in on your back and we'll both get in that way."

Uncle Sambo agreed to that and thought it would be a good idea. So the Republican got up on Uncle Sambo's shoulders and went back to the gate of Heaven. He knocked and the saint came and opened the door again and said, "Who is there?" The Republican told him.

"Are you riding?" asked the saint.

"Yes," replied the old Republican.

"Well, just hitch your horse outside and come right in."

So he had to leave the poor old colored man outside. He got in, but the colored man didn't. That's just the way you're doing. You still want to ride into office on the back of Uncle Sambo. When you get there, you go in and he has to be hitched outside like a mule.

* * *

I extend to the Senators who are candidates the warm hand of fellowship. We want to keep them here. It would be lonesome without my distinguished friend, the Majority Leader [Senator Lyndon Johnson], and without my distinguished friend from Massachusetts [Senator John F. Kennedy], with whom it has been my honor and pleasure to work on the Senate Labor Committee. My affection is as high as the sky and it is as deep as the sea—and I do not want sixteen blocks to intervene.

Senator Everett M. Dirksen of Illinois in his "adjournment conversations," September 2, 1960

* * *

At one place where I was booked to speak there was a man in the crowd crazy drunk, who made frequent interruptions and who was finally carried away. He escaped from his captors later in the evening and, hunting through the crowd until he found me, drew a revolver which he flourished about his head. Then pointing the weapon directly at my stomach he said: "I'm going to blow out your brains." And I think that he knew where he was aiming.

Senator George G. Vest of Missouri, 1890

* * *

The dealer in the products of labor fixes the value of what shall be received for them. A woodchopper on the banks of the Mississippi near the close of the Civil War, when hailed by a steamboat captain who asked whether his wood was for sale, answered, "Yes." The captain inquired, "How much a cord?" Asked the woodchopper, "How do you propose to pay?" "In Confederate money." "Then cord for cord."

Representative Galusha A. Grow of Pennsylvania

* * *

Two old drunkards were in the habit of coming to Lebanon, Kentucky, twice a week to get drunk together. They would buy a two-gallon jug of whiskey and get out in some old house and lie around until the last drop was gone. They kept this up for awhile, but in the course of years one of them died. His old friend came in on Saturday and inquired about him. The boys told him, "He is dead; have you not heard of it?" "Oh, no. What killed him?" "Well, you know he has been drinking hard for a good many years, and the doctors say that the whiskey was taken into his circulation, and so saturated his breath and his blood that one night the old man before going to bed went to blow out the candle, and his breath caught on fire and he was burned to death." "Gracious heavens!" said the surviving friend. "What a horrible death! Boys, send for a preacher, give me a Bible, and bring me in a magistrate, and let me take the oath quick." This request was complied with. The old man took hold of the holy volume, kissed it, lifted his hand and his eyes, and began: "I swear before Almighty God and these witnesses that I will never, during life, blow out another candle."

Senator John S. Williams of Mississippi, 1902

* * *

IN THE POETIC VEIN

A little thieving is a dangerous art,
But thieving largely is a noble part;
'Tis vile to rob a henroost of a hen,
But stealing largely makes us gentlemen.

Representative Samuel S. Marshall of Illinois in a speech in 1868

For ways that are dark
And tricks that are vain,
I name Speaker Blaine,
And that I dare maintain.

Representative Benjamin F. Butler of Massachusetts in a controversy with Speaker James G. Blaine, Representative from Maine

When we've been there ten thousand years,
And sucked from sun to sun,
'Tis just as hard to quit the teat
As when we first begun.

Representative John McSweeney of Ohio in describing the length of time the Republican party had been "sucking at the public teat"

Taxed on the coffin, taxed on the crib,
On the old man's shroud, on the young babe's bib,
To fatten the bigot and pamper the knave
We are taxed from the cradle plumb into the grave.

Representative Thomas R. Hudd of Wisconsin, 1888

* * *

Every man can think, even if he does not speak, and do his own thinking, like the man whose lawyer was not talking exactly to suit him in the courtroom so he stood up to make a few remarks himself. The judge, of course, made him take his seat. He got up again and the judge made him take his seat again. A third and a fourth time this happened, and finally the gentleman got up and said, "Judge if you will not let me talk, won't you let me think?" "Why, certainly," said the judge. "Well, Judge," said the man, "I think you and all these lawyers are a set of grand rascals."

Representative W. Jasper Talbert of South Carolina, 1897

* * *

I desire now to say a few words for the benefit of our Northern and Western farmers. I know the gentleman from Massachusetts (Mr. Lodge) complained yesterday of so much talk about the farmers, and he reminded us that there were other people in this country besides farmers. That is true; but he ought to permit us to talk for the farmers, for talk is all the farmer gets. (Laughter and applause.) The other fellows get the "provisions" in the bill.

Representative John M. Allen of Mississippi, commenting on the McKinley Tariff Bill, 1894

* * *

It may be remembered that Horace Greeley once wrote a book entitled *What I Know About Farming*. Subsequently it became fashionable to perplex him with all sorts of queries about agriculture. One man wrote him inquiring the best way to cure a dog of killing sheep. Greeley promptly answered, "Cut off his tail just behind his ears." It seems to me, Mr. President, that the proper way to cure the Wilson bill which proposes to kill all the sheep in this country and rely upon other countries for wool, is to amputate this bill just below the enacting clause.

Senator Shelby M. Cullom of Illinois, 1894

* * *

Why, in 1873 Uncle Sam was healthy and doing well in all particulars. The country was prosperous. You commenced doctoring him in that year with your vaunted gold standard, and I'm afraid if you keep up your gold cure, you will find that the epitaph that was placed on the tombstone of the man who died in Maine many years ago, and which read:

I was well. I wanted to be better.
I took physic and died.

will apply to the United States under your financial mismanagement.

Representative James A. Johnson
of California

* * *

Senator Zebulon B. Vance of North Carolina, upon being asked where he stood on the subject of prohibition, said, "I will reply to the gentleman's question by saying that my head is strongly inclined to the great policy of prohibition, but my stomach yearns the other way. I may say therefore I truthfully declare myself as being divided on the issue."

* * *

The great Tom Corwin, in a speech in the Senate one day, told this one on himself. Corwin, called "Black Tom" because of his dark, swarthy countenance, was interrupted while speaking in Ohio as candidate for Congress, by a listener who sought to upset him with the inquiry: "Are you in favor of a law permitting colored people to eat at the same tables with white folks, in hotels and on steamboats?"

Corwin had to do some quick thinking. If he said Yes, he'd lose the proslavery votes; if he said No, the abolitionists would go all out to defeat him.

"Black Tom's" answer was nimble. "Fellow citizens: I submit that it is improper to ask such a question of a man of my color."

* * *

A bull-whacker whose wagon got stuck in the mud was cussing and lashing his team for all he was worth. The Yankees were closing up and the Grays were taking to their heels. His general rode up and rebuked him for being cruel to his horses. "You're spoiling a good team by being a mighty poor driver," said the general. "Well, General, they tell me—God knows I don't know, though—they tell me that this is a good army that is being spoiled by a mighty poor general. But, as I said, General, God knows I don't know."

Representative Charles T. O'Ferrall of Virginia, 1885

* * *

When I first came to Congress I felt very much like the old farmer who went into a courtroom for the first time to see what a court was like. They were trying an action of replevin about a cow, and the third day of the trial had been reached when the old gentleman, becoming impatient that the valuable time of the court should be wasted on such a trivial matter, shouted out at the top of his voice, and pulling out his purse at the same time, "Judge, what is this old cow worth? I'll pay her value, and let the court proceed to something of importance." So when I came here and listened day after day to long speeches about slavery in the District of Columbia, I felt like asking what this District could be bought for.

Representative Benjamin F. Junkin of Pennsylvania, 1861

* * *

This conversation was overheard once between two newly-elected members of the House.

"How did you ever come to run for Congress, anyhow?"

"Well, sir, I did it to bring disgrace on an uncle of mine up in New York. You see he treated me very badly when I was a boy, and I took a fearful vow that I would humiliate him, and I have done it."

"What business is your uncle engaged in?"

"He's making shoes in Auburn penitentiary."

* * *

I read with great interest a few years since some of the private writings of Daniel Webster, and remember that I was much amused in reading one of his letters in which he said that in his college days he used to write theses for some of the young men who were his classmates, for, he said, they thought he was a promising young man. "And so," he said, "have my creditors thought ever since."

Representative Thomas J. Henderson of Illinois

* * *

Rely upon it that to love a woman as a mistress, although a delicious delirium, an intoxication far surpassing that of champagne, is altogether unessential, nay pernicious, in the choice of a wife, which a man ought to set about in his sober senses—choosing her, as Mrs. Primrose did her wedding gown, for qualities that wear well.

John Randolph of Virginia

* * *

In 1869, when Senator George F. Hoar was a "freshman" in the House, Ben Butler of Massachusetts was the most quarrelsome buffoon in the lower chamber. Observed Senator Hoar to General Nathaniel Banks one day, "Don't you think it quite likely that Butler will be the next President of the United States?"

"Never," replied Banks flatly.

"Why, the papers are full of him every day," interposed Hoar. "People seem to be reading about nobody else. Wherever he goes crowds throng about him. Nobody else gets such applause, not even General Grant."

"Mr. Hoar," said Banks, "when I came down to the House this morning there was a fight between two monkeys on Pennsylvania Avenue. There was an enormous crowd, shouting, laughing, cheering. They would have paid very little attention to you and me. But when they come to elect a President of the United States they won't take either monkey."

* * *

During the Eighty-sixth Congress, while the Budget and Housing Acts were being debated, the Majority Leader of the Senate (Lyndon Johnson of Texas) and the Minority Leader (Everett Dirksen of Illinois) swapped a variety of amusing anecdotes, of which these four are fair examples.

I think sometimes of the fellow who saw an automobile accident out home when he was put on the stand to testify. Counsel said, "Did you see the accident?" He said, "Yes, sir." Counsel asked, "How far away were you when the accident happened?" Witness said, "Twenty-two feet, nine and three-quarter inches." Counsel looked at the court and looked at the jury and said, "Well, Smartie, tell the court and jury how do you know it was twenty-two feet, nine and three-quarter inches?" Witness replied, "When it happened I took out a tape measure and measured from where I stood to the point of impact, because I knew some darned lawyer was going to ask me that question."

Senator Everett M. Dirksen of
Illinois, during the debate on the
Housing Act of 1959

* * *

Former Vice President Barkley used to tell about the cuckoo clock a fellow had in the hills of Kentucky. Some of his neighbors wanted him to get rid of it because they did not think it was keeping good time. He said, "It keeps good time. When the hands point at two and the clock strikes four it is half past six." That is comparable to what the other side [Republican] is saying about the reductions made by Congress in the appropriations.

Senator Lyndon B. Johnson of Texas, 1959

* * *

The statement made by the majority leader [Lyndon Johnson of Texas] on a number of occasions on the floor and in the tables he inserted in the Record, are quite correct so far as they go. As I said before, however, it is like the man who fell off the twentieth floor of a building. As he passed the sixth floor a friend shouted to him, "Mike, so far you're all right." (Laughter.) So, I believe in the interest of the whole rather than in the fraction of the story.

Senator Everett M. Dirksen of Illinois, 1959, during debate on the budget

* * *

During the early days of the depression, a poor schoolteacher in search of a job applied to the hill country school board. The board was rather impressed by his presentation. He was eloquent; generally, he was factual; he was impressive. So the members of the school board said to him, "Well, we think we would like to have you teach and we would like to retain your services. But tell us this: there is some difference of opinion in our community about geography; and we want to know which side you are on. Do you teach that the world is round, or do you teach that the world is flat?"

The eloquent applicant responded immediately, "I can teach it either way."

Mr. President, notwithstanding everything that has been said here today, and the stirring statement which has been made, the Minority Leader has demonstrated he can "teach it either way."

Senator Lyndon B. Johnson of Texas

* * *

Mr. CANNON. I called together all the chairmen of committees that had appropriation bills to consult as to what the revenues were and see if we could not come to an agreement. Nothing doing. Each chairman was like a hen with one chicken. You know a hen with one chicken makes more fuss than a hen with sixteen chickens. The mother hen with sixteen chickens marches with dignity and clucks occasionally and the little chicks follow; but the hen with one chicken runs the legs off her poor little chick, worrying and bothering around, and does not have any regard for any other mother hen with sixteen chickens.

Mr. BUTLER. How about a hen with no chicken at all?

Mr. CANNON. The gentleman is an expert in poultry matters, and I will not answer his question according to the facts. I prefer to answer him in private. (Laughter.)

* * *

Rivalry between regiments in the Civil War often led to good-natured flings at each other. On one occasion a Virginia cavalry regiment and a North Carolina regiment were passing each other. A Virginian, catching the eye of a North Carolinian, inquired if he had been home lately. "Oh, yes," replied the North Carolinian, to which the Virginian inquired, "Did you bring any tar back with you?" "Sure did. Our general ordered us to bring a carload back with us." Inquired the Virginian, "What for?" Smiled the North Carolinian, "To give it to your general to put on your heels to make you stick in the next fight."

Representative Charles T. O'Ferrall of Virginia, 1889

* * *

I do not know that I see before me one individual who I believe can write an English sentence of twenty words that I cannot give more than one meaning to. It is an exceedingly difficult thing to use the English language in such a way that ingenious carping cannot find fault with it. My friend here has undoubtedly heard the story of the little girl who at her prayers in the morning said, "Good-by, God; we are going to move to Missouri." Her wicked brother, who happened to overhear her, and who was jubilant at the idea of the journey, used the very same sentence, but he said, "Good! By God, we are going to move to Missouri!"

Representative W. Bourke Cockran of New York, 1906

* * *

It is said that anxious and nervous political aspirants sometimes find it necessary, before voting on a question, to go out and not only consult the signs of the zodiac, but see how the tin roosters on all the barns stand, so as to know exactly which way the wind blows.

Senator Roscoe Conkling of New York, 1879

* * *

Mr. President, I remarked the other day that the question as to whether this was a protectionist or a revenue reform measure was an interesting discussion. A little incident occurred in my state a few years ago that might illustrate. We had a noted character there known as Sailor Stevens. One day, while in a state of utter inebriation, he undertook to saddle a horse, and he had the pommel towards the horse's tail. I called the gentleman's attention to it, when he looked at me in utter disgust, and with great indignation in his voice, said, "Mind your own business, sir. How do you know which way I'm going to travel?"

Senator Jacob H. Gallinger of New Hampshire

* * *

This is a measure from the Judiciary Committee, composed, of course, entirely of lawyers, and they are divided on it. There is an old saying that "when rogues fall out, honest men get their dues." I am reminded, Mr. Speaker, by the lawyers, from the way they have changed front on this question, of a discussion I once heard, and an explanation was given of the question, "Why is a lawyer like a restless man on a bed?" Can you tell me why? Because "he lies first on one side and then turns over and lies on the other."

Representative W. Jasper Talbert of South Carolina

* * *

"What sort of a fellow is this new Virginia Senator?" asked Senator Daniel Webster of Colonel Preston of South Carolina. "Do you know him?"

"Yes," replied Colonel Preston, "very well; and a very clever fellow he is. What do *you* think of him?"

"Why," said Mr. Webster, "I dined with him today, and think him a preposterous aggregation of heterogeneous paradoxes and perdurable peremptorences."

* * *

An Irishman up in my state was testifying in a controversy as to whether a certain Mr. A. was drunk or not. Twenty witnesses had gone on the stand and sworn that A. was drunk, but Pat, when he was put on the stand, swore A. was practically sober. They wanted to ascertain Pat's method of determining the soberness of the man and asked him the question, "Pat, when do you think a man is drunk?" He replied, "I never think a man is drunk as long as he can lay on the ground and hang on to the grass."

Representative Samuel L. Powers
of Massachusetts, 1904

* * *

I recall a story in regard to President Jackson. He was riding one day with the French Minister around the environs of Washington. Jackson did not understand any French, but he had an interpreter, a secretary, riding at his side who did the French act for him, and while this secretary and the French Minister were conversing very animatedly, old Jackson, with his cloak wrapped around him, was in a state of quietude. After a while, however, he turned to the secretary and asked, "What is he jabbering about?" The secretary replied, "Mr. President, he was telling me how a French fleet could come up the broad sweep and reaches of the Potomac, get within gunshot of the capital, and how easy it would be for such a foreign fleet to take Washington." Old Jackson turned round to the secretary and said, "Take hell!"

Senator Joseph T. Robinson of
Arkansas, 1925

* * *

During World War II, Quaker antiaircraft guns were mounted on the roof of the Capitol. This excerpt from an exchange between Representatives Fred L. Crawford of Michigan, Harold D. Cooley of North Carolina, Clarence J. Brown of Ohio, and Hamilton Fish, Jr., of New York is typical of the furor aroused in the House by the wooden artillery.

Mr. CRAWFORD. I am not concerned about how many wooden guns, but how many wooden Congressmen they have got around here.

Mr. COOLEY. Those decoys would probably indicate we have some lame ducks in Congress. I think the time has come when the Members of this House ought to know what is being done around this city of Washington. It is unfortunate that this city, the capital of the greatest republic of the earth, is being protected by wooden guns and decoy soldiers.

Mr. BROWN. We have heard a good deal about wooden guns and wooden soldiers, but is not the real danger from wooden heads?

Mr. FISH. I think the gentleman is right—wooden heads and bureaucratic government.

* * *

I recollect a story that John O'Neill told me many years ago. He was an Irishman who represented a St. Louis district, and he had all the brightness, wit, and humor that Irishmen generally have. One day, sitting in the cloakroom, when the conversation was running, he said: "When I was at home last week, having leave of absence for a few days, an Irish client of mine was about to die. He had no relatives in this country, and all his relatives in Ireland had crossed over, and he sent for me to write his will. I had been his attorney. He gave so much for the repose of his soul, so much to this hospital, and so much to that hospital, and so much for various charities. He knew exactly what he had, and I wrote the will and read it over to him, and he discovered when he came to make the addition that there was ten dollars left over that had not been disposed of.

O'Neill said the dying Irishman realized that his time was short, and asked if there was time to write the will over. O'Neill said to him: "Oh, I can fix it all right. I will just put in what we call a 'codicil.' What do you want to do with the ten dollars?" He thought a minute and said, "I'll not be knowin' what I want to do with the ten dollars exactly—but, yes; it can be invested in whiskey, to be drank at my funeral." "Going or returning?" asked O'Neill. "Going, of course. I'll be wid 'em then." (Laughter.)

Representative Joseph G. Cannon of Illinois, 1916

* * *

Mr. Speaker, by the remarks which have been made here in reference to political "combines," I am reminded of the witty clergyman who said that his "doxy" was orthodoxy and that all other "doxies" were heterodoxy. We all believe in the "combine" that we ourselves belong to, and the bad fellows are always in the other "combine."

Representative Galusha A. Grow of Pennsylvania, 1896

* * *

Pericles used to say that his baby governed Athens. Pericles governed the Athenian Assembly. His wife, Aspasia, governed Pericles, and the baby governed Aspasia. The Senate is governed by the Finance Committee. The Finance Committee is governed by its Democratic majority, and the Democratic majority is governed by that trinity of wisdom and patriotism —the junior Senator from Missouri, the senior Senator from Arkansas, and the junior Senator from Texas—and to judge from their product, that one among those Senators who is nearest to the baby stage in knowledge and reflection upon the tariff governs the senatorial trinity.

Senator George F. Hoar of Massachusetts, 1884

* * *

I remember a few years ago there was a run on a savings bank not far from my own residence. Some little distrust arose, and I remember during the progress of the run a Quaker friend of mine drove into town, lashing his horse. Rushing into the bank, he threw his deposit book down, saying, "I want my money." There was the cashier sitting before him, and he immediately counted out the amount of his deposit. "Why, of course, we have an abundance of money. We'd be glad to have you take your money." "Well," said the old Quaker, "if thee has the money, I don't want it—but if thee hasn't it, I want it right off." Now that illustrates the basis of confidence.

Representative Nelson Dingley, Jr., of Maine, 1896

* * *

My colleagues will recall former President Calvin Coolidge, who was once asked the question, "Mr. President, do the people where you come from say 'A hen lays' or 'A hen lies'?" Mr. Coolidge replied, "The people where I come from, sir, lift her up to see."

Representative Sidney R. Yates of Illinois, 1956

* * *

Mr. CONNALLY of Texas. The Senator from Connecticut (Mr. Danaher) said, "Well, just take out section 7 or 8 of the amendment proposed by the Senator from Ohio (Mr. Taft) and it will be a fine bill." That, Mr. President, reminds me of a story which our old friend, Senator Tom Heflin of Alabama, used to tell in the cloakroom. I shall tell it on the Floor. Uncle Remus went fishing. He caught a little perch about two inches long, and took the little perch home to trim and clean it. It was slimy and still alive, and it began to flirt and flip and jerk around.

Uncle Remus exclaimed, "Little fish, what in the world is the matter with you? Why are you cutting up so much? I ain't going to do nothin' to you but gut you." Mr. President, that is the situation with respect to the motion to recommit. The proponents of that motion have the complacency to say to the Senator from Texas and to the Senator from Ohio and to every other member of the Senate, "Why are you worrying about this little bill? We want to recommit it. We ain't goin' to do a thing to it but gut it; that's all."

* * *

The speculators get it [the farmer's crop] at the depreciated price–then they deflate the currency and, turning it loose, sell it back at three times what they paid. This is the system we are living under today. It is not the Sherman Act. That has done the sick man a great deal of good. If it is a cowardly makeshift, it has acted like a little quinine. It will cure chills, but they will come back after a while. The people have been quiet too long. They have stayed quietly at home, trusting to their representatives at Washington to do the nice thing for them. Every once in a while they send up to ask "What of the night?" and the good gentlemen here, the great big bushy-headed statesmen, fattening and feasting on the best in the land, would reply, "All is well. Plow on, boys! We will be down again in the fall. We will want your votes and the fried chickens as usual."

Representative W. Jasper Talbert
of South Carolina

* * *

I am reminded of the old colored preacher who, speaking of the Bible, said he believed in it. "Whatever is commanded in this book," he said, "I will do. If I should read in this Bible that it was my duty to jump through a stone wall, I would try. Jumping at the stone wall belongs to me—going through it belongs to the Lord."

Representative James A. Johnson
of California

* * *

Mr. Speaker, some of the statements that have been made here remind me of the story of the old maid, away up in the seventies, who was standing before a burning furnace and the poor old woman began to cry, when someone standing near her asked what was the matter, why was she crying. "Why," she said, "I was just thinking that if I should ever get married and should have a child and it should fall into the furnace, what a fearful thing it would be."

Representative Seth Milliken of
Maine

* * *

There are some things that I can understand and some that I cannot. As the traveler said, after traveling all over the world, he understood many things—why rivers flow downhill, why the moon shines by night and the sun by day—but on passing a tannery and seeing as the sign of the tannery a cow's tail in an auger hole, he said he could not see how that cow could jump through that hole and leave her tail behind. I cannot see how the committee, who have signed this report, can ask this House to give a pension of seventeen dollars to this lady.

Representative W. Jasper Talbert
of South Carolina, 1897

* * *

I think I told this story when I appeared before the Interstate Commerce Commission with regard to this bill, about the Irishman who was about to be hanged. The sheriff asked him whether he would like to inspect the gallows and he said he would not mind. After Mike was done inspecting, the sheriff asked him whether he had anything to say, and he said he thought the damn thing was not safe.

Representative Franklin Menges
of Pennsylvania, 1926

* * *

"Mr. Speaker, can there be anything brought into this House that will not be repealed sooner or later?" asked Representative John F. Potter of Wisconsin during the Thirty-seventh Congress. "Yes," replied Representative William E. Lansing of New York, "a skinned orange."

* * *

If I am not mistaken, this House did pass, at the last term of Congress, a resolution of sympathy, not of sincere sympathy, for the farmers. I understood they actually had the word "sincere" stricken out so as to give them simply sympathy. Now I say that the farmer is tired of this kind of sympathy. I am a farmer myself. When the farmer, at the end of the year, goes to the merchant and pays his bill, the merchant says to him, "I sympathize with you. You are the bone and sinew of the country," while at the same time he is poking the money down into the bottom of his pockets, and tells him as he goes out of the store, "Stay out of politics." Then the farmer goes to his lawyer and the lawyer tells him as he pays him a nice, big fee, "I hope you will have a better crop next year," and all the time he is poking the money away down into his pocket; and so it is when he goes to the doctor. And finally he goes to the good old minister, but the good old minister, he, too, takes the contribution, and while he puts it in his pocket he says, "Brother, if you do not get your reward in this world, you will in the sweet by-and-by." And that's all we get.

Representative W. Jasper Talbert
of South Carolina

* * *

The remarks of the gentleman from New York remind me of a story of an old colored man down in Virginia who was riding a mule, and who was caught in a violent thunderstorm while passing through a dense forest. Being unable to make any headway, except through the agency of the fitful flashes of lightning which occasionally revealed his surroundings, and becoming greatly alarmed at the loud and terrible peals of thunder which shook the earth and reverberated over his head, he at last appealed to the Throne of Grace in this fashion: "O Lawd, if it's jest the same to you I'd rather have a little less noise and a little mo' light!"

Now we have had a hogshead of noise, and would be thankful for a thimbleful of light on this important subject.

Representative Charles T. O'Ferrall of Virginia

* * *

It reminds me of the old fellow out in Texas who wrote back to a friend in Tennessee. He said: "Dear Bill: If you have not started for Texas, don't. This is the most hellacious climate in the world. Only yesterday, while driving a yoke of steers across the prairie, one of them had a sunstroke and while I was skinning him, the other one froze to death." That was a quick change in the weather, Mr. President, but not much quicker than the changes of my friend from Tennessee.

Senator J. Thomas Heflin of Alabama during an altercation with Senator Kenneth D. McKellar of Tennessee

I never visit the White House. I am a spring chicken in this House and do not go there unless sent for to be consulted about great matters of state, and I do not suppose the gentleman from Michigan does. I do not know anything about what they have there to eat. But a spring chicken had better stay away. I have only been there once or twice, and I do not know that I will ever go there again. (Laughter.)

Representative Peter J. Otey of Virginia, 1897

* * *

Cromwell looked to the Lord—had great confidence in the Great Ruler of the universe—but he had a certain confidence in charcoal and saltpetre when it was kept dry.

Representative Thomas Corwin of Ohio, 1861

* * *

WAYSIDE FLOWERS, FLINGS AND FUN

The Democratic party is like a mule without pride of ancestry or hope of posterity.

Representative Emory Speer of Georgia, 1880's

* * *

The basic principle that will ultimately get the Republican party together is the cohesive power of public plunder.

Senator Anselm J. McLaurin of Mississippi

* * *

I believe if we introduced the Lord's Prayer here, Senators would propose a large number of amendments to it.

Senator Henry Wilson of Massachusetts

* * *

History is but little more than a graveyard in which one reads the epitaphs of buried states.

Senator Edgar Cowan of Pennsylvania

* * *

A President without both Houses of Congress back of him doesn't amount to much more than a cat without claws in that place that burneth with fire and brimstone.

Representative Joseph G. Cannon of Illinois

* * *

His face is livid; gaunt his whole body,
His breath is green with gall; his tongue drips poison.

John Quincy Adams on John Randolph of Roanoke

* * *

Mr. President, I never quarrel, sir. But sometimes I fight, sir, and whenever I fight, sir, a funeral follows.

Senator Thomas Hart Benton of Missouri, 1850

* * *

A member from North Carolina was once asked to explain what he meant by a "third head speech." Replied the lawmaker: "Gentlemen, first I'll tell you what I know and you don't know; second, I'll tell you what you know and I don't know; and third, what neither you nor I know anything about. The last is a third head."

* * *

Mr. President, the mammoth chimney called the Washington Monument is a meaningless and unsightly thing; its foundations are insecure; and we have buried a hundred thousand dollars in the ground. Assuming that we succeed in founding or establishing the foot of the monument so that it will not give way, it will still remain as I have described it.

Senator Roscoe Conkling of New York, 1876

* * *

Now, Mr. Speaker, I undertake to predict that this world in which we live will not go on permanently under a system like that. It will not go on forever buying coffee grinds delicately moulded out of blue mud. It will not go on buying tea that has been generously commingled with the dried leaves of the forest. It will not go on drinking wine that has been manufactured in a cellar without the intervention of grapes, nor those other and more penetrating beverages that have entered into partnership with such a fatal assortment of explosive chemicals as to greatly facilitate the descent of our fellow citizens, as the old Negro preacher expressed it, down the lubricated steps to the opaque profundity of damnation.

Representative Jonathan P. Dolliver of Iowa

* * *

There is a story told of a man and his wife who quarreled as to what they should have for dinner. The one wanted terrapin stew and sherry, and the other wanted canvasback duck and champagne. They wrangled and quarreled and finally compromised on cabbage. We have had the terrapin stew of the Senate and the canvasback duck of the House, and now we come in and compromise on cabbage.

Representative Peter J. Otey of Virginia, 1897

* * *

Our city of Washington is filled with officials who have new duties to perform, offices to be made for them. You may go to any of the departments of the government and walk through during business hours, and you will not find one clerk in five who has any business to do except smoke a cigar and enjoy conversation with his friends.

Senator James A. McDougall of California, 1866

* * *

I might call your attention to what is happening to sheep. All the ewes have gone to the blue heaven or to the ewe heaven. I do not know which, because the sheep population has been reduced thirty-five percent. If we keep on with this policy, you will have to take your grandchildren down to the zoo, because there is the only place where you will find a sheep. There will not be any found on the farms of the United States.

Representative Reid F. Murray of Wisconsin, 1948

* * *

How "Private" John Mills Allen of Mississippi got to be a national lawmaker at Washington has been often told on the floor of the House. In the 1884 elections Allen took the stump to unseat former Confederate General Tucker who had two terms in Congress to his credit.

One night during the campaign General Tucker wound up his speech with a rousing flourish: "My fellow citizens, twenty years ago last night, after a hard fought battle on yonder hill, I bivouacked under yonder clump of trees. Those of you who remember, as I do, those times that tried men's souls will not, I hope, forget their humble servant when the primaries are held."

It was appealing medicine in those days, but Allen went the General one better: "My fellow citizens, what General Tucker says to you about having bivouacked in yonder clump of trees on that night is true. It is also true, my fellow citizens, that I was a vidette picket and stood guard over the general while he slept. Now then, fellow citizens, all of you who were generals and had privates stand guard over you while you slept, vote for General Tucker; and all of you who were privates and stood guard over the generals while they slept, vote for Private John Allen!"

It delighted the audience, devastated the General, and swept "Private" John Allen on to Washington.

* * *

Mr. CONNALLY of Texas. The [Committee] leadership did not want even a mild bill considered by the Senate. They taunted me here saying, "Why, your bill does not amount to anything. Why bring it up? There is nothing to it. Why don't you put some teeth in it?"

Then, Mr. President, just so soon as we put a couple of little milk teeth in it, they want to call in the dentist and have him pull out the two teeth we have in it, by sending it back to the Committee on the Judiciary as a nursing home.

Mr. BARKLEY of Kentucky. Mr. President, will the Senator yield?

Mr. CONNALLY. I yield.

Mr. BARKLEY. The mere operation of taking out a couple of milk teeth does not necessarily justify putting in two sets of false teeth.

Mr. CONNALLY. Well, Mr. President, the Senator from

Kentucky is more familiar with false teeth than is the Senator from Texas.

Mr. BARKLEY. I am willing to undergo an inspection on the premises if the Senator desires it.

Mr. CONNALLY. I do not care to undergo an inspection of the Senator from Kentucky.

* * *

"LOQUACITY, CONFUSION, AND CHAOS"

This amusing little colloquy between Senator Matthew M. Neely of West Virginia and Senator Everett M. Dirksen of Illinois brightened the interminable debate that led to the liquidation of the Reconstruction Finance Corporation in 1952.

Mr. NEELY. Mr. President, I ask unanimous consent, first, that in the distant future or on whatever date we finally vote on this measure in the Senate, no Senator be allowed to offer more than twenty amendments.

Secondly, that no Senator be allowed to speak more than forty times on either the bill or any amendment that may be offered; and that during the tedious, tasteless, dreary, weary period of loquacity, confusion, and chaos no Senator be allowed to speak more than one minute under any of the forty recognitions by the chair.

SEVERAL SENATORS. Vote! Vote!

Mr. DIRKSEN. Mr. President, there are some things which have been confused this afternoon. Strangely enough, I think we are in the situation of the man in the penitentiary, under sentence of death. He wrote the Governor and said, "Dear Governor: They are fixing to hang me on Friday, and here it is Tuesday."

That is about the situation in which we find ourselves. Every conceivable point is brought up. If disaster is an emergent matter, I am not going to confess my own inepitude, nor the inepitude of the Senate. I am not going to confess that there is something so decadent about the activities of the Congress that it cannot deal with this question.

* * *

Mr. Speaker, I want to tell a little story if I can in my time. I knew Judge Holman of Indiana very well. I served here with him for many years. He was one of the most distinguished men who ever served in Congress from that state, but he had the reputation of being the "Watchdog of the Treasury." Once in a while I would meet him and we would take a drink together. Now I can take a drink and it will not affect me much, but if ever he took one or two he became exceedingly bright and would reminisce. One day he met an old friend of his from Vermont who had served with him in former years, who was second auditor under Grant. I forget his name. He shook hands with us but he did not drink. [Judge Holman] said to this gentleman, "Oh, I recollect our service with great pleasure. We were both called 'Watchdogs of the Treasury.' So we were, so we were, but we always had sense enough not to growl when our friends were around." (Prolonged laughter [so says the *Congressional Record*])

Representative Joseph G. Cannon of Illinois

* * *

LINCOLN AND THE GENERAL'S APPETITE

Representative Abraham Lincoln of Illinois delighted in twitting his Democratic opponents in the House. He took particular sport in shooting his barbs at General Lewis Cass of Michigan, Democratic candidate for president in 1848 whose military abilities were somewhat suspect. On this occasion Mr.

Lincoln centered his ridicule on the general's accounts with the government in 1831.

Mr. Speaker, I adopt the suggestion of a friend, that General Cass is a general of splendidly successful charges–charges, to be sure, not upon the public enemy, but upon the public treasury.

I have introduced General Cass's accounts here chiefly to show the wonderful physical capacities of the man. They show that he not only did the labor of several men at the same time, but that he often did it at several places many hundred miles apart, at the same time. And at eating, too, his capacities are shown to be quite as wonderful. From October, 1821, to May, 1822, he ate ten rations a day in Michigan, ten rations a day here in Washington, and near five dollars' worth a day besides, partly on the road between the two places.

We have all heard of the animal standing in doubt between two stacks of hay and starving to death; the like of that would never happen to General Cass. Place the stacks a thousand miles apart, he would stand stock still midway between them, and eat them both at once; and the green grass along the line would be apt to suffer some too, at the same time. By all means, make him President, gentlemen. He will feed you bountifully–if–if there is any left after he shall have helped himself.

* * *

Mr. President, if a stranger, ignorant of the events that have transpired in our country during the last ten years, had been in this chamber as a listener during the progress of this debate, and had heard a part of the speeches which have been delivered, he would hardly have been led to believe that a great war had existed for four years in this land; and when told that such was the fact, he would have been inclined to ask: Who surrendered at Appomattox?

Senator John M. Thayer of Nebraska during debate on the readmission of Georgia in March 1870

* * *

In 1852 when Franklin Pierce was nominated for President of the United states it was said of him that Mr. Pierce was a very large man in the State of New Hampshire, but when you came to spread him over all the United States the ground showed up in some spots. And so of our Navy. It is a very good Navy as far as it goes.

Representative James A. Johnson of California, 1896

* * *

Somebody estimates that getting born costs the people of the United States two hundred and fifty million dollars annually, getting married three hundred million and getting buried seventy-five million. But, Mr. Speaker, that is absolutely nothing. The cost of being governed by this Administration, the extra cost to business and to commerce and to labor over and above what it ought to be, would marry and bury every man, woman and child in America every month, and then pay the cost for every one of them to be born again in the latest and most approved fashion.

Representative Robert G. Cousins of Iowa, 1900

* * *

I do not want the House to be so very polite as was a young lady of whom I once heard, who, when the house was on fire, when she was cut off by the flames and stood at a window, the only mode of escape being by means of a ladder, when a brawny, grimy fireman came up through the smoke and flames, with the ladder crumbling under his feet, and offered to save her, said, "No, sir. You cannot take me down that ladder. I have never been introduced to you and I cannot get into your arms. I prefer to burn."

Representative James A. Johnson
of California, 1870

* * *

Mr. UPSHAW of Georgia. Does not the gentleman think that the gentleman who depends upon the keg of liquor should be put out of politics?

Mr. GALLAGHER of Illinois. Oh, that is cheap talk. We hear that line of talk from men who think they are making friends by going around speechifying and pretending to work for the general welfare of the people and the good of the public.

Unto those who talk and talk,
This proverb should appeal:
The steam that blows the whistle
Will never turn the wheel.

Men who do the greatest good for the community in which they live, as a rule, do not blow about it. Professional agitators shout about anything they think will make them popular.

* * *

You all remember that Frederick the Great was against dueling although the spirit of his time was in favor of it, and that when an officer came to him—an officer with whom he was intimate and friendly—and told him that he must accept a challenge to fight a duel, the great king replied, "Yes, you can fight your duel." But on the morning when they came they found upon the dueling ground a scaffold erected. So they asked, "For what purpose is that scaffold erected?" The answer was given to them, "Whoever survives the duel shall be hanged on the spot!"

Representative Franklin Bartlett
of New York, 1896

* * *

OH! HOW THEY LOVE THE PEOPLE!

In this bit of satire, J. Proctor Knott of Kentucky painted a heartwarming picture of the burning love of the politician for "the people"—and their votes.

Mr. Speaker, I have been satisfied for a long time that the affection of a young mother for her first-born bears no sort of comparison to the love which gentlemen on this floor entertain for the people. To do anything like justice to the depth of that sentiment would bankrupt all the resources of the most pathetic eloquence or the most stirring poetry. If we speak of the law, it is "the people's law"; if we speak of ourselves, it is as "the people's Representatives"; if we allude to the Constitution, it is "the people's Constitution"; if we have anything to say about the government, it is "the people's government." Everything belongs to them, and their interests are paramount to every other consideration. Gentlemen love them—love them as they do the apple of their eyes. They would undergo any sacrifice for them. There is not an office, from President down, that any of us would not relieve the people of the trouble of holding, and of which we would not heroically shoulder the emoluments.

* * *

I think that when God created this country He certainly intended to see, or at least had an idea, that the people should have some rights of self-government. But about the only thing they have left in the country in the way of self-government is how many children the women shall have, and I suppose after a while they will want to regulate even that.

Senator Coleman L. Blease of South Carolina, 1926

* * *

Let me repeat that we ought to consider the people's side of this question a little more than some of you seem inclined to do. We ought to be as generous toward them, at least, as the Jewish waiter toward the hen who, when his customer refused to take a fried egg after he had ordered it because the waiter charged him ten cents for it, which, he said, was too much, the Jewish waiter replied, "But, my dear sir, you must be reasonable and look at the other side of it. You must remember that an egg represents a whole day's work for the hen."

Representative John W. Langley of Kentucky, 1919

* * *

I do not believe it is necessary for me to say that the people are fed up with political favoritism, with influence peddling, with unearned fees, with natural royal pastel mink coats, with free luxury hotel accommodations for government officials. People from all over the nation write to members of Congress asking "Have morals gone out of style in Washington?"

Senator James P. Kem of Missouri, 1952

* * *

Liberties and rights are never taken from a people by action that is so labeled. It is invariably an oblique attack. The technique is to represent that a poor job is being done and that a better one can be done with the new proposal at hand.

Senator Roman L. Hruska of Nebraska, 1955

* * *

The maxim of Jefferson should be written in letters of gold and placed over every legislative hall in this broad land, "That government is best which governs least." Let the people be self-reliant, not slaves. Let them govern themselves, make as few laws as possible. That is the way to do your duty to the people whose servants you are. You are not sovereigns. The people of the United States are sovereigns, not we; not the gentleman who lives at the other end of the Avenue; he is their chief servant, not their sovereign.

Senator William W. Eaton of Connecticut

* * *

It is to be hoped that our people will soon grow tired of wasting much blood and treasure in foreign lands in which they have no interest and from which no good to them can ever come. Why not spend our lives and our money in trying to make our people prosperous and happy instead of wasting them on foreign races? Why should America not be satisfied with America, where, with good government and conditions, every citizen may become prosperous and happy under his own vine and fig tree?

Representative James R. Williams of Illinois, 1898

* * *

The American people are loyal. They stand by the law and the rights it guarantees. They are patient. They are forbearing. They are conciliatory. Let me say to my friend, they feel like the Indian chieftain. "Metamora is like flint," exclaimed the old chief. "Grate on him and he will bear it; but strike too hard, he will burst and show his heart is fire."

Representative George M. Robeson of New Jersey, 1883

* * *

I wish he [President Wilson] was back home because I do not want to entangle this great, free Republic, this owner of a hemisphere, this people sufficient within themselves; I do not want them to mix up in a card game where there are more kings and queens than there are presidents. You know we do not stand to get anything out of these entanglements except more entanglements. England, as has been well said, gets predominancy. France gets *revanche*. Italy gets back the Adriatic. But what does Uncle Sam get except a burden and a mortgage upon the resources of this country?

Representative Martin Dies of Texas, 1919

CLASSICS OLD AND NEW

ROSCOE CONKLING ACQUIRES HIS TURKEY-GOBBLER STRUT

Nothing ever uttered in the American Congress quite matches James G. Blaine's plastering of Roscoe Conkling of New York before an enthralled House one day in 1866. At issue between the two statesmen, both Republicans, were the military abilities of a Civil War general. For days arrogant, swaggering Conkling had needled the man from Maine. Suddenly Blaine let fly the words that dogged Conkling the rest of his life. The gulf between the two men was never bridged. Cartoonists forever after depicted Conkling as a strutting turkey cock.

As to the gentleman's cruel sarcasm, I hope he will not be too severe. The contempt of that large-minded gentleman is so wilting, his haughty disdain, his grandiloquent swell, his majestic, supereminent, overpowering turkey-gobbler strut, has been so crushing to myself and all the members of this House, that I know it was an act of the greatest temerity for me to venture upon a controversy with him.

But, sir, I know who is responsible for this. I know that within the last five weeks, as members of this House will recollect, an extra strut has characterized the gentleman's bearing. It is the fault of another. That gifted satirical writer, Theodore Tilton of the New York *Independent*, spent some weeks recently in this city. His letters as published in that paper embraced, with many serious statements, a little jocose satire, a part of which was the statement that the mantle of the late Henry Winter Davis had fallen upon the member from New York.

The gentleman took it seriously, and it has given his strut additional pomposity. The resemblance is great; it is striking. Hyperion to a Satyr; Thersites to Hercules; mud to marble; dunghill to diamond; a singed cat to a Bengal tiger; a whining puppy to a roaring lion! Shade of the mighty Davis! Forgive the almost profanation of the jocose satire!

* * *

You can take the heart even out of an elephant, the stomach out of an ostrich, and you may finally pierce the hide of a rhinoceros, if you keep at him so great a time as the long and weary months that I have been practically on the gridiron, trying to prevent the great injustice this bill would perpetrate against Arizona.

Senator Henry F. Ashurst of Arizona while filibustering against the Boulder Dam Bill in 1928

* * *

J. Thomas Heflin of Alabama was one of the rearguard of the swallow-tail statesmen. He could work up a sweat on almost anything, but outdid himself on tariffs and trusts, rich folks and Republicans. Here's a 1910 sample:

Mr. Speaker, I have seen the women of your tariff barons and trust magnates, in gorgeous apparel and flashing jewels, speeding along Pennsylvania Avenue and through the streets of New York in ponderous automobiles, not with little children at their sides, but instead a bull pugdog sitting on the seat and wearing a gold collar around his neck. And on the same street I have met half-clad, hollow-eyed, hungry people begging for bread, and yet you talk about prosperity in the face of these horrible Republican conditions. It is prosperity for bull pugs and millionaire's pets of the Republican party, but misery and want among many of God's plain people.

* * *

"THIS SOAKED MASS OF DEMOCRACY"

The great Sergeant S. Prentiss of Mississippi served one term in the House, in the 1830's, but this echo—still heard in the House—is a sample of the brilliant wit for which he is remembered. He once engaged in a joint debate with Governor M'Nutt, who took the rostrum ahead of Prentiss and made the mistake of deploring the latter's love of John Barleycorn. In his turn, Prentiss first depicted the delights to be found in a jug of firewater. Then, turning to his opponent, he said:

Now, fellow-citizens, during this ardent campaign, which has been so fatiguing, I have only been drunk once. Over in Simpson County, I was compelled to sleep in the same bed with this distinguished nominee, this delight of his party, this wonderful exponent of the principles and practices of the unwashed Democracy, and in the morning I found myself drunk on corn whisky. I had lain too close to this soaked mass of Democracy, and I was drunk from absorption!

* * *

Mr. President, the sun has set for the last time upon the guaranteed and certain liberties of all the unsettled and unorganized portions of the American continent that lie within the jurisdiction of the United States. Tomorrow's sun will rise in dim eclipse over them. How long that obscuration will last is known only to the Power that directs and controls human events. For myself, I know only this, that no human power will prevent its coming on, and that its passing off will be hastened and secured by others than those now here, and perhaps by only those belonging to future generations.

Senator William H. Seward of New York at midnight, May 25, 1854, just before final passage of the Kansas-Nebraska Bill

* * *

It is recorded that on the entry of Louis XVIII into Paris, after the fall of the great Napoleon, an old marshal of the empire who stood in the vast throng, unknown, was addressed by an ardent Bourbon who expatiated on the gorgeous splendors of the scene and exclaimed, "Is not this grand! Is it not magnificent! What is there wanting to the occasion?" "Nothing," said the warworn veteran as his mind wandered over Lodi and Wagram and Austerlitz and a hundred fields where he had fought beneath the eagles of his now exiled chief. "Nothing," he said in a tremulous voice "nothing is wanting to the occasion but the presence of the brave men who died to prevent it."

Representative William Elliott of South Carolina, 1891

* * *

"USELESS?"

In 1825, when Senator Mahlon Dickerson of New Jersey ridiculed the idea of establishing a military post on the Oregon coast as "useless and impracticable" and charged that Oregon could never become a state, Senator Thomas Hart Benton of Missouri rose swiftly to dispute the assertion.

Useless? I answer, the advantages will be the securing of the fur trade on the Columbia, the Rocky Mountains, and the upper Mississippi; preventing the Russians and British getting control of the Indians on the Columbia; a naval station for us on the Pacific; communication between the valley of the Mississippi and the Pacific; and, chief of all, the exclusion of foreign powers from Oregon. Within a century from this day a population greater than that of the present United States will exist on the west side of the Rocky Mountains.

* * *

"OLD SOLDIERS NEVER DIE"

On April 19, 1951 General of the Army Douglas MacArthur returned from his conquest of Japan to receive the rare honor of addressing the Joint Congress of the United States. In a moving farewell scene this great soldier sheathed his sword. His closing words on this occasion brought tears to many eyes.

I am closing my fifty-two years of military service. (Applause.) When I joined the Army even before the turn of the century, it was the fulfillment of all my boyish hopes and dreams. The world has turned over many times since I took the oath on the plain at West Point, and the hopes and dreams have long since vanished. But I still remember the refrain of one of the most popular barrack ballads of that day, which proclaimed most proudly that, "Old soldiers never die; they just fade away." And like the old soldier of that ballad, I now close my military career and just fade away—an old soldier who tried to do his duty as God gave him the light to see that duty.

Good-by.

* * *

My colleague, Judge De Armond, has been trying to have the capital moved. Eastern people make fun of him on that account. I am on his side. His head is level. I would like to see it moved to the place where it ought to be, on top of the Ozark Mountains, in the commonwealth of Missouri. I do not care particularly where it is, but put it in the right place. The government of the United States ought to buy a reservation for it, pass a law, when the capital is established there, that there should not be a private dwelling or business house within ten miles of it—keep the lobbyists, keep the jobbers, keep the pressure of outside influences away from it absolutely.

Representative Champ Clark of Missouri, 1894

* * *

MOVE IT TO JACKASS GULCH!

The idea of moving the nation's capital out of Washington to a safer place was considered by Congress the moment the government moved it in 1801. The War of 1812, when Washington was so easily captured and burned by the British, brought on a chorus of demands for moving. The Civil War, when threats of capture hung over the capital for four years, roused the capital-movers to a high pitch. In 1870, Representative James A. Johnson of California came up with a suggestion that, for originality, walks off with the honors. Here it is, in part.

Mr. Speaker, the question of the removal of the capital is one of grave importance. Let us select a place with an appropriate name for the capital of that nation with the best government the wisdom of man ever devised. Let us go to the Pacific, where pacification may be found in our soil, our air, our fruits and juices, and in our ledges and placers.

Sir, let us locate the capital at RED DOG, among the breezy pines whose long slanting shadows fall with witchery to charm upon the surrounding hills; where the mountain streams babble music to the glass-slippered fairies, and invite the howling coyote to lap their waters. If this grand site, seated in a saddle in the mountains, pleases not your fancy, then YOU BET is a fitting place. No hostile fleet can ever there ascend. YOU BET is too high. YOU BET, our future capital, can never be shaken by mortal foe. YOU BET is above tidewater. But if you like it not, YUBA DAM is a favorable place. But still further and last, if you will select none of these for safety or for beauty, then JACKASS GULCH is an appropriate place. There every ass can bray with no one to molest or make him afraid.

But why should I take time to present the advantages of RED DOG, YOU BET, and YUBA DAM when I know JACKASS GULCH can hardly meet with opposition. Jack is a jolly fellow. Ass is the superlative stentorian verbose orator. Gulch means a nice shady place with rippling waters, where gold may be found. Who could wish for more–jolly fellows, long thundering speeches, plenty of money, and lying in the shade? Every gentleman could speak his well-digested piece in peace. He of the true Bashan thunder could roar and make his tale ring about your ears to his heart's content.

* * *

On March 2, 1901 retiring Senator William E. Chandler of New Hampshire fired this Parthian shot at William Clark, Montana copper king, who was charged with buying his seat in the United States Senate. Clark's repeated efforts to get into the Senate, and the lavish use of money in these attempts, got thumbs-down from the Senate itself. On his sixth knock at the door, he was admitted, March 4, 1901. The art collection to which Senator Chandler referred was truly magnificent. Today it may be seen in the Corcoran Gallery of Art.

Mr. President, on Monday next will come the sequel to the six chapters in the Senatorial candidacies of William A. Clark. He may again enter the Senate, and if he does he can make reply to these remarks of mine, and I shall not be here to make rejoinder. He will stand up before the Vice President—if the Senate shall permit—and will make oath faithfully to perform the duties of the office (which has cost him $2,000,000) in company with William P. Frye, George F. Hoar, and Shelby M. Cullom, with John T. Morgan, Augustus O. Bacon, and Benjamin R. Tillman, and with other Republicans and Democrats whose elections did not cost one of them so much as $200.

His castle in Dupont Circle he will decorate with statues and paintings which are among the marvels of modern art, in the presence of which his fellow Senators, with their families and the elite of Washington society, will eat, drink and be merry. The most observed picture to be seen in the gallery, painted by a competent artist, will be that of a man with a mute inquiry on his face, holding in his hand two papers, and every guest will see that one paper is a certificate and the other an expense account—in 1890, $150,000; in 1893, $300,000; in 1895, $50,000; in 1899, $330,000; in 1900, $1,230,000; and that this is his agonizing inquiry: "Is it worth all this and all besides which I have parted with and lost?"

This is a true picture which not all the pigments which millions can buy, nor all the painters whom money can hire, will be able to obliterate; and the title thereof will not be "One scoundrel disposed of," but, if the Senate shall permit, it will be "One—one—one—Montana gentleman not disposed of."

* * *

Every man's home is his castle! So said the great Englishman who said that the homely Latin in the Magna Carta was worth all the classics: "Every man's house is his castle—not that it is surrounded by walls and battlements. It may be a straw-built cottage. Every wind of heaven may whistle through it; all the elements of heaven may enter it; but the King cannot, the King dare not enter it." This is the language of an Englishman speaking of Englishmen; and we descend from that blood, and speak that language, and have cabin castles as well as they. The king cannot force a possession—cannot violate a possession—might be shot and killed if he attempted it. So with us. Every man has a right to defend his possession—to keep intruders out of his house—to warn them out of his fields—to warn them off his land; and if a contest comes on in defense of his possession, he has a right to defend it unto the death—a right to kill.

Senator Thomas Hart Benton of
Missouri, 1851

* * *

I do not think the argument can be defended other than upon the ground assumed by a justice of the peace, well known to my distinguished friend from Illinois (Senator Douglas), old Bolling Green, in answer to a little law advice that I gave him on one occasion when the Senator and I were both very young men and very poor lawyers. Old Bolling Green, then a magistrate, came to me and said, "Baker, I want to know if I have jurisdiction in a case of slander."

I put on a very important air; looked at him steadily—looked as wise as I could, and said to him, "Squire, you have no such authority; that is reserved to a court of general jurisdiction." "Well," he said, "think again; you have not read law very well or very long; try again. Now, have I not jurisdiction? Can I not do it?" "No," I said, "you cannot; I know it; I have read the law from Blackstone to—well, I have read Blackstone, and I know you cannot do it."

"Now, sir," said he, "I know I can. For, by God, I've done it!" I understand now that the sum total of the answer which is made to my objection as to the constitutionality of the Missouri Compromise touching the consciences of the gentlemen who proposed to pass it without power, is just the reply of my friend Bolling Green. They say, "Theoretically, we have not the power; constitutionally, we have not the power; but, by God, we have done it."

Senator Edward D. Baker of Oregon, 1861

* * *

Dawn, March 3, 1854, and Senator Sam Houston of Texas held the floor. About him Senators, grim and haggard, slumped in their chairs waiting for the oratory to cease. Houston was the final speaker on the bitterly fought Kansas-Nebraska Bill that would scrap the Missouri Compromise and open up a vast new territory to slavery. Fateful it was, but now assured of passage before sunrise, with a coalition of Democrats and Southerners riding herd to force it. But Sam Houston, Southerner in all the word implied, was against it—the lone one of his party. In the gray dawn that streaked into the dim-lit Senate Chamber he stood erect, resolute, like the Cherokee chief whose adopted son he was, picturesque, with his panther-skin waistcoat and a colorful Mexican blanket over his shoulders. It took courage to say what Houston said. The South wanted the bill to pass, as did his state and his people. But Sam Houston didn't. Why? Already Southern voices were charging him with treason to his people. Hero of San Jacinto, first President of the Texas Republic, first Senator from the state of Texas, Democrat to the core, he offered no expiation for his bold stand against scrapping the solemn compact between North and South, the Missouri Compromise of 1820.

This is an eminently perilous measure; and do you expect me to remain here silent, or to shrink from the discharge of my duty in admonishing the South of what I conceive the results will be?

I will speak in spite of all the intimidations, or threats, or discountenances that may be thrown at me. Sir, the charge that I am going with the Abolitionists or Free-Soilers affects me not. The discharge of conscience duty prompts me often to confront the united array of the very section of the country in which I reside, in which my associations are, in which my affections rest. When every look to the setting sun carries me to the bosom of a family dependent upon me, think you I could be alien to them? Never! Never!

Sir, if this is a boon that is offered to propitiate the South, I, as a Southern man, repudiate it. I will have none of it. Our children are either to live in aftertimes in the enjoyment of peace, of harmony and prosperity, or the alternative remains for them of anarchy, discord, and civil broil. We can avert the last. I trust we shall.

I adjure you to regard the contract once made to harmonize and preserve the Union. Maintain the Missouri Compromise! Stir not up agitation! Give us peace!

* * *

"LAWS ENOUGH FOR TEN THOUSAND YEARS"

So proclaimed Senator James Alexander Reed of Missouri in his magnificent appeal for less law. Each year sees the volume of legislation mounting. It was this ceaseless spinning of the web of controls around the American people that gave Reed the theme of his warning against its continuance. The date was June 4, 1926.

Oh, but somebody says—and we have heard it *ad nauseam*, indeed, until the gorge would rise in the gizzard of an ostrich at the sheer idiocy of the statement—"We must speed up the public business. We must enact more laws. We must not consider them. We must not analyze them. We must not talk about them." Of course, if we can not talk about them we ought not to think about them. There are a good many men who do a good deal of talking in favor of stopping talking who never stop long enough talking themselves to do any thinking themselves.

My friend from Alabama (Mr. Underwood) waxed eloquent and told us the Lord's Prayer was very short—and he might have added that in modern days it is seldom repeated. He told us that Lincoln's Gettysburg speech only occupied two minutes. He might have added that the Ten Commandments of Moses could be printed on a single page. I do not know what application that may have to the question in hand, except it be the thought that it is not necessary to have many laws, that brevity and limitation of laws is a desirable thing. Well, Mr. President, while we are talking about not having enough legislation, let me call your attention to the thing that I hold in my hand. It is the new condensed code of the United States, on which we are all afraid to vote because we do not know what is in it. We are not going to vote on it either just at present if some of us can help it.

I wish I could find out how many words there are in it. I have made a quick estimate. It may be a little inaccurate, but it will not be any more inaccurate than some statements we have heard from the advocates of more laws. It contains, sir, 1,706 pages very finely printed. As nearly as I can make out there are in it over 14,000 sections. There are written here for the regulation of the American people, by this single body of lawmakers, 2,388,400 words, and the whole of the law and the gospel was put in the Ten Commandments!

Mr. NEELY of West Virginia. If the Jews had had to carry this thing around with them through the wilderness instead of the Ten Commandments, does the Senator think they would have gotten out in forty years? (Laughter.)

Mr. REED of Missouri. I think the Jews would have had too much sense to have toted it around. We are weeping here because we can not do anything but vote. We vote too much.

We deliberate too little. We have brought within the scope of the federal jurisdiction a vast number of subjects that do not belong here, but are nevertheless here.

What we need to do is to stop passing laws. We have enough laws now to govern the world for the next ten thousand years. Every crank who has a foolish notion that he would like to impose upon everybody else hastens to some legislative body and demands that it be graven upon the statutes. Every fanatic who wants to control his neighbor's conduct is here or at some other legislative body demanding that a law be passed to regulate that neighbor's conduct. So we have people who want to regulate the woman who is about to give birth to a child. We once had here a bill that came near passing—I talked it half to death, and I wish to the Lord I had had sufficient physical strength to have talked the rest of it to death, but we took half of its enormities out of it—that could have been so used that governmental agents could have demanded that every woman about to give birth to a child should register the fact at a public registry, so that a public snooper could come around and investigate to see whether the woman was really fit to give birth to a baby. It was proposed to regulate the selection of her midwife or her doctor; and when we ran the thing to earth, these extraordinary powers were to be put in the hands of a board every member of which was a spinster beyond the age of hope.

What is it has made this race great? It has not been the proud blood of an illustrious ancestry; it has not been because we could trace our lineage back to kings and a royal household; it has not been because of the peculiar graces or abilities of those emigrants who came to our shores and from whose loins we are sprung. It is simply because for once in the history of the world the chains were taken from the arms, the shackles from the brain, the shadows of fear were dissipated by the sunlight of liberty and freedom, and every brain of every human being, great or small, was at liberty to function, every arm and every limb was at liberty to move. So we unleashed the latent powers of a race of people; and from the cottage of poverty there came forth the genius, and from the house of the man of humble estate there emerged the child who could turn the dull and inexpressive canvas into pictured harmony of color, light, and shade, and paint the rainbow's mingling hues and marvelous tints. From the cottages of the impoverished, from the homes of ancestors who had been enslaved and enthralled, there came forth children who in the full liberty of our civilization were able to attack every problem and to undertake every great vocation of life; so that within one generation of time we produced here orators whose words of flame could fire the hearts of all the people of this land; poets whose words will be read so long as men shall love the music of our tongue, and a citizenry who have defended our soil and our flag with unexampled valor in every contest of this Republic. All these triumphs of intellect, all these great advances in the arts and in the sciences, all our wondrous advance in wealth are due to one great fact: that we have allowed the individual in this land the opportunity to develop, the opportunity to express himself.

But here are men and women coming constantly to the legislative halls wanting to tie around the liberties of the American people first this thread and then that thread, until finally, as the Lilliputians bound the full-sized and athletic Gulliver with threads until he was inert and helpless on the ground, we ourselves will be bound.

Sir, what we need is less law, less interference, less legislative guidance. What boots it to be called a free man if when you are born you fall into a legislative cradle, your swaddling clothes are regulated by statute, your steps through life are all in accordance with the law and a policeman is there to see that you take them, your course in life is marked out for you from the cradle to the grave, all the time you have moved in gyves and all the time you have been a slave to the laws of a Republic? And one might as well be a slave to the decrees of a tyrant as to the decrees of a Senate or of a House of Representatives.

* * *

When, in May 1872, radicals in Congress proposed a bill giving the President virtually despotic power over the Southern states, Senator Thomas F. Bayard of Delaware challenged the measure as perilous, revolutionary, and aimed at crushing the very breath out of the South. An advocate of the bill even taunted the Southern people for weeping over the graves of their fallen dead in the War between the States. Bayard's reply to this unmanly scoff still rings clear and challenging.

Yes, Mr. President, and should it ever come to pass that the graves of the Southern dead should be neglected by their kindred, kind Nature herself will take their place, and the Southern earth in which the dead sleep will yield its lilies and its daisies to wreath their places of rest, and the soft winds of the South will gently wave the grass above them, and the dews of her starry nights will keep grass and flower fresh in memory of her brave children who died in defense of the soil which now contains them.

Why, sir, can it be that a mind can be so darkened by prejudice and party spirit as to forget the very echoes of human nature itself? If these people did not weep over their loved and their lost, they would be something more or less than human; much more likely less than more. Such a speech and such sentiments sound to me like the report of some Russian commander writing from Warsaw to the Czar, followed by an order forbidding the women of Poland to wear mourning for their dead. Is it the feeling or the language of an American senator directed toward those who are his fellow citizens, and who it is the hope of the country will be a source of happiness and strength to our Union? Certainly men can not be won back from error by such sentiments as these, and by such condemnation. They never can be made friends by such processes.

The law now proposed is an act of assault; it breathes of violence. It works upon no emotions but those of fear. It will cause hatreds. It will produce no good will either between citizens or toward the government. It is, as I have tried to show, a plain violation of the limits of our written charter of power, and, even if it were not so, it is unwise and unjust. Cease, then, I beg of you, this maleficent, odious system, so foreign to the genius of American government, called "reconstruction," and adopt now and from this time forth the true, the wise, the Christian policy of "reconciliation" between the states of this Union.

* * *

On May 19, 1856 Senator Charles Sumner of Massachusetts delivered his highly polished speech, "The Crime Against Kansas," before packed galleries in the Senate Chamber. His target was slavery in Kansas. Courtly, supremely gifted, deadly foe of slavery, Sumner poured out his scholarly wrath for hours. He closed his violent outpouring with an unworthy exchange of personalities with the man who, Sumner charged, fathered the "Crime" against Kansas, Senator Stephen A. Douglas, the Little Giant from Illinois. This sequel to Sumner's famous philippic is the skunk-iest in Senate history.

Mr. DOUGLAS. I shall not detain the Senate by a detailed reply to the speech of the Senator from Massachusetts. Indeed, I should not deem it necessary to say one word, but for the personalities in which he has indulged, evincing a depth of malignity that issued from every sentence, making it a matter of self-respect with me to repel the assaults which have been made.

The libels, the gross insults which we have heard today have been conned over, written with cool, deliberate malignity, repeated from night to night in order to catch the appropriate grace; and then he came here to spit forth that malignity upon men who differ from him—for that is their offense.

Mr. President, I ask what right has that Senator to come here and arraign three fourths of the body for a dereliction of duty? Has he a right to arraign us because we have felt it to be our duty to be faithful to that Constitution which he disavows—to that oath which he assumes and then repudiates?

Mr. SUMNER. To the Senator from Illinois I should willingly leave the privilege of the common scold—the last word; but I will not leave to him, in any discussion with me, the last argument, or the last semblance of it. He has crowned the audacity of this debate by venturing to rise here and calumniate me.

Perhaps I had better leave that Senator without a word more; but this is not the first, or the second, or the third, or the fourth time, that he has launched against me his personalities. Since he has presumed to touch me, he will not complain if I administer to him a word of advice.

Sir, this is the Senate of the United States, an important body, under the Constitution, with great powers. Its members are justly supposed, from age, to be above the intemperance of youth, and from character to be above the gusts of vulgarity. They are supposed to have something of wisdom and something of that candor which is the handmaid of wisdom. Let the Senator bear these things in mind, and let him remember hereafter that the bowie-knife and bludgeon are not the proper emblems of senatorial debate. Let him remember that the swagger of Bob Acres and the ferocity of the Malay cannot add dignity to this body. The Senator has gone on to infuse into his speech the venom which has been sweltering for months—ay, for years; and he has alleged facts that are entirely without foundation, in order to heap upon me some personal obloquy. I will not go into the details which have flowed out so naturally from his tongue. I only brand them to his face as false. I say, also, to that Senator, and I wish him to bear it in mind, that no person with the upright form of man can be allowed—(Hesitation).

Mr. DOUGLAS. Say it.

Mr. SUMNER. I will say it—no person with the upright form of man can be allowed, without violation of all decency, to switch out from his tongue the perpetual stench of offensive personality. Sir, that is not a proper weapon of debate, at least, on this floor. The noisome, squat, and nameless animal, to which I now refer, is not a proper model for an American Senator. Will the Senator from Illinois take notice?

Mr. DOUGLAS. I will; and therefore will not imitate you, sir.

Mr. SUMNER. I did not hear the Senator.

Mr. DOUGLAS. I said if that be the case I would certainly never imitate you in that capacity, recognizing the force of the illustration.

Mr. SUMNER. Mr. President, again the Senator has switched his tongue, and again he fills the Senate with its offensive odor.

Mr. DOUGLAS. I am not going to pursue this subject further. I will only say that a man who has been branded by me in the Senate, and convicted by the Senate of falsehood, cannot use language requiring reply, and therefore I have nothing more to say.

* * *

"THE HABITS OF THE HYENA"

Senator Daniel W. Voorhees of Indiana, "The Tall Sycamore from the Wabash," went into verbal battle with Senator James G. Blaine of Maine over—of all things—the flight of an Indiana Regiment at the battle of Buena Vista in the Mexican War.

Blaine had accused the Second Indiana of taking to their heels under fire and being rescued by Colonel Jefferson Davis and his Mississippians.

Mr. VOORHEES. Mr. President, in the order of divine providence nothing is made in vain, and in the physical world every object has its sphere. This is eminently true in the world of men, and having known the Senator from Maine a long time I had assigned him a higher, a better, and a more useful sphere in public affairs than he seems determined to occupy. For many years I have looked upon him as fitted by nature to fill that place among men which the eagle occupies among the birds of the air. I have fondly hoped to see him soar toward the sun in the clear, upper atmosphere of an exalted statesmanship; but if as a matter of choice he adopts the part of the scavenger bird, hunts for offal, the cast off and putrefying matter of past years, I may deplore but I cannot prevent such a course. If he prefers to abandon the pursuits of the lion, and follow the habits of the hyena, to dig into the graves of the past for loathsome and offensive things, I deeply regret it but it is a matter for him alone to decide.

Mr. BLAINE. Offensive to whom?

Mr. VOORHEES. Offensive to the public interests, if not to common decency. The Senator from Maine has seen fit to resurrect an old, stale, and exploded charge against an Indiana Regiment on the field of Buena Vista.

Mr. BLAINE. No, sir. One moment. I disclaim the charge. It was a scandal against the Indiana Regiment, and I showed that the Southern friends of the Senator from Indiana were perpetuating that and teaching it to their children.

Mr. VOORHEES. I have no such Southern friends, and I find no such miserable literature. I do not burrow in the sewers where such cast-off slanders are to be found. A Senator of the United States can give a calumny, however gross, an air of probability without a direct indorsement, if he is simply willing to pollute his fingers by bringing it into this presence. While the Senator from Maine may say that he does not make this charge against the troops of Indiana or indorse it, I know him too well to be deceived as to his purpose in parading it here.

* * *

" 'TIS GREECE BUT LIVING GREASE NO MORE"

"Sunset" Sam Cox of Ohio, and later New York, was the mighty midget of the House for thirty years. As leader of the "loyal opposition" on the House floor during the Civil War, he called them as he saw them. His rousing description of how a "few Congressmen won the battle of Bull Run against our own soldiers" was a satirical masterpiece. His forensic set-to with Roswell G. Horr, corpulent, 250-pound Representative from Michigan, reduced the House to stitches. Cox was touchy about his small size, and Horr, in the debate on the 1880 Harbor and River Bill, had needled Cox as "my genial little friend."

Mr. COX. Was it logical for my friend the other day to call the attention of the House to my body? Suppose I am little, was it logical, or parliamentary, or kind to say it? It was done without malice, but it permeated every one of my two million pores.

Now, sir, I submit, was my size a subject for any gentleman's logical laughter? I never claimed, because of its smallness, exemption from the demands of courage or in the arena of debate. Laughter is health. It oils the joints (laughter) and the countenance, causing it to shine. But where is the point of making my small person—though I carry the weight of the average man, one hundred and forty pounds—the butt of his ridicule? Why should smallness, in such an immensity of creation, and when everything may be reduced to atomies, be accounted contemptible?

My friend evidently meant to be familiar with me in two respects: first, to humble me for my size; and second, to be witty over what I cannot help, my stature.

I never knew till the other day when I failed to recognize him, how imperfect was my body. Yet, on my failure to recognize him, he called me, first, "genial," and second, "little."

I endeavor to debate here impersonally; never refuse to yield; never invade another's right; always consider my person almost as an abstraction. I am not proud of my appearance as some men are who swell. (Laughter.) Why, sir, I argued against making Congress too big ten years ago. Two hundred and fifty was enough. Had I known the advent of this leviathan into our troubled waters, I should have favored two hundred as our number. (Laughter.) Corpulency is not strength. Let us remember that!

I represent large folks, fighting folks (laughter), good folks; they did not measure my girth or take my altitude when they sent me here. They did not think me unconstitutional. (Laughter.) They did not think blubber indicated brains; nor meat manhood; or that tumors necessarily tend to intellectuality. They did not regard me as unworthy of their trust, because I had not layers of lard over immense adominal muscles. (Prolonged laughter.) They are intelligent; they know that tissues of fat do not control issues of fact or of politics. A man may be five hundred and seventy pounds, or several gentlemen rolled into one, yet he might still be as a tallow candle to the sun. (Laughter.)

Suppose he be six feet high, and have an abdomen ten feet in girth. Does the gentleman tell me that therefore he can assume airs of superiority, "genial" airs? Suppose he has a longer oscoxygis (laughter) and his ancestors had a firmer prehensile grip to a Darwinian limb. (Great laughter.)

Perhaps next he will raise the point of order on me that I

cannot vote, because my esophagus is not as magnificent as his own (laughter), or his phalanges or metacarpus, or, rather, corn-stealers, are bigger than those of any other member. (Laughter.)

Why should such a one be proud? Falstaff weighed about as much as my friend, but he took care not to make his hilarity too loud—when the prince was about. Will the gentleman still insist on raising the point on my size? Is it raised as to my sternum? (Laughter.) If so, I ask him boldly the size of his duodenum? How is the nature of his body different that his pericardium should take on airs over my medulla oblongata? (Great laughter.)

I fear my friend's latter end will come sooner than he knows. Corpulence is disease. I am tired of making obituaries here. But if I am called on to speak his eulogy I would draw on two eminent poets who will combine for such an occasion. One is the sweet singer of Michigan and the other Byron. Over his grave let there be inscribed:

Here lies the body
of
Congressman *Horr;*
'Tis Greece,
But
Living Grease
no more!
Requiescat!

Mr. HORR. I wish to say in defense of myself that those words, "genial little friend," were used in the heat of debate. (Laughter.) And had I known the sensitiveness of the gentleman from New York, had I known the poetry of his nature, I certainly never should have used the language I did at the time. I should have addressed him in the language of one of our modern poets, "Dear little Buttercup, sweet little Buttercup, I."

Some poet has told us that "a thing of beauty is a joy forever." How simple the statement, and yet how true it is! Now, with all the gentleman's transcendent loveliness, I would wish to make this one suggestion which I think, if he will follow, will add much to his already exceeding grace and beauty. My idea is that Brother Cox should part his hair in the middle, and wear bangs. (Loud laughter).

I have a few words to say to the democracy of this country. Gentlemen, you are partly to blame for the trouble I am in. A gentleman from New York informed me this morning that my friend (Mr. Cox) once stated in his presence, or in the presence of a gentleman who told him, that if he had been six inches taller he would have been President of the United States today. Now I have no doubt that six inches would help the gentleman if you put it on the upper story, although it would not help to make him a better Democrat. Why, only think of it. He would have been Speaker of the House if he had only had three inches more on his head and a lot more votes; for he did lack votes. (Laughter.)

I wish to say in conclusion that whatever I may say hereafter in debate, I beg that gentleman to understand I have no malice nor any hardness of heart in me. I do not suppose that the half hour of billingsgate that he piled up on me was called for. But he is a high literary man and I am a poor, unsophisticated boy. He was kind enough to give you yesterday an epitaph for me. I am not a poet. I may say there are many things I wish I was that I am not; but there is a friend of mine who furnished me an epitaph for my friend from New York, and I will say for him that I think it covers the case:

> Beneath this slab lies the great SAM COX,
> He was wise as an owl and grave as an ox;
> Think it not strange his turning to dust,
> For he swelled and he swelled till he finally "bust."
> Just where he's gone or just how he fares
> Nobody knows and nobody cares.
> But wherever he is, be he angel or elf,
> Be sure, dear reader, he's puffing himself.

* * *

GEMS AND JABS BY JOHN RANDOLPH OF ROANOKE

That most delicious of all privileges—spending other people's money.

No man was ever satisfied to be half a king.

The three degrees of comparison—begging, borrowing and stealing.

Clay's eye is on the Presidency; and my eye is on him.

Against eight hundred ships in commission we enter the lists with a three-shilling pamphlet. [Of Madison's pamphlet on neutral rights.]

Never were abilities so much below mediocrity so well rewarded; no, not when Caligula's horse was made Consul. [Of the appointment of Richard Rush to be Secretary of the Treasury.]

He is like a carving knife whetted on a brickbat. [Of Ben Hardin of Kentucky, powerful backwoods orator.]

Life is not so important as the duties of life.

Time is at once the most valuable and the most perishable of all our possessions.

Stick to a friend a little in the wrong.

Asking one of the States to surrender part of her sovereignty is like asking a lady to surrender part of her chastity.

He rowed to his object with muffled oars. [Of Martin Van Buren.]

An English noble has but one son. All the rest are bastards.

All of us have two educations: one which we receive from others; another, and the most valuable, which we give ourselves.

* * *

A GOOD, FAT GOVERNMENT JOB

Before the House in 1876 was a bill to elect the President of the United States for six years and limit him to one term. In opposing the measure, J. Proctor Knott of Kentucky delivered the following oft-quoted speech, one of three that established him as one of the all-time great humorists in Congress.

Mr. Speaker, it has been many and many a time remarked that an incumbent of a good fat office seldom dies, and never resigns; and, sir, it is true. There is scarcely anything within the range of human affection which under some circumstances may not be surrendered with cheerfulness. Friends, home, country, and even life itself may be given up without a murmur; but the disinterested patriot once in possession of a good paying public office hangs on to it with a grim determination and a deathless constancy that would have added a brighter halo to the crown of a Christian martyr—especially when his salary is $50,000 a year; when he is supplied with a palace maintained in a style of luxury of which Lucullus himself never dreamed: furnished, repaired and heated at an annual expense of $25,000; where the very air he breathes is redolent with the perfume of rare exotics propagated in a $55,000 greenhouse, maintained out of the public Treasury at an expense of $5,000 per annum; an office in which his writing is done by a private secretary on a salary of $3,000 a year, with an assistant secretary on a salary of $2,500 to do the writing of the private secretary, and two clerks at $4,500 to do the writing of the assistant secretary; where he has a steward at $2,000 per annum to purvey for his table the choicest wines and daintiest viands that can either tempt or satiate the appetite, and where he is allowed $6,000 a year for books, papers, periodicals, telegrams, and "general contingencies." What the "general contingencies" may include I do not know, but let us thank God for the contingencies anyhow.

Why, Mr. Speaker, if the children of Israel sighed for the flesh-pots, the leeks and onions and garlic and other beggarly concomitants of their bondage in Egypt, what must be the emotions of a sensitive and patriotic soul on contemplating a last, long farewell to a salary and perquisites like these? Now, sir, I ask gentlemen who would lengthen the present term of the presidential office to go home to their honest-hearted, hardworking, overtaxed constituents and explain to them if they can why it is that four years are not a sufficient length of time for any one American citizen to enjoy the luxuries I have mentioned.

Ah; but say the gentlemen on the other side, we want the benefit of the President's experience after a four-year term for another of similar duration; that of all the offices in the gift of the American people there is no other in which experience is so necessary as in the office of President; that the greater experience the incumbent may have had as President the better President he will make. But I ask gentlemen to point out a solitary instance in which the last year of the administration of any President has been more satisfactory to the people than the first.

Sir, I call attention to these facts not only to illustrate the enormous power of money as well as of numbers now wielded by a single hand of this government, but to furnish another answer to the objections which gentlemen have urged against the report of the majority of the committee that four years is too short a time for one man to occupy the presidential chair.

And besides, sir, it may be possible—I do not say that it has ever happened or that it will happen—yet it may be possible that at some time or other we may be so unfortunate as to elect a bad man to the Presidency, of whom we would wish to be rid as soon as consistent with public convenience; consequently the shorter the term the better in that respect.

ON IMMIGRATION AND MARRIAGES "PROPERLY CONSUMMATED"

Senator Hubert H. Humphrey of Minnesota has the gift of ready wit. Witness this tidbit from the debate on the McCarran Immigration Bill in 1952.

Mr. HUMPHREY of Minnesota. Do I understand correctly that under the terms of the bill the Attorney General is to have something to say about whether or not a marriage relationship has been fulfilled and is satisfactory? That certainly smacks of something new in legislation.

Mr. MOODY of California. It is certainly smacks of something. The bill provides that if a bride and bridegroom come into this country under a marriage relationship and fail to fulfill the marital agreement to the satisfaction of the Attorney General . . .

Mr. HUMPHREY. Just a moment. Let us stop there.

Mr. MOODY. I do not know why the Attorney General should be interested in that, but perhaps he is.

Mr. HUMPHREY. I do not believe Congress should put the burden upon the Attorney General as to whether a marriage relationship is satisfactory or has been properly consummated.

Mr. MOODY. That is my point.

Mr. HUMPHREY. What is the express language of the bill?

Mr. MOODY. "Failure to fulfill marital agreements to the satisfaction of the Attorney General."

Mr. HUMPHREY. I think we should ascertain from the sponsors of the bill just what that means. It sounds very interesting.

Mr. MOODY. It would be interesting to know.

Mr. HUMPHREY. The Attorney General is going to be

a very busy man under this bill. Not only that, he is going to be in on some secrets he ought not to be in on.

Mr. [John O.] PASTORE of Rhode Island. As a matter of fact the McCarran Bill may become the best-seller of the year.

Mr. HUMPHREY. It will certainly become a sort of Kinsey report.

WORDS OF WISDOM

"A CLEARER OF THE INTELLECT"

Mr. Speaker, I recollect reading once in an old book a comment on logic. One of the old philosophers said, "If you will give me Aristotle's system of logic, I will force my enemy to a conclusion: give me the syllogism, and that is all I ask." Another philosopher replied, "If you will give me the Socratic system of interrogatory, I will run my adversary into a corner." Another old philosopher standing by said, "My brethren, if you will give me a little ready cash, I will always gain my point. I will always drive my adversary to a conclusion, because a little ready cash is a wonderful clearer of the intellect."

Representative John S. Little of Arkansas, 1899

* * *

As a nation we think not of war but of peace; not of crusades of conflict but of covenants of cooperation; not of the pageantry of imperialism but of the pride of new states freshly risen to independence. We like to look with Mr. Justice Holmes beyond the vision of battling races and an impoverished earth to catch a dreaming glimpse of peace. In the words of Edmund Burke we sit on a "conspicuous stage," and the whole world marks our demeanor. In this year and this Congress we have an opportunity to be worthy of that role.

Senator John F. Kennedy in behalf of his resolution to close the economic gap between the "developed and the undeveloped nations" and, specifically, to extend economic aid to India's 400,000,000 people, 1959

* * *

I would with great pleasure vote for a law by which every President, upon closing his administration, should be placed upon the retired list with such allowances as are fitting for the rank of Commander-in-Chief of the Army and Navy given him by the Constitution. Nor do I see any sectional feature in this measure. It threatens danger to no Southern interest; it does not impair any Southern right; it ought not to be considered as wounding any Southern sentiment. I am in favor, as was done with those who had completed their service under the Roman eagles, of writing opposite the name of General Ulysses S. Grant, *Emeritus*.

Senator Lucius Q. C. Lamar, of Mississippi, 1881, in supporting a motion to place General Ulysses Grant on the retired list as a General of the Army. His was the only Southern vote in the Senate to support the measure.

* * *

I repeat it again, there are but two things necessary to make a man a despot: the purse and the sword. The Congress gives to the President the power of the latter, and is about to give the power of the former into his hands; when this is done the liberties of the people are surrendered to his discretion.

Senator James Jackson of Georgia, 1789

* * *

What do we want with this vast, worthless area? This region of savages and wild beasts, of deserts, of shifting sands and whirlwinds of dust, of cactus and prairie dogs? To what use could we ever hope to put these great deserts, or those endless mountain ranges, impenetrable and covered to their very base with eternal snow? What can we ever hope to do with the western coast, a coast of three thousand miles, rock-bound, cheerless, uninviting, and not a harbor on it? What use have we for this country?

This example of great wisdom was expounded by the Great Expounder, Daniel Webster, in denouncing a measure, in 1829, to establish a mail route from Missouri, across the plains and mountains to the West Coast.

* * *

Let me tell you, you may defeat it today, but you only postpone it. You may postpone it for a few months, it may be possibly for a year, but this Congress, as it is gradually dying, has this opportunity to make itself immortal. If you do not pass this joint resolution the incoming Congress will pass it. You cannot prevent the passage of the joint resolution. You cannot prevent giving women the right to vote. They are going to have it. It is just a question whether you will do it today or whether you will do it a little later.

Senator William P. Pollock of South Carolina, 1919, in behalf of a joint resolution giving women the right to vote

* * *

Mr. President, I wish to make clear that the budget is the nation's purse. The very word budget means "purse." It is derived from the old French word "bouge," which means "purse" or "pocketbook." Our budget is our national pocketbook. What goes in is part of the budget; what is taken out is part of the budget. And it can come out in many ways.

Senator Everett M. Dirksen of Illinois, 1959, during the debate on the Budget

* * *

One day General Lee was walking down the streets of Richmond during the War between the States, when it looked as if the South was going to win. One of his enthusiastic supporters met him and said, "General, as soon as this war is over we are going to elect you President to succeed Jefferson Davis." If you remember, we had a six-year term provided for in the constitution, and the President could not succeed himself. General Lee replied, "No, sir; I do not believe in military Presidents or political generals."

Representative John E. Rankin of Mississippi during the debate on the Marshall Plan, 1948

* * *

WHO OWNS FORMOSA ANYWAY?

On June 27, 1955 a mutual defense treaty with Nationalist China on the island of Formosa was engaging the wisdom of the Conscript Fathers. In a skirmish with Senator George H. Bender of Ohio, Senator Wayne L. Morse of Oregon elucidated the status of Formosa.

Mr. MORSE. The time has come to make it clear to the American people that this government is not going to war to protect Chiang on the Quemoys and Matsu. If he wants to stay there, let him stay there and take the consequences. We're not going to sacrifice American boys to keep him there.

Mr. BENDER. Is Chiang less reprehensible in Formosa than in the Quemoys? The Senator is painting a dreadful picture of Chiang, but Chiang is running the show in Formosa. When do we love Chiang and when do we stop loving him?

Mr. MORSE. I will not vote to get my country involved in civil war in China over Chiang. Formosa has nothing to do with the civil war in China. Formosa involves a territorial obligation of the United States, who are caretaker over that area until the United Nations disposes of Formosa. As a matter of international law we have not the slightest right to defend the Quemoys and Matsu because we have no sovereign right in them. They belong to China.

Mr. BENDER. Is it not a fact that Formosa was part of the Chinese Empire?

Mr. MORSE. Not at all.

Mr. BENDER. Seventy or eighty years before the Japanese took over.

Mr. MORSE. But China ceded it to the Japanese under solemn treaty.

Mr. BENDER. She ceded it to the Japanese when she had a pistol at her head.

Mr. MORSE. It was in settlement of a war.

Mr. BENDER. Formosa, on that basis, was certainly a part of the Chinese Empire.

Mr. MORSE. Not after she ceded it.

Mr. BENDER. The fact of the matter is that it was a part of the Chinese realm.

Mr. MORSE. Decades and decades ago, of course, it was, but it ceased to be when, by solemn treaty, Japan and China entered into a territorial settlement. Unfortunately, throughout history, the animalistic side of man has caused him to fight wars, and as a result of those wars there have been treaty settlements. Formosa thus became Japanese territory, and we joined in taking it away from Japan as a result of the peace treaty with Japan.

* * *

The very essence of a free government consists in considering offices as public trusts, to be bestowed for the good of the country, and not for the benefit of an individual or a party; and that system of political morals which regards offices to be used and enjoyed as their proper spoils, strikes a fatal blow at the very vitals of free institutions.

Senator John C. Calhoun of South Carolina, 1834

* * *

Why keep a minister resident at Liberia and have none at Hayti? My answer is this: that the colony of Liberia upon the African coast was planted by us; that it is one of the offsprings of the humanity of our people; that it was established under the auspices of some of the best and purest men of the past age; that it has encountered serious obstacles; its inhabitants were natives of our country; and, if by any means a representative of the United States can render assistance to these remote people struggling to establish a republic in Africa, I say we should extend to them all the aid in our power. We leave that mission untouched.

Representative William S. Holman of Indiana during the debate on the Diplomatic and Consular Appropriation, 1876

* * *

The law has been a little slow in coming to the protection of cheese—probably because many varieties of cheese have been thoroughly able to take care of themselves. It would seem, for example, that limburger cheese is endowed by nature with means of defense that require very little assistance from an act of Congress.

Representative Jonathan P. Dolliver of Iowa

* * *

Gentlemen, when you stand against this, you are standing against an elemental force as restless as the Gulf Stream; when you stand against this, you are standing against an enemy that is as powerful as the processes of nature. More than that, you are standing against a thing which, from a moral and intellectual point of view, is fundamentally right.

Senator Albert J. Beveridge of Indiana speaking in favor of the election of Senators by direct vote, 1901

* * *

While we have been "evoluting" toward a gold basis we have been evoluting toward that condition which has confronted all the nations of ancient times just before they lost their liberties. Evolution! It has been said that evolution comes from a full stomach, but there is another thing that comes from an empty stomach, and it is called Revolution.

Representative Joseph C. Sibley of Pennsylvania

* * *

"THERE IS NO SAFER INVESTMENT THAN BOOKS"

The bill authorizing construction of the Library of Congress had some difficulty in passing the legislative shoals and reefs of the House. Among its ardent supporters was the former

Confederate cavalry chieftain, Representative Joseph Wheeler of Alabama. His magnificent plea, in February 1883, for a building to accommodate the fast expanding library, might be said to have clinched the passage of the bill—and the erection of the wondrous Library of Congress. He closed his plea with his justly celebrated dissertation on books.

Wisdom is wealth, and every good book is equivalent to a wise head—the head may die, but the book may live forever.

The man Homer, the man Demosthenes, the man Plato, the man Burke, the man Clay, and the man Webster may die, but their books will live forever.

The wise economist, when he invests his money, wishes first to be safe. There is no safer investment, for a private or a public man, than books. A good book, in the hands of a studious and ambitious boy, is better for him than money at interest in a bank.

We are throwing off millions of money daily. Many of these millions go down into the waters of oblivion. We have millions of money for rivers and harbors; let us make one safe investment for books. We can do this by laying the foundation of this contemplated structure so deep and solid that it will endure for all time and still subserve the holy purposes for which it was erected.

You give millions of money for a great ship of war; that is a public necessity. No patriot complains at the cost. Yet that ship is a thing of frailty, and goes upon the waters with its doom written in advance, "*in gurgite vasto*." It may or may not make a history and save a state; but history or no history, its end is inevitable—to be buried in the deep or to rot in a dock. The millions that built it are gone forever, and there is absolutely nothing left of it but its name and the history of its cruises.

Not so with a great temple whose foundation is upon a solid rock, and whose materials are of imperishable substance.

Old Cheops lives in every slab that, inch by inch, rears the colossal pyramid. Nor winds, nor rains, nor storms, nor wars can move it from its base. There stands the original investment. Give us, not such a temple as that, to be forever shrouded in impenetrable mystery, but give a grand, solid, colossal structure, within whose marble arms we may safely hope to see, still preserved, in 1983, seventeen million of copyrighted American books.

* * *

You cannot fail to see the deep significance of the words once uttered by President Lincoln. One day shortly before his death after the commencement of his second Administration, he pointed out to a friend the crowd of office-seekers besieging his door and said to him, "Now we have mastered the rebellion; but there you see something that in the course of time may become far more dangerous to this Republic than the rebellion itself." And indeed, sir, he had a prophetic mind.

Senator Carl Schurz of Missouri, 1873

* * *

If we would pass fewer laws, and better mature those we do pass, it would be far better for the American people. Sir, this disregard for vested rights, this wild, reckless legislation under the whip and spur of your previous question, this usurpation of power by Congress, if persisted in, will certainly end in the overthrow not only of our great network of railroads, but will eventually result in injury to private as well as public rights, and change this government, with all its checks and balances, into a consolidated imperialism.

Representative Benjamin T. Biggs of Delaware, 1870

* * *

Mr. President, when a man becomes obsessed with the idea that he is running for President of the United States, he is all too apt to be influenced by some vain delusion, and is likewise too apt to think he promotes one vain delusion by exploiting another.

Senator William J. Stone of Missouri, 1916

* * *

The trouble with this resolution is that it comes nine years too late, and promises to hang the wrong outlaw in the event of a raid on Formosa. We are like the timid sheriff in a western town who is eager to string up the minor cattle thieves, but avoids any harsh words with the boss rustler who directs the whole thieving operation. Red Russia, of course, is the boss outlaw.

I have never known a real outlaw in my life to reform, and I don't expect that from the world's top outlaw, Russia. But Russia being the outlaw she is, is all the more reason why we should break off diplomatic relations with her now, send her spies and agents packing, and put her American agents in jail where they belong. That would have a more salutary effect on Red China than all the resolutions we could adopt in the Eighty-fourth Congress.

Senator George W. Malone of Nevada on a Resolution to use armed forces to defend Formosa, 1955

* * *

LIPSTICK, COLD CREAM, AND THE MARSHALL PLAN

The Marshall Plan for reviving the industrial life of war-torn Europe was running the Senate gantlet in 1948. Just why over a billion dollars worth of cigarettes, lipstick, and cold cream were included in this vast giveaway was not quite clear to all. Hence this pertinent query.

Mr. JENNER of Indiana. I like cigarettes, but I should like to have the Senator tell me what $900,000,000 worth of tobacco has to do with rebuilding the economy of Western Europe to withstand the onslaught of communism.

Mr. MALONE of Nevada. That's a tremendous lot of tobacco.

Mr. JENNER. Another item in this program is lipstick and cold cream. Does the Senator know about that one?

Mr. MALONE. The only lipstick in the Russian program that I recall reads like power machinery—high octane gas, refineries, tool steel, and so forth.

Mr. JENNER. I know of the British loan and the way it worked out. A great percentage of the money, which in all amounted to approximately four billion dollars, was for movies, cigarettes and cosmetics. In Indiana we like our women to look pretty, we like lipstick on them and we like rouge on them, but I want to know what lipstick and rouge have to do with rebuilding the productive ability of a nation to withstand communism.

Mr. MALONE. I cannot say how the State Department works, no. As the State Department now stands it is not bipartisan. It is a two-headed monstrosity.

Mr. KNOWLAND of California. As to the particular question raised by the Senator from Indiana, I think there is a legitimate place in the appropriations for something as incentive goods. In the Ruhr, the industrial heart of Germany, I checked to ascertain whether they had made any investigation as to the reason for the high rate of absenteeism.

They told me that in making a survey in one of the large Ruhr coal mines they went to the home of one of their miners to discover why he worked only two days a week, which was enough to give him the heavy miner's ration. A miner made about ten marks a day, which if he worked six days a week would mean sixty marks. As was found on investigation, this miner owned a hen. The hen laid five eggs a week. He ate one egg. The other four eggs he traded in the black market, five cigarettes for each egg. That gave him twenty cigarettes. He then traded in the black market the twenty cigarettes for eight marks apiece, and that gave him 160 marks. So his hen was earning two and a half times a week what he could earn by working in a coal mine.

I feel there is a legitimate need in this program of incentive goods—for a certain amount of tobacco, because if we can increase the productivity of the mines and industrial plants in the Ruhr Valley and other parts of Europe, so that more steel shall be produced, I think that will be a constructive solution.

Mr. JENNER. I think the reasoning which the able Senator from California has indulged in to the effect that furnishing of American cigarettes would increase productivity, also would apply to lipstick and cold cream, because I think the people of Europe would like to have their ladies beautiful. So I think it would be a further incentive for the people of Europe to produce more, if we were to include lipstick and cold cream in what we furnish to them. I think it might be well to include these two items in the Marshall Plan.

* * *

From the Seven Hills of Rome, down through the corridors of time, comes the story which Cicero relates from Thucydides: that a brazen monument was erected by the Thebans to celebrate their victory over the Lacedaemonians, but it was regarded as a memento to civil discord, and the trophy was abolished, because it was not fitting that any record should remain of the conflict between Greek and Greek.

Representative Samuel S. "Sunset" Cox of Ohio on the abolishment of test oaths and proscriptive laws, 1880

In my judgment, Mr. Speaker, there is but one standard in which the difference can be marked in the social standing of the human family, and I wish to draw that standard here, before the young men of the House, who, I trust, will be in it, its pride and glory, perhaps long years after many of us who are older have gone to the other land. There is just one standard of distinction, appropriately speaking, between the men in this world, and that is greater knowledge and better morals. To know more and do better. Everything else is subordinate to that. I do not care to go beyond that. Beyond that Mat Pryor's epitaph is good enough for me:

Here lie the bones of Mat Pryor,
Descended from Adam and Eve;
If anyone can rank higher,
I'm willing to give him leave.

Representative Jonathan S. Willis of Delaware

* * *

In the Lord's Prayer the sentence that always appealed to me stronger than any other is, "Lead us not into temptation," because if you are not led into temptation to do improper things you will get along very well.

Representative Joseph G. Cannon of Illinois

* * *

A TIME FOR DECISION

On June 14, 1960—with the Democratic presidential nomination virtually in the bag—Senator John F. Kennedy of Massachusetts rose to announce a twelve-point agenda for America that foreshadowed the pattern of world action he would propose should he be elected President. Not all who listened agreed with the Senator from Massachusetts, in particular Senator Homer E. Capehart of Indiana, who said as much.

Mr. KENNEDY. Mr. President, May 17, 1960, marked the end of an era—an era of illusion, the illusion that personal good will is a substitute for hard, carefully prepared bargaining on concrete issues, the illusion that good intentions and pious principles are a substitute for strong creative leadership.

For on May 17, 1960, the long-awaited, highly publicized summit conference collapsed. That collapse was the direct result of Soviet determination to destroy the talks. The insults and distortions of Mr. Khrushchev and the violence of his attacks shocked all Americans, and united the country in admiration for the dignity and self-control of President Eisenhower. Regardless of party, all of us deeply resented Russian abuse of this nation and its President, and all of us shared a common disappointment at the failure of the conference. Nevertheless, it is imperative that we, as a nation, rise above our resentment and frustration to a critical reexamination of the events at Paris and their meaning for America.

Thus, neither our smiles nor our frowns have ever altered Mr. Khrushchev's course, however he may alter his expression. His real goals have remained unmoved, his interests unchanged, his determination unending. And so long as Mr. Khrushchev is convinced that the balance of world power is shifting his way, no amount of either smiles or toughness, neither Camp David talks nor kitchen debates, can compel him to enter fruitful negotiations.

So let us abandon the useless discussion of who can best "stand up to Khrushchev," or whether a hard or soft line is preferable. Our task is to rebuild our strength and the strength of the free world—to prove to the Soviets that time and the course of history are not on their side, that the balance of world power is not shifting their way—and that, therefore, peaceful settlement is essential to mutual survival.

The hour is late, but the agenda is long.

First. We must make invulnerable a nuclear retaliatory power second to none—by making possible now a stopgap air alert and base-dispersal program, and by stepping up our development and production of the ultimate missiles that can close the gap and will not be wiped out in a surprise attack.

Second. We must regain the ability to intervene effectively and swiftly in any limited war anywhere in the world, augmenting, modernizing, and providing increased mobility and versatility for the conventional forces and weapons of our Army and Marine Corps.

Third. We must rebuild NATO into a viable and consolidated military force capable of deterring any kind of attack, unified in weaponry and responsibility.

Fourth. We must, in collaboration with Western Europe and Japan, greatly increase the flow of capital to the underdeveloped areas of Asia, Africa, the Middle East, and Latin America—frustrating the communist hopes for chaos in those nations.

Fifth. We must reconstruct our relations with the Latin American democracies, bringing them into full Western partnership.

Sixth. We must formulate, with both imagination and restraint, a new approach to the Middle East—not pressing our case so hard that the Arabs feel their neutrality and nationalism are threatened, but accepting those forces and seeking to help channel them along constructive lines, while at the same time trying to hasten the inevitable Arab acceptance of the permanence of Israel.

Seventh. We must greatly increase our efforts to encourage the newly emerging nations of the vast continent of Africa.

If our policies toward Africa are to be effective, we must extend this aid in terms of America's desire to bring freedom and prosperity to Africa—not in terms of a narrow self-interest which seeks only to use African nations as pawns in the cold war.

Eighth. We must plan a long-range solution to the problems of Berlin. We must show no uncertainty over our determination to defend Berlin and meet our commitments.

Ninth. We must prepare and hold in readiness more flexible and realistic tools for use in Eastern Europe.

Tenth. We must reassess a China policy which has failed dismally to move toward its principal objective of weakening communist rule in the mainland—a policy which has failed to prevent a steady growth in communist strength.

Eleventh. We must begin to develop new, workable programs for peace and the control of arms. We have been unwilling to plan for disarmament.

Twelfth, and finally, we must work to build the stronger America on which our ultimate ability to defend ourselves and the free world depends.

Mr. CAPEHART. Is it not a fact that practically all the problems that have been confronting this administration for the last eight years, such as the Berlin situation, the East German situation, the cold war, and all the problems that the able Senator from Massachusetts has discussed in his speech were inherited by the present administration, which has been endeavoring to solve the problems which existed eight years ago?

Mr. KENNEDY. Yes, I agree that the problem of Berlin was inherited. I would also agree that nothing has been changed, except a diminishing of the ability to bring about any difference in the status of Berlin and to insure greater security to the people.

Mr. CAPEHART. I do not find anything in the Senator's speech which is particularly new. I do not particularly find anything which he said that was not a problem eight years ago, following the recognition of Russia in 1933, the conferences which were held at Tehran and Yalta, and the concept of an administration which created the situation in which Berlin now is. Part of the control of Berlin was given to the communists, and the entire city of Berlin was surrounded by East Germany, which is controlled by the communists.

Those are things which were accomplished by former administrations. The present administration has tried to do something about them for eight years. Frankly, I will admit that the efforts of this administration have not been very successful.

Mr. KENNEDY. That is correct.

Mr. CAPEHART. I do not know of anyone at the moment who has any idea how to handle them.

I cannot quite compliment the Senator from Massachusetts, as some Senators did, upon his speech. I think he covered the entire waterfront. I think he promised something to everybody in the world. He covered the entire field.

I do not know where we would get enough money to do the things he talks about. I do not know how we could do them. Frankly, I believe that kind of speech leaves false hopes in the minds of the world. I think that is what has got us into trouble today.

In my opinion, we ought to quit promising a world with a fence around it to the people of the globe. I do not believe we have the resources to do that. We do not have the money or the resources.

If I understood the Senator's speech correctly, he was promising everything to Latin America, to Africa, to India, and to nations all over the world. He was going to solve the problems of those people. I think that leaves false hopes. It does more harm than good.

Mr. KENNEDY. I understand. In fact I am complimented by the fact that the Senator from Indiana has not complimented my speech. (Laughter.)

* * *

Was President Lincoln very wrong when once, in a moment of despair, he said with a grim humor, "I have discovered a good way of providing officers for this Government: put all the names of the applicants into one pepper-box and all the offices into another, and then shake the two, and make appointments just as the names and the offices happen to drop out together."

Senator Carl Schurz of Missouri, 1870

* * *

When the Athenians had suffered under the harsh laws of Draco they asked Solon to prepare for them a code of laws, and when they were completed they asked him, "Have you prepared for us the best laws which you could?" He replied "No, I have not, but I have prepared the best laws that the Athenians are able to bear." We are precisely in that situation today, and I hope my friend from Boston, the modern Athens of America, will yield to the example of the men who made Athens so distinguished.

Representative Newton M. Curtis of New York, 1893

* * *

Mr. President, it may be a defect in my education, but I have always believed that the humblest man in America had upon him the same obligations to do his duty at the general election that a Senator in the Congress of the United States has to do his duty here. There may be something that elevates a man above the great mass of humanity when he is elected to the Senate. Some of them seem to think so. I have read in a very excellent play by an immortal author of the man who climbs,

> But when he once attains the utmost round
> He then unto the ladder turns his back,
> Looks to the clouds, scorning the base degrees
> By which he did ascend.

But as for my part, the people who sent me to the Senate have exactly the same rights, duties, and responsibilities at home as I have here, and if the American citizen in the primary of his own party and at the general election does not do his duty, it is of small consequence how we do ours. Concede that we are the head—they are the heart and blood. Corrupt and stifle that, and the Senate becomes a matter of no national consequence. The attempt to differentiate between the duty of a Senator from the duty of a constituent when it comes to deciding the great affairs of this Republic will not be accepted by the American people.

Senator Joseph W. Bailey of Texas, 1907

* * *

A MISSOURI RECIPE FOR BANISHING CARE

No one could have depicted the homely virtues of "Missouri meerschaum" better than did Representative Clarence Cannon of Missouri during a 1960 session of Congress.

Mr. CANNON. Mr. Speaker, the repeal of this unnecessary and inequitable tariff on pipestems for corncob pipes further reduces the price of the components of this indispensable adjunct to human happiness.

Mr. Speaker, when the earliest pioneers from Virginia and the Carolinas first migrated to the motherly bosom of Missouri a century and a half ago, each settler brought with him a rifle, his Bible, and his pipe, and was equally proficient in the use of all three.

There on the fertile alluvial Mississippi and Missouri River bottoms and the rich loam of the Missouri uplands he found Indian maize yielding corn with cobs of such durable texture and generous proportions that he abandoned the colonial clay and briar bowls of the Old Dominion and adopted the Missouri meerschaum, which has become today the standard of pipe comfort, luxury, simplicity, economy, and enjoyment throughout the world.

Whether in London, or Shanghai, or San Francisco Bay, or the sidewalks of New York, buy a pipe at the nearest tobacconist's, and on the bottom of it you will read "Made in Missouri."

Fill it up with the golden flakes of your favorite smoke, preferably old homespun from a Missouri hillside, aged and ripened and mellowed in the top rafters of an ancient log tobacco barn, and it will give you such joy and solace as it is seldom human privilege to enjoy.

Mr. Speaker, I have placed an assortment of this exceptional product of Missouri's soil and industry in the cloakroom, and shall be glad to have the members of the House avail themselves of the opportunity to sample one of them. When you get crosswise with life, or digestion is bad; when things go wrong and you want to kick the dog; when the wife is critical and your best friends are out of town, tamp down an extra-heavy charge in one of these friendly pipes and light it with a coal from the fireplace, and peace and contentment will attend you like a benediction. Cares will vanish in dissolving rings of fragrant blue, and life once more will be worth the living.

* * *

Mr. President, I remember a story about the first Napoleon which I am sometimes reminded of in these criticisms of the Chief Magistrate. He was walking one day with a beautiful lady of high rank, when a workman came along with a heavy burden on his shoulder. The haughty beauty kept the narrow path and was for making the poor man step out of the way, that she need not soil her dainty shoes by stepping in the mud. "Madam," said the Emperor, "respect the burden."

Senator George F. Hoar of Massachusetts, 1896

WHAT? CENSOR "MY OLD KENTUCKY HOME"?

In 1957 when the broadcasting networks decreed censorship for Stephen Foster's exquisite songs, a son of Old Kentucky in the House, Frank L. Chelf, rose to protest. Nor was he alone.

Mr. CHELF. Mr. Speaker, it has just come to my attention that the songs written by that great and outstanding composer, Stephen Collins Foster, most especially "Swanee River," "My Old Kentucky Home," and "Ol' Black Joe," three magnificent, beautiful, sweet, and lovely old songs, have been censored, and if not rewritten, they are to be banned from the air by the two big networks.

For anybody to say that the words of that beautiful old folksong, "Swanee River," and the gentle, kind, sympathetic, heartwarming, refreshing, dedicated words, penned by Foster, to that melodious tune known as "My Old Kentucky Home" —the state song of my beloved Kentucky—are detrimental or harmful to the colored race or to any race, contains about as much fact and truth as the gold fillings that are to be found in the teeth of a dead dickey-bird.

"My Old Kentucky Home" is more than just a song, a tune; it is a ritual; it is an integral part of America; it is part of her background, her folklore, her culture, her customs, her foundation, her very being, but yet these uninformed New York officials say it has to be rewritten. If we are going to change every song that has something in it that somebody does not like, there are not enough rewrite men in America to even get the project started.

* * *

Mr. Speaker, since I have been a member of this House I have repeatedly heard the merchants, bankers, and businessmen of my state called shylocks, extortioners, gold bugs, monopolists, robber barons. I threw back these epithets to the men who made them, and I say that there are not on the face of the earth more honorable, enterprising, just, and honest men than bankers, merchants, and businessmen of Massachusetts.

When the yellow wings of pestilence flap themselves in a Southern sky, when earthquake, or fire, or famine, or flood overtake any sections of the country, North or South, where do they go for relief? Who pours out its treasure like water to relieve the distressed? Why, those same "gold bugs," "shylocks," "extortioners," and "robber barons." Who builds your Western and Southern railroads? Who laid the iron rails across the continent? Why, these same "robber barons" that we hear denounced on this floor. Why, this talk makes me tired.

Representative Elijah A. Morse
of Massachusetts, 1895

* * *

Historians have noted that the highest civilization was reached in rainless lands. There is a reason for that, Mr. President, because in lands where God sends the rain to enrich the soil the tiller of the soil is enervated. He goes out and looks up to the sky and says to his sons, "Well, please God, send a rain storm and we will make a crop," or "Please God, no more rain and our crop will be saved." But in rainless lands, where irrigation is practiced, the husbandman at six o'clock in the morning says, "Up boys and turn the water on, and by our own energy we will make a crop," and crop failures are never known. There is thus a significant physical reason why in rainless lands men should develop to a stancher and more self-reliant type.

Senator William V. Allen of
Nebraska

* * *

WHERE IS BEHIND BULL RUN?

They called it the Third Battle of Bull Run, the interminable debate on restoring Major General Fitz-John Porter to rank. Porter was charged with disobedience at Second Bull Run and cashiered on the spot. It took twenty years to win vindication at the hands of Congress; the whole battle was refought on the floor of the Senate and House in the 1880's. In the Senate John A. Logan of Illinois, himself a Civil War general of no mean ability, fought Porter's vindication every step of the way. Here is an exchange with Senator William J. Sewell of New Jersey.

Mr. LOGAN. The joint order, which the Senator tries to confine me to, is the joint order to Generals Porter and McDowell, requiring them not to go beyond a certain distance on the road to Gainesville, so that they could that night, if necessary, fall behind Bull Run. The Senator knows, if he will examine the map, that Manassas Junction is not behind Bull Run.

Mr. SEWELL. It is in the direction of Bull Run.

Mr. LOGAN. I beg your pardon. I state it as it is. He was to fall behind Bull Run.

Mr. SEWELL. I would state to the Senator from Illinois that I have been up and down that country one hundred times and I probably know as much about it as he does.

Mr. LOGAN. It is very likely. Well, is Manassas behind Bull Run?

Mr. SEWELL. No, sir. It is in the direction of Bull Run.

Mr. LOGAN. That is what I was saying, is it not?

Mr. SEWELL. It was the line of retreat of Porter.

Mr. LOGAN. I say it is not behind Bull Run. He had no order to fall back to Manassas. He had orders of the kind that they should go on the road to Gainesville and make connection with the left of Pope's army, and to make connection in such a way they could fall behind Bull Run that night. Is not that so?

Mr. SEWELL. Yes.

Mr. LOGAN. Manassas was not behind Bull Run. Bull Run was over to the right and to get behind Bull Run they would have to go down the Warrenton Pike. This is an entirely different road, going in a different direction, not going towards Bull Run. Bull Run was over to the right.

Mr. SEWELL. Does the Senator from Illinois wish to convey the impression that you could not get to Bull Run by Manassas?

Mr. LOGAN. I try to convey the impression that Manassas is not behind Bull Run. Does the Senator pretend the troops were required to fall behind Bull Run that night? They had no orders to fall behind Bull Run. And when the whole army of Pope was engaged in battle, when none of them fell behind Bull Run, but remained on the battlefield and fought the battle of the 30th—south of Bull Run, not behind Bull Run—will the Senator claim that Porter must fall behind Bull Run when the whole army was engaged and none of them went back? If that is the construction of this order, that construction would have put the whole army behind Bull Run that night, for it was intended when the order was given that the whole army might fall back behind Bull Run if it had to fall back.

* * *

The most interesting character which has ever been portrayed by human genius and germane to this discussion is Wilkins Micawber. He was always indulging in long, windy speeches; always voraciously hungry; always hounded by numerous creditors; always expecting something to turn up to relieve his situation; always paid his debts by giving his note, and when the note fell due always gave a new note in exchange, exclaiming as he did so, "Thank God! There's another debt paid!" He was the type and ideal of a vast number of the financiers of the world, and if his life-size bust does not adorn the room of the Committee on Banking and Currency there has been a gross disregard of the eternal fitness of things.

The history of the world is filled with Micawbers, who have discharged their debts by promises to pay, and nations have been the chief imitators of this historical character. The Carthaginians wrote their promises on leather; the Romans, in their palmiest days, on strings of wood; the Moguls, on mulberry bark; the semi-civilized citizens of sundry lands on the skins of animals; and their lineal successors in the Bureau of Engraving and Printing put theirs on paper. The greatest of all the apostles of paper money was old Kublai Khan, whom Coleridge has immortalized, who issued during his brief reign more than $600,000,000 of mulberry bark legal tender notes, which went:

> Where Alf the sacred river ran,
> Through caverns measureless to man
> Down to a sunless sea.

The fiat money of all ages and climes has gone down the same dark and fathomless abyss.

Representative Frank E. Beltzhoover of Pennsylvania, 1895, during the interminable silver-gold debates

* * *

"FIRST CAST OUT THE BEAM OUT OF THINE OWN EYE"

The blockade mounted by the Southern Senators against civil rights legislation in March 1960 brought on many a skirmish and occasionally a splotch of humor. Even the Bible got into the debate. In a crossfire between Senators Russell B. Long of

Louisiana and Paul H. Douglas of Illinois, the former demonstrated that he knew his Bible as well as had his uproarious uncle who had preceded him in the upper chamber.

Mr. LONG. I hope I can find the quotation from the Sermon on the Mount. I think it so aptly applies to the situation involved in the civil rights case. I do not want to make a mistake in quoting the Bible. I think when we quote Jesus, we ought to try to be accurate about it. I am quoting from the Holy Word itself, Matthew, Chapter 7, the Sermon on the Mount:

> Judge not, that ye be not judged.
>
> For with what judgment ye judge, ye shall be judged; and with what measure ye mete, it shall be measured to you again.
>
> And why beholdest thou the mote that is in thy brother's eye, but considerest not the beam that is in thine own eye?

Mr. President, some folks who may not be Bible readers may not know what a mote is. A mote is a teeny, teeny speck of dust. "Teeny" means it is almost impossible to see with the naked eye. If a person can see it at all, he is lucky.

On the other hand, the beam, the other Biblical term referred to, is a fairly good-sized piece of wood, I suppose about the size of a splinter. Jesus said to the people, in his Sermon on the Mount:

> And why beholdest thou the mote–

this little speck of dust–

> that is in thy brother's eye, but considerest not the beam that is in thine own eye?
>
> Or how wilt thou say to thy brother–

Jesus goes on to say:

> Or how wilt thou say to thy brother, Let me pull out the mote out of thine eye, and, behold, a beam is in thine own eye?
>
> Thou hypocrite–

That is not addressed to any Senator; that is Jesus talking to the people in general—

> Thou hypocrite, first cast out the beam out of thine own eye; and then shalt thou see clearly to cast out the mote out of thy brother's eye.

The Senators from New York State tell us that we ought to do something about four little parishes in Louisiana where twenty thousand colored persons do not qualify as voters. Yet in their own state of New York there are 618,000 Puerto Ricans who cannot qualify because the laws of the state prohibit them from doing so.

Jesus said:

> Thou hypocrite, first cast out the beam out of thine own eye; and then shalt thou see clearly to cast out the mote out of thy brother's eye.

In other words, let New York State first take care of its 618,000 Puerto Ricans. After New York has done that, she will be better able to tell the folks in Louisiana how to deal with four little river parishes where twenty thousand colored folks live.

Mr. DOUGLAS. I have been greatly impressed with the Biblical knowledge exhibited and the evangelical discourse given by my great friend from Louisiana in quoting from the sayings of Jesus. But I think the Senator also realizes, does he not, that Jesus did not say, "Thou shalt not cast the beam out of thine eye because there is a mote in thine eye"?

Mr. LONG. No. The Senator is quite correct. Jesus said, "First cast out the beam out of thine own eye." One had to do that first. That is what I am trying to tell the Senator.

Look; here is the Civil Rights Commission's report. I did not have anything to do with it. I did not even vote for it. Senators stood here and fought this thing for months, and forced some of us to submit ourselves to it. We did not approve of it.

Look what this commission said about Chicago, from whence comes the distinguished Senator from Illinois.

I skip a couple of paragraphs, and find it says:

> The general metropolitan residential pattern shows Chicago . . . on the basis of census maps, to be the most residentially segregated city in America.

Imagine that. We have an area where they say segregation is evil, and the largest city up there, the second largest city in the entire United States, is said to be the most segregated city in America. Look at the map, and there it is. Some persons talk about segregated schools. That is what they have in Chicago.

Mr. DOUGLAS. The segregation which does exist in Chicago is not a legal segregation. People are free to live as they wish, and though there is opposition to Negroes moving into white neighborhoods, they are accorded police protection. The segregation which exists in many of our southern states—and I am not indicting the South—is a legal segregation, and there is a great deal of difference between these two types of segregation.

Mr. LONG. Mr. President, I wish I could quote the language, which I learned from the Senator from Illinois, the distinguished scholar and student, who tells us of the magnificent impartiality of the law, which prevents princes and paupers alike from sleeping under bridges and permits them to walk in the rain for lack of shelter.

Mr. DOUGLAS. Mr. President, the Senator is more an expert on the Bible than he is on the writings of Anatole France. The quotation which I gave was from Anatole France's novel, *The Red Lily*, which speaks of the majestic equality of the laws, which prohibit the rich as well as the poor from sleeping under bridges and begging in the streets for bread.

Mr. LONG. I am glad the Senator quoted correctly, because I want it for the *Record*. The point I am getting to is this: Look at Chicago; look at it. Look where the colored men live, and look where the white people live. The colored go to segregated schools; there are nobody but colored folks in the schools, because they keep all the colored in the same areas.

Mr. DOUGLAS. Mr. President, I must protest. We do not keep Negroes in segregated districts. They are free legally to move.

Mr. LONG. They just cannot get there. (Laughter.) What I am trying to say is this: If segregation is evil, why do you practice it in Chicago?

Mr. DOUGLAS. Mr. President, may I make a reply? It so happens, in the section of Chicago in which my wife and I live, that about fifty percent of the persons who reside in that area are Negroes, and that in the public school which is nearest to our apartment, the students are perhaps sixty percent Negroes.

It is an integrated community. I frankly admit that over the years that this has been happening, we have had our difficulties. But we have carried through with it. We believe we shall be successful in it. And the relationships between the races are much better than they would have been if we had used either force or the pressure of law to maintain it as an all-white community.

Mr. LONG. All I did was read the report.

It asks where segregation exists. It says more is found in the second largest city in the country—Chicago. And the report also describes the practices in New York.

I think the Senator will be fair enough to admit that in most instances the colored children in Chicago are going to schools in the areas shown in black on the map, where the schools are practically confined to Negro children.

Mr. President, I have had occasion to speak to people from

various large cities who tell us how the school-board members gerrymander the school districts, so that almost all the white children attend white schools, and almost all the colored children attend colored schools, Negro schools.

But the Good Book tells us that Jesus said:

> Thou hypocrite, first cast out the beam out of thine own eye; and then shalt thou see clearly to cast out the mote out of thy brother's eye.

Mr. DOUGLAS. Well–

Mr. LONG. Mr. President, I have not been quoting any remarks by the Senator from Illinois. I have been quoting what Jesus said, as it is recorded in the Bible, in the Book of Matthew.

Mr. DOUGLAS. But I remind the Senator from Louisiana that he should worry more about removing the beam from his own eye.

Mr. LONG. But, Mr. President, I have not urged the enactment of five pounds of bills, in an effort to tell someone else how to run his own business.

I ask Senators just to look at all these five pounds or more of bills–bills introduced and proposed and urged by certain Senators who are trying to tell someone else how to run his own business.

Mr. President, some of these bills are so-called antilynching bills. But there has been only one lynching in the Southern states in the last five years.

Mr. DOUGLAS. Two.

Mr. LONG. Well, certainly there has been only one in the last three years; I know that, for sure.

Mr. President, I ask Senators to consider that situation–one lynching in three years, contrasted with an annual average of six thousand murders in the United States. Murders occur daily in New York City. I should imagine that even a colored man would be much more interested in protection from a mugging—which is likely to happen to him at any moment in New York City—rather than to have further protection by law against a lynching, inasmuch as only one lynching has occurred anywhere in the entire nation in the last three years.

Yet certain of the laws now proposed, by means of these more than five pounds of bills, are designed to provide further protection by law against lynching—which is the rarest sort of crime—whereas in the nation there are an average of six thousand murders a year. But, despite that, some persons hope to send agents of the federal government into the South, to protect against one lynching in three years, whereas six thousand murders are occurring in the nation each year. Furthermore, there seems to be very little interest in calling in the FBI to solve the six thousand murders each year. Certainly I would be much more interested in protection against a mugging or a cutting or a killing—any one of which is very likely to happen to me if I live in one of the large northern cities—rather than in having further protection by law against a lynching, inasmuch as only one lynching has occurred in the entire nation in the last three years.

So, Mr. President, why should anyone be anxious to urge the enactment of an antilynching law? Well, Mr. President, the reason is politics—politics.

* * *

I will tell you about judges. You can take the most mild-mannered and tender-hearted man you ever saw, make him a judge for life, and his disposition to tyrannize over people will grow with what he feeds on.

Representative Champ Clark of
Missouri, 1919

* * *

"Good men" are sometimes prophets of evil. During our Revolutionary War, good men predicted that it would result in the destruction of what few liberties our ancestors then enjoyed. During the formation of our Constitution, "good men" predicted that instead of being the shield of liberty it would prove to be the sword of tyranny. When Washington was President some "good men" declared he was no better than a king. And when Jefferson became President some "good men" branded him as an emperor. Some "good men" denounced Andrew Jackson as a tyrant and a usurper. Some "good men" charged that Abraham Lincoln was a despot. Some "good men" predicted that if Grant were elected President he would overturn the Constitution and we would never elect another President.

And now, Mr. Speaker, some of these same "good men" are calling William McKinley an "emperor," and are prophesying that he will destroy our Constitution and rob us of our liberties.

Representative Henry R. Gibson
of Tennessee, 1900

* * *

There is implanted in the breast of man a monitor called conscience. Its prickings may be deadened and its voice stifled for the time, but its presence and power will ever and anon proclaim itself.

> The secret which the murderer possesses soon comes to possess him, and like the evil spirit of which we read it overcomes him and leads him whithersoever it will. He feels it beating at his heart, rising in his throat, demanding disclosure. He thinks the whole world sees it in his face, reads it in his eyes, and almost hears its workings in the very silence of his thoughts. It has become his master. It betrays his discretion, it breaks down his courage, it conquers his prudence. When suspicions from without begin to embrace him, and the net

of circumstances to entangle him, the fatal secret struggles with greater violence to break forth. It must be confessed, it will be confessed; there is no refuge from confession but suicide, and suicide is confession.

Thus spoke the immortal Webster while painting the powers of conscience!

Representative Edward S. Bragg
of Wisconsin, 1884

* * *

In 1935 President F. D. Roosevelt sent a message to the Senate urging entry into the World Court. Presidents Harding, Coolidge, and Hoover had stumbled over the same hurdle. More than sixty thousand telegrams of protest against President Roosevelt's proposal flooded Congress. Senator Hiram W. Johnson of California voiced his opposition in these prophetic words.

We are dealing today with one simple proposition: Shall we go into foreign politics? Once we are in, it does not make any difference whether we are in a little way or whether we are in a long way, or whether we have gone into one appendage of the League of Nations or whether we have gone into the League–once we are in, we are in. And when we are in, then, of course, all the internationalists in this land will tell the necessity that exists for us to perform our moral obligations and, if necessary, become a part of the intrigue, the controversies, the broils, and ultimately the wars on the other side of the ocean.

Less elegantly, Senator Huey Long of Louisiana exclaimed:

We are being rushed pell-mell to get into this thing so that Señor Ab Jab or some other something from Japan can pass upon our controversies.

Blind Senator Thomas D. Schall of Minnesota put it even more succinctly:

To Hell with Europe and the rest of those nations.

* * *

THEY LAUGHED IN DECEMBER 1899

John J. Fitzgerald of Massachusetts was not elected to Congress for his ability as a prophet, but he apparently struck a vein in the last sentence of his salutation to the departing Nineteenth Century.

Think for a moment what a hundred years has brought forth. This century received from its predecessor the horse; we bequeath the bicycle, the locomotive, and the automobile. We received the goosequill; we bequeath the typewriter. We received the scythe; we bequeath the mowing machine. We received the sickle; we bequeath the harvester. We received the hand printing press; we bequeath the Hoe cylinder press. We received painted canvas; we bequeath lithography, photography, and color photography. We received the cotton and wool loom; we bequeath the factory.

We received gunpowder; we bequeath nitroglycerine. We received the tallow dip; we bequeath the arc light. We received the flintlock; we bequeath the automatic firing gun. Receiving nothing, we bequeath the anaesthetic properties of sulphur ether, by means of which to a great extent human life has been saved and pain prevented. We received the beacon signal; we bequeath the telephone and wireless telegraphy. We received ordinary light; we bequeath the X-ray. We received the old-fashioned sailing ship; we bequeath the ocean greyhound and freight leviathan.

Perhaps with the coming of the twentieth century airships

may be invented to sail from this country to other parts of the world. (Laughter.)

* * *

The communist threat is a global one. Its successful advance in one sector threatens the destruction of every other sector. You cannot appease or otherwise surrender to communism in Asia without simultaneously undermining our efforts to halt its advance in Europe. (Applause.)

It has been said in effect that I was a warmonger. Nothing could be further from the truth. I know war as few other men now living know it, and nothing to me is more revolting. I have long advocated its complete abolition, as its very destructiveness on both friend and foe has rendered it useless as a means of settling international disputes.

But once war is forced upon us, there is no other alternative than to apply every available means to bring it to a swift end. War's very object is victory—not prolonged indecision. (Applause.) In war, indeed, there can be no substitute for victory. (Applause.)

General of the Army Douglas MacArthur, 1951, before the Joint Congress

* * *

Do you not see what my constituent asks me to do? He wants Congress to act as censor and take out the objectionable parts of television programs. Well, I do not know the people who are putting out the comic strips. I do not read them. So I could not write them and in that way stop the practice. Nor do I think Congress can do an effective job. Why doesn't Dad just turn off the objectionable programs and say to the kids, "Now, you have seen enough for tonight," instead of writing to his Congressman?

Congress should not be required to enter the house, and,

assuming the duties of parents, tell the children what they can or cannot see or hear. Should we attempt to censor all these things we could get into a terrific fix. We do not have to buy them for the child. We do not have to permit them to look at television when we think it is wrong.

Representative Clare E. Hoffman of Michigan, 1952, commenting on the idea of investigating the immoral matter in "certain phases of current literature"

* * *

I do not want to weary the House. You may say, here is a great capitalist and his children do not do anything. They grow up in the main men of no account, but the men who are doing things in the United States—four fifths of them today in the House—very largely are the children of what are called poor parents. They contributed their effort to keep the wolf from the door, and frequently got far better education than they can get in any high school or college in this country.

Go about your streets here; take the boys that we are sorry for. I am not sorry as a rule for the poor man's children—children that hustle to earn the value of a dollar or a nickel. I am sorry for the rich man's children that do not do something by honest toil to help support the family. (Applause.)

Representative Joseph G. Cannon of Illinois, 1901

* * *

THE GREENBACK DISTANCE TO THE MOON

If the imagination of Representative J. Proctor Knott of Kentucky reeled before the magnitude of the national debt in 1875, one wonders what it might do today.

We are informed by the Secretary of the Treasury that our bonded debt amounts to about $2,500,000,000. Have you, sir, any conception of the magnitude of that sum? Has any gentleman here? I make no imputation upon your intellect when I say you do not. Try if you can realize it unit by unit. Can you do it? Sir, it is not within the power of the human intellect. The brain reels beneath the immensity of the conception. You had as well undertake to number the seconds on the dial of eternity.

There is one way, however, and only one way by which the human intellect can approach a realization of the magnitude of this sum; and that is by comparison. Each greenback dollar bill is about seven inches in length. Now, place two thousand five hundred millions of them in a line, and you will find it will be over two hundred and fifty thousand miles long! Geographers tell us it is twenty-five thousand miles around the earth. Our public debt would therefore make a band of greenback dollars that could encircle this globe more than ten times. It is said to be two hundred and forty thousand miles from the earth to the moon. If this is so, our debt would make a rope of greenback dollars long enough to cable the moon to the earth, and have over ten thousand miles to sag!

* * *

THE FAMOUS FIVE

On March 2, 1959 the Senate stood in a body in the Reception Room to dedicate portraits of the most famous five in its history. These portraits were painted to adorn five unfilled spaces on the walls of the reception room. Chairman of the committee charged with the selections was Senator John F. Kennedy of Massachusetts. Ordered the Senate, "It shall be the duty of the committee to select five outstanding persons from all persons, but not a living person, who have served as Mem-

bers of the Senate whose paintings shall occupy these spaces in the Reception Room." Senator Kennedy thus announced the selection of the Famous Five:

These are the five men whom the Senate honors today. This nation, I know, will honor for all time to come these men and all those who seek to follow in their hard path. (Applause.)

Henry Clay of Kentucky, probably the most gifted parliamentary figure in the history of the Congress, whose tireless devotion to the Union demonstrated that intelligent compromise required both courage and conviction.

Daniel Webster of Massachusetts, the eloquent and articulate champion of "Liberty and Union, now and forever, one and inseparable."

John C. Calhoun of South Carolina, the intellectual leader and logician of those defending the rights of a political minority against the dangers of an unchecked majority.

Robert M. La Follette, Sr., of Wisconsin, a ceaseless battler for the underprivileged in an age of special privilege, a courageous independent in an era of conformity, who fought memorably against tremendous odds and stifling inertia for the social and economic reforms which ultimately proved essential to American progress in the twentieth century.

And, finally, Robert A. Taft of Ohio, the conscience of the conservative movement and its most constructive leader, whose high integrity transcended partisanship, and whose analytical mind candidly and courageously put principle above ambition.

BITS OF GIVE-AND-TAKE

THE BRITISH RETREATED

Senator Henry Clay of Kentucky delighted in interrupting the grave routine or heated debate in the chamber with gibes at Senator James Buchanan of Pennsylvania for the latter's supposed disloyalty in the War of 1812. On one occasion, Buchanan, an old Federalist, to prove his loyalty, stated he had joined a volunteer company and marched to the defense of Baltimore.

Mr. BUCHANAN. True, I was not in any engagement, as the British had retreated before I got there.

Mr. CLAY. You marched to Baltimore, though?

Mr. BUCHANAN. Yes, sir.

Mr. CLAY. Armed and equipped?

Mr. BUCHANAN. Yes, armed and equipped.

Mr. CLAY. But the British had retreated before you arrived?

Mr. BUCHANAN. Yes.

Mr. CLAY. Will the Senator from Pennsylvania be good enough to inform us whether the British retreated in consequence of his valiantly marching to the relief of Baltimore, or whether he marched to the relief of Baltimore in consequence of the British having already retreated?

* * *

In 1846 William Sawyer, a member of the House from the Ohio backwoods, who brought a snack of sausage and hominy each day, soon acquired the nickname, "Sausage." He rose one day to protest that the Democrats had spent lots of time and money to elect President Polk, but that the Whigs still held 235 of the 730 clerkships in Washington. He was interrupted.

A MEMBER. How do you know they are Whigs?

Mr. SAWYER. Don't I know a Whig from a Democrat as far as I can see him? (The House in a roar.)

A MEMBER. How can you tell one from the other?

Mr. SAWYER. Just as easy as you can tell one of your sheep from the others; or just as well as you can tell a racehorse from a workhorse. A Whig always dresses up fine, or better than Democrats do, and looks like he thought he knew more and was a great deal better than a Democrat. They ain't plain folks like we are.

(Roars of laughter from all sides, and the galleries.)

* * *

Representative William D. "Pig Iron" Kelley of Pennsylvania added a laurel or two to his fame in this brief exchange with Kentucky Democrat William C. P. Breckinridge.

Mr. KELLEY. We made in 1887 more than half the steel that was made on the face of God's footstool. More than half!

Mr. BRECKINRIDGE. How much does my venerable friend say the half of the steal was?

Mr. KELLEY. Oh, that is a beautiful pun, that is a sweet play upon a word, and if there was a prohibitory duty on the flowers of rhetoric, my friend from Kentucky would have much cause to complain.

* * *

PIGS IN THE PARLOR IN THE NINETIES

Mr. MILLIKEN of Maine. My friend from Mississippi has reflected upon me because I said I would not put a hogpen in the parlor. He seems to disagree with me in that respect. He and I have different tastes. Possibly there is a difference of taste between his people and mine. We do not do that in my state. He cannot go through my state as I have gone through his from the south end to the north, and seen pigs running into the dooryards and kitchens. We do not have that in my state.

Mr. STOCKDALE of Mississippi. What were you doing in the kitchens of my state?

Mr. MILLIKEN. I have to say that what I saw in the gentleman's state was what I saw riding along in the cars. I did not get off the cars and so did not go into any of the kitchens. Indeed there was nothing enticing, to induce a person to go in, which I saw.

Mr. STOCKDALE. Now, so far as the gentleman from Maine has described his trip, I did not object to that. He said he did not see anything enticing in the kitchens; that was because he did not look anywhere else. (Laughter.) I want to say that the people do not eat clams down there, and if you speak to a man from Maine about making a meal on anything but clams it turns his stomach. I do not object to the gentleman going through without getting off the train in Mississippi —I only sympathize with the people where he was going.

Mr. MILLIKEN. I do not desire to insult the people of the state of Mississippi through my good friend from Mississippi, and therefore I will not reply to him in the manner of his own speech. I might possibly say that it would be good for the yellow in his eyes and in his complexion, if he could get down into the fresh sea breezes of Maine and eat our clams instead of the hog and hominy he eats in his own state, but I will not say that because it would not be very respectful to him or to his people. I have been through his state, and he has not been within five hundred miles of mine.

* * *

The gentleman from Ohio said that the sheep of Ohio were better than the sheep of Texas, and he presumed that it was because they were better civilized. Mr. Speaker, I thank the gentleman for the compliment which followed it. He then said that the delegation from Texas—I appropriate none of it to myself—was one of the best in this body. It explains, Mr. Speaker, the difference between Ohio and Texas. While Ohio has cultivated the civilization of her sheep, Texas has cultivated the manhood and the civilization of her citizens under free institutions.

Representative Joseph C. Hutcheson of Texas replying to an invidious remark about Texas mutton by Representative George W. Wilson of Ohio

* * *

WHO SURRENDERED AT APPOMATTOX, LEE OR GRANT?

There seemed to be a divergence of opinion in the House as to what happened at Appomattox in 1865. Witness this skirmish in 1895 between W. Jasper Talbert of South Carolina and William P. Hepburn of Ohio.

Mr. TALBERT. I want to deny that the South was responsible for the war.

Mr. HEPBURN. Ah, in the light of history, do you say that?

Mr. TALBERT. I do.

Mr. HEPBURN. Yet, notwithstanding all, when you were crouching at the feet of our power, not "worn out trying to whip us" as the gentleman from South Carolina said but when your power was utterly annihilated, when there was no man in all your borders who was not ready to accept any terms, you were reestablished in all your old forfeited rights, not a man was punished, you were given absolute amnesty, your states were permitted to be represented, not a dollar's worth of confiscation was made, but everything restored to you in the same ample manner as though it were Grant who had surrendered at Appomattox instead of Lee.

Mr. TALBERT. Were not those the terms of the surrender?

Mr. HEPBURN. No, sir.

Mr. TALBERT. I thought those were the terms.

Mr. HEPBURN. The terms were unconditional surrender, the only terms Grant ever accepted. In his first experience with you three years before, he demanded unconditional surrender at Fort Donelson and you complied. He demanded the same kind of surrender at Appomattox and again you yielded.

Mr. TALBERT. I thought the war was over.

Mr. HEPBURN. Yes, it would be if you people would let it.

* * *

THERE WAS NO ANSWER

Believe it or not, the House was debating the Chinese Exclusion Act in 1893 when the Pilgrims suddenly appeared on the scene.

Mr. [Elijah A.] MORSE of Massachusetts. Mr. Speaker, a great son of my state, John A. Andrew, the great war governor of Massachusetts, a man of giant mind and genius, the great Andrew, said shortly before his death, "I know not what record of sin awaits me in another world, but this I do know: I never despised any man because he was poor, black, or ignorant." And I think he spoke the sentiment of the people of Massachusetts.

Mr. [John L.] WILSON of Washington. The gentleman must know in speaking of the red man, or perhaps he remembers the fact in history—that the first thing the white people did in his region of the country was to fall on their knees and then on the aborigines.

Mr. MORSE. That is a slander on the good old Pilgrims of Massachusetts. Has the gentleman read the history of the country? Does he know the facts?

Mr. WILSON. Yes, sir. I have read the history of the Pequots and the Narragansetts and some other Indians who inhabited that region.

Mr. MORSE. Has the gentleman read that for fifty years after the Pilgrims landed at Plymouth Rock they had a treaty with Massasoit, the great chief, and for all time lived in peace and quiet with him and the Indians of Massachusetts? Has the gentleman read the history of the great commonwealth of Massachusetts?

Mr. WILSON. I have. Nothing is further from my thoughts than to misrepresent the good old commonwealth, but when you drove the Narragansetts and Pequots and others, with their friends, west of the Mississippi River you put the burden of caring for them upon us. Let me ask the gentleman: where are the descendants of the Pequots today?

Mr. MORSE. The discussion of the North American Indian is hardly germane to this discussion.

* * *

"WHO STAYED AT HOME AND PLEADED THE BABY ACT"

Senator and former Confederate general John Tyler Morgan of Alabama was a fearless scrapper. He graced and enlivened the Senate for nearly thirty years; the news that he was to speak packed the galleries. The year 1893 saw him in a historic clash with New York's Senator David Bennett Hill, himself a sharpshooter in any fight. In a filibuster against the silver purchase repeal bill, Senator Morgan vowed to die in the breach. Hill struck back at him viciously, "below the belt" some said, with a reference to Morgan's disattachment from the United States Constitution for four years of civil war. Here are the final volleys in this memorable tilt.

Mr. HILL. Mr. President, the Senator from Alabama spoke —yea, boasted—of his lifelong devotion to the Constitution of the United States. It may be so. I supposed that for a very brief period my friend was supporting another constitution, but I may be mistaken. (Laughter and applause in the gallery.)

The Senator spoke of the wrongs that were about to be perpetrated by this body in the passing of the pending bill. If his contention about these rules is correct, then there is no possible danger of any wrong being perpetrated, because if the view taken by him is correct there seems to be no method provided by which we can reach a result. Therefore, if that is true, he can with the utmost safety repeat the statement in imitation of another distinguished Senator from that state, that if we pass the pending bill in the manner suggested by me and under a construction of the rules, we must walk over his dead body. I do not believe it. It is an idle threat. I have heard of statesmen before who were going to die in the last ditch, but there are some of them alive now.

Mr. MORGAN. Mr. President, I do not have so much respect for those men who are constantly quoting that difficulty whenever they have an opportunity to make a point on a brother Senator or anybody about it, but who did not have the pluck to shoulder a gun to go out to fight. My respect does not extend to that class in the cordial way that it does to men like Morrison, Randall, Palmer, and Sickles, and hundreds of others whose names I might call in the northern states, who came out and took their muskets in their hands and said:

"We will try the question with you upon the issue of battle." I am not alarmed lest one of these gentlemen should quote upon me my attitude in 1860 to 1865, for an honest soldier who fought me in the war never does it; only those who hired substitutes and stayed home and pleaded the baby act, or something like that, for an excuse for patriotic delinquency, are in the habit here and elsewhere of quoting upon me the fact that I belonged at one time to the secession and rebel government of the South. I did belong to it, and when a blush of shame comes over my cheek to condemn me for the part I took in that struggle, I shall still be more ashamed of the poor, craven creature who can undertake to impose that as a disgrace upon me; for if there is a man in the world who is entitled to any consideration from the human family, it is one like old John Knox, or John Wesley, or Martin Luther, and men of that kind, who fought the battles of Christianity and who fought for freedom of conscience against the strength of the greatest combination of political and civil and religious power which ever existed in the world. These are the men whom I revere in history, not those petty politicians whose figures rise suddenly to the surface like bubbles on a stagnant pond, and explode and leave nothing behind them but mephitic odors.

* * *

SHAKESPEARE STRUTS THE SENATE STAGE

In his "Party Dishonor and Perfidy" letter in 1894, President Cleveland blasted Democratic Senators for violating promises and lining up with Republicans to emasculate the Wilson-Gorman Tariff Act. In a blistering retort, Maryland Senator Arthur P. Gorman charged the President with lack of veracity and called on four Senators—Jones of Arkansas, Vest of Missouri, Voorhees of Indiana, and Harris of Tennessee—to back him up, which they did. In passing, Gorman took a sideswipe at Senator David Bennett Hill of New York, whom he accused of playing the role of Iago (Othello's faithless friend) in the tariff drama. Next day, July 24, 1894, Hill retaliated with a brilliant adaptation of the stabbing scene from Shakespeare's Julius Caesar.

Mr. GORMAN. I said a moment ago that the Senator from New York has been consistent from the day the bill came up for consideration in his efforts to defeat the bill. He has made every motion which it was possible for him to make to defeat it. He would defeat it now. He is playing his hand well. He is stirring up passion here. It is the role of Iago played by a man not suited to the part.

Mr. HILL. Mr. President, I have discharged my duty from my standpoint. The Senator from Maryland yesterday started to describe me as the Iago of Shakespeare, and then he withdrew the comparison. That reminds me of the senatorial cabal conspired to assassinate the great Roman emperor. If I were disposed to make comparisons, I might speak of the distinguished Senator from Maryland as the "lean and hungry Cassius." (Laughter.) You recollect what Caesar said of him. He said:

> He thinks too much; such men are dangerous.

(Laughter.)

I might speak of the Senator from Arkansas (Mr. Jones) as Marcus Brutus—"honest Brutus." Right here I want to say a word. During all the tariff debate, during all the preparation of this bill, that Senator has exhibited most wonderful patience and sagacity; he has treated every citizen and every Senator with the greatest respect. No matter how this debate may terminate, no matter whether this bill passes or not, I say the Senator from Arkansas—and in paying this compliment I do not discriminate against anyone else—has won the esteem and respect of his countrymen everywhere. I will call him "honest Brutus." Cassius I have already referred to. (Laughter.) Casca was the distinguished Senator who struck the first blow last Friday (Mr. Vest). Trebonius, the Senator from Indiana (Mr. Voorhees)—testy, probably a little petulant—"good Trebonius." Metellus Cimber, the distinguished Senator from Tennessee (Mr. Harris). (Laughter.)

Mr. President, when yesterday they stabbed at our President, and sought to strike him down, they made the same plea as did the conspirators of old, that they struck for Rome—for their country. They said they did it, not that they loved Caesar less, but that they loved Rome more; not that they loved the President less, but they loved their party and this Senate bill more. (Laughter.) I can say with Mark Antony:

> What private griefs they have, alas, I know not,
> That made them do it; they are wise and honorable.

* * *

WAS THE SENATE "CONFEDERATE"

In 1878 President Hayes appointed Henry "Hangman" Foote of Mississippi, former U. S. Senator and member of the Confederate Congress, Director of the Mint at New Orleans. It infuriated Republicans in general and brought on many a spirited tilt on Capitol Hill. In the Senate, powerful James G.

Blaine of Maine clashed often with the "Southern brigadiers" who were—for Blaine and his colleagues—already too numerous. Witness this exchange between Blaine and Senator George Graham Vest of Missouri.

Mr. VEST. I had the honor, whatever gentlemen may think of it on the other side, of serving in the Confederate Congress with Governor Foote. He had the same extraordinary facility then of being on one side and talking on the other side, that he has now. (Laughter.) He is now an appointee of President Hayes, confirmed by a Confederate Senate, and has taken up his residence in the city of New Orleans as Director of the Mint.

Mr. BLAINE. "Confirmed by a Confederate Senate?" (Laughter.)

Mr. VEST. By this Senate. (Great laughter.)

Mr. BLAINE. The Senator says he was confirmed by a Confederate Senate.

Mr. VEST. Mr. President, if I have heard one thing since I have been on this floor, it has been from the Senator from Maine that this was the Confederate Senate.

Mr. BLAINE. And the gentleman now owns that it is. (Laughter.)

Mr. VEST. No, sir.

Mr. BLAINE. I am glad to be vindicated by the testimony of so valuable a witness.

Mr. VEST. I used the word "Confederate" in juxtaposition to my statement that Governor Foote had been a member of the Confederate Congress, and I answer the gentleman by stating that he has made the charge over and over again that this was the Confederate Senate and controlled by Confederate influence. I know that it is not true, and I know that the gentlemen on this side of the Chamber who sit around me are as true to their oaths to support the Constitution and the Union of the States as the gentleman from Maine or any

Senator who sits upon that side of the Chamber. The Senator from Maine is apt in his play upon words, and he seeks nothing better than a syllable out of which to make a harangue to fire the Northern heart and bring about a Republican victory.

Mr. BLAINE. I hope the honorable Senator from Missouri will never say that I called this a Confederate Senate. I said it was the United States Senate controlled by Confederates. That is what I said.

Mr. VEST. Yes, sir; I understand. If it were ruled by the true and gallant and honest men who risked their lives and all they had for the people with whom they lived, what a slur that would be upon this Senate! It would be ruled by gentlemen, by true men, and by brave men, and the country would be safe in their hands under their oaths of office.

* * *

DID THE STATESMAN HAVE A VISION OF THE FUTURE?

During the debate in the House in April 1908 on the naval construction bill, two Southern statesmen disagreed sharply on whether the United States should build two or more battleships at the same time. Representative John Sharp Williams of Mississippi favored two at a time, because they would be so quickly outmoded by nations trying to surpass one another in their navies. Representative Richmond Pearson Hobson of Alabama thought otherwise and propounded a jesting, prophetic question about aerial armadas.

Mr. WILLIAMS. Not only do ships sail the seas to fight one another now, but we are informed by a good many hopeful gentlemen who are expert on matters of this aerial sort that it will not be long before ships are sailing through the air; and when they do begin to sail through the air, we all know human nature—its barbarity, cruelty, and violence—well enough to know that it will not be long before we are equipping, perhaps armoring, ironcladding, and officering, and manning dirigible balloons for the purpose of destroying—no, not for the purpose of destroying anything, not for the purpose of making war at all, but for the purpose of preparing for peace (great laughter), for the purpose of filling the minds of the world with the idea that it is the ardent desire of the American people to go armed in order that it may have no occasion or opportunity to attack anybody. (Great laughter.)

Mr. HOBSON. Will the gentleman allow me to ask him a question?

Mr. WILLIAMS. Yes.

Mr. HOBSON. It is simply to ask the gentleman if he were going to be in a fleet of balloon ships, and were going to meet another fleet of balloon ships, whether, being in the American fleet of balloon ships, and the enemy being in another class of balloon ships (laughter), he being desirous of keeping his own lofty altitude, and not wishing his tire to be punctured at ten thousand feet in the air, whether he would not prefer to have balloon ships of a little different and better type and a few more of them than the other fellow? (Laughter.)

Mr. WILLIAMS. Mr. Speaker—

Mr. HOBSON. And further, if you could judge by the oratorical powers displayed whether, with a puncture, there would not be, perhaps, danger of more hot air escaping than there is today. (Great laughter.)

Mr. WILLIAMS. More than there is today, but not more than there was yesterday and the day before. (Great and continued laughter.) Mr. Speaker, I do not want you to understand—for I have the highest regard for your good opinion—I do not want you to understand that I am uselessly consuming the time of this House, and I would not have you or this House to understand, as probably you might from the nature of the question propounded by my young kinsman, the gentleman from Alabama, that I was up in the air in this argument. I am not. I have been merely referring him to the proposition that if fellows are ever to fight battles in the air, with air guns or other aerial weapons, that the eloquence and the oratory of my friend from Alabama will keep pace with the altitude of the other fellow. (Laughter.) And yet there never will be a time when his eloquence could exercise the influence upon him that it did upon me the other day.

I tell you, Mr. Speaker, when he described to me and you how the Japs are yearning for my blood and the blood and property of my children, and in blood-curdling vein how the great yellow race is prepared to inevitably conduct a war upon the great white race, and how we must prepare to take care of ourselves, after we got through with that argument I feared very much for all mankind and for myself and had to retire to the cloakroom for five or ten minutes to smoke, in order that my affrighted imagination could settle down and my reason once more take cool possession of me. (Great laughter and applause.)

* * *

Gentlemen say this is a small amount. If you continue to heap up these little things you will be like the old antediluvian of whom the story is told that when that great and good man Noah built his ark and took into it all the things and persons that God Almighty desired to have saved, when the fountains of the great deep were broken up and the rains descended and the ark began to float, this old fellow swam up to the window and said, "Mr. Noah, please take me in there." "No," said Noah, "it is too late; you can't get in here now." The fellow turned away and said, "Well, you can go to hell. There ain't going to be much of a shower anyway." But, gentlemen, there was a good deal of a shower and that man and all the other people outside were drowned.

Representative W. Jasper Talbert
of South Carolina

* * *

A Congressman comes in here newly elected and mantled with a brand-new authority, booted and spurred by gifts of confidence from whatever political party gave his name the life, the required boost, that placed him high enough to strike out for Congress. So he comes here an heir to party enthusiasm. This alone is natural, healthy, and proper, of course, but did you ever see the swelling and inspired patriot breeze into Congress fresh and green from his home town with a new vision, a new commission, and a new necktie, a gleam in his eye, a well-worded, highsounding speech in his mouth, feeling fully qualified to shed any light needed on any subject arising, whether or not connected with any committee with which he is connected—and scarcely has he warmed his seat—his seat in Congress, till the lightning speed of his expanding scope is such that he announces as a candidate for the Senate of the United States. Oh, mores! Oh, tempora! Personally I have doubts as to its being any advantage or promotion to go from this body to the Senate.

Representative Luther Patrick of
Alabama, 1940

* * *

BRIGADIER GENERAL OF BEAN SOUP

Mr. LOGAN of Illinois. The great difference between our staff corps and the staff corps of other armies is caused thus: you have to graduate a man at West Point to make him a quartermaster. Think of it! In order to make a man competent to issue shoes, boots, pork, sugar, coffee, and molasses, you have to educate him in engineering and in artillery, cavalry and infantry tactics, at West Point. What an absurdity!

Then again, sir, if you put a man in the quartermaster's department to take charge of it, you must make a brigadier general of him. Brigadier general of what? Of boots and shoes, coats, tents, wagons, and mules. If you put a man in charge of the commissary department, you have to make him a brigadier general. Brigadier general of what? Of beef and molasses and pork and beans.

A MEMBER. Brigadier general of bean soup! (Laughter.)

Mr. LOGAN. Yes, sir. The gentleman is right, a brigadier general of bean soup.

* * *

NO APPLESAUCE, PLEASE

In 1945 Speaker Sam Rayburn cracked down on a long-cherished prerogative of the House: the use of words, in the Congressional Record, *indicating any demonstration or applause following speeches by members. The ruling rather robbed the* Record *of its touches of drollery. Here's what the Speaker said.*

The SPEAKER (Mr. Rayburn of Texas). The Chair does not intend to be facetious, but the Chair would like to give the House his reaction to the expressions "Hear! Hear!" and "Applause" in the *Record.* When I came here thirty-two years ago on Sunday last, a gentleman had been elected by a split in the Republican party in a particular state, and he had come here with Democratic and Progressive votes. He made a speech in the House. Whether it went into the permanent *Record* I do not know, but I know it went into the temporary

Record. It closed in this fashion: "Loud and prolonged applause among Democrats and Progressives, followed by much handshaking."

In times past there appeared in the *Record* the word "Applause" where a member spoke. In another place there was "Loud applause." In another place there was "Loud and prolonged applause, the Members rising." If I had made a speech and had received "Applause," and some member had followed me immediately and had received "Loud and prolonged applause, the Members rising," my opponent in the next primary might have called attention to how insignificant I was, because I only received "Applause," and the other member had received "Loud and prolonged applause, the Members rising."

The Chair has held that demonstrations in the House are not a part of the *Record*, and shall continue to hold that until the rules of the House are changed.

Mr. RANKIN of Mississippi: The unusual cases to which the Speaker refers were exceptions and not the rule and, in my opinion, do not justify excluding all demonstrations on the part of the members from the *Record*.

* * *

BLACK AS SIN AND HOT AS HELL

True, but the statesman—Representative T. Hale Boggs of Louisiana—did not say Hell. Rules of the House forbade it. So he compromised with Hades while the House was putting on the free tariff list of 1960 that ne plus ultra *ingredient of New Orleans coffee—chicory. When it came to what is a good cup of coffee, statesman Boggs stood his ground.*

Mr. HAYS of Ohio. So if this bill were defeated would it be possible to get a cup of coffee in New Orleans?

Mr. BOGGS. Yes; but not as good as coffee with chicory. That, of course, is the best coffee on earth.

Mr. HAYS. There is a difference of opinion about that.

Mr. BOGGS. I admitted that there is a difference, but the gentleman understands that is the best coffee on earth.

Mr. HOFFMAN of Michigan. I understood the gentleman to say this is an additive to coffee.

Mr. BOGGS. That may not be the proper word.

Mr. HOFFMAN. The gentleman meant an adulteration.

Mr. BOGGS. Oh, no. It improves the coffee. It makes it delicious. We prefer our coffee as strong as love, as black as sin, and as hot as Hades.

* * *

"WORDS OF BRILLIANT, POLISHED TREASON"

On August 1, 1861, the dark cloud of defeat at Bull Run hung over Congress. The fate of the Union dangled in the balance. On this day Kentucky's Senator John C. Breckinridge (former Vice President and soon to wear the gray) rose to denounce Lincoln's war measures. His brilliant tongue framed biting, dangerous words. Tension ran high. He was virtually one man against the Senate, but he was still Kentucky's Senator and he would be heard. As he swept along, into the chamber strode Senator (then Colonel) Ned Baker of Oregon. Unbuckling his sword, he laid it on his desk and waited for the Kentuckian to finish. Then he rose to answer.

Mr. BRECKINRIDGE. Sir, this drama is beginning to open before us, and we begin to catch some idea of its magnitude. We are on the wrong tack; we have been from the beginning. The people begin to see it. Here we are hurling gallant fellows to death, and the blood of Americans has been shed—for what?

I have said, sir, that we are on the wrong tack. Nothing

but ruin, utter ruin, to the North, to the South, to the East, to the West, will follow the prosecution of this contest. You may look forward to innumerable armies; you may look forward to countless treasures—all spent for the purpose of desolating and ravaging this continent.

If the forces of the United States are successful in ravaging the whole South, what on earth will be done after that is accomplished? Are not gentlemen now perfectly satisfied that they have mistaken a people for a faction? Are they not perfectly satisfied that, to accomplish their object, it is necessary to subjugate, to conquer, ay, to exterminate nearly ten millions of people?

Let the war go on, however, and soon, in addition to the moans of widows and orphans all over this land, you will hear the cry of distress from those who want food and the comforts of life.

The Pacific slope now, doubtless, is devoted to the Union of States. Let this war go on till they find the burdens of taxation greater than the burdens of separate condition and they will assert it. Let the war go on until they see the beautiful features of the old Republic beaten out of shape and comeliness and they will turn aside in disgust from the sickening spectacle, and become a separate nation.

Fight twelve months longer, and the already opening differences that you see between New England and the great Northwest will develop themselves. You have two confederacies now. Fight twelve months longer, and you will have three; twelve months longer, and you will have four.

Mr. BAKER. Mr. President, the honorable Senator says there is a state of war. What then? There is a state of public war; none the less war because urged from the other side; not the less war because it is unjust; not the less war because it is a war of insurrection and rebellion.

It is still war, and I am willing to say it is public war. What then? Shall we carry that war on? Is it his duty as a Senator to carry it on? If so, how? By armies, under command; by military organization and authority, advancing to suppress insurrection and rebellion. Is that wrong? Is that unconstitutional? Will the honorable Senator tell me it is our duty to stay here, within fifteen miles of the enemy seeking to advance upon us every hour, and talk about nice questions of constitutional construction as to whether it is war or merely insurrection?

No, sir. It is our duty to advance, if we can; to suppress insurrection; to put down rebellion; to dissipate the rising; to scatter the enemy; and when we have done so, to preserve the liberty, lives and property of the people of the country.

The Senator from Kentucky stands up here in a manly way in opposition to what he sees is the overwhelming sentiment of the Senate, and utters reproof, malediction, and prediction combined. Well, sir, it is not every prediction that is prophecy.

I confess, Mr. President, that I would not have predicted three weeks ago the disasters that have overtaken our arms, and I do not think, if I were to predict now, that six months hence the Senator will indulge in the same tone of prediction which is his favorite key now.

I would ask him what you would have us do now—a Confederate army within twenty miles of us, advancing or threatening to advance, to overwhelm your government; to shake the pillars of the Union; to bring it down around your head, if you stay here, in ruins? Are we to stop and talk about an uprising sentiment in the North against the war? Are we to predict evil, and retire from what we predict?

These speeches of his, sown broadcast over the land, what clear distinct meaning have they? Are they not intended for disorganization in our very midst? Are they not intended to dull our weapons? Are they not intended to destroy our zeal? Are they not intended to animate our enemies?

Sir, are they not words of brilliant, polished treason, even in the very Capitol of the Republic?

What would have been thought if, in another capitol, in another republic, in a yet more martial age, a Senator as grave, not more eloquent or dignified than the Senator from Kentucky, yet with the Roman purple flowing over his shoulders, had risen in his place, surrounded by all the illustrations of Roman glory, and declared that advancing Hannibal was just, that Carthage ought to be dealt with in terms of peace?

What would have been thought if, after the battle of Cannae, a Senator had risen there in his place and denounced every levy of the Roman people, every expenditure from its treasury, and every appeal to the old recollections and the old glories?

Mr. FESSENDEN of Maine. He would have been hurled from the Tarpeian Rock!

Mr. BAKER. Mr. President, a Senator, himself learned far more than myself in such lore, tells me, in a voice that I am glad is audible, that he would have been hurled from the Tarpeian Rock. It is a grand commentary upon the American Constitution that we permit these words to be uttered. I ask the Senator from Kentucky to recollect, too, what, save to send aid and comfort to the enemy, do these predictions of his amount to.

Every word thus uttered falls as a note of inspiration upon every Confederate ear. Every sound thus uttered is a word (and falling from his lips, a mighty word) of kindling and triumph to a foe that determines to advance. For me I have no such words as a Senator to utter. For me, amid temporary defeat, disaster, distraction, it seems that my duty calls me to utter another word, and that word is, bold, sudden, forward, determined war, by armies, by military commanders, clothed with full power, advancing with all the past glories of the Republic urging them on to conquer.

Sir, it is not a question of men or of money. All the money, all the men, are well bestowed in such a cause. When we give them we know their value. Knowing their value we give them with the more pride and the more joy. Sir, how can we retreat? Sir, how can we make peace? Upon what terms? Where the end of the principles we shall have to give up? What will become of constitutional government? What will become of public liberty?

What of past glories? What of future hopes? Shall we sink into the insignificance of the grave—a degraded, defeated, emasculated people, frightened by the result of one battle, and scared at the visions raised by the imagination of the Senator from Kentucky on this floor? No, sir; a thousand times, no, sir!

We will rally, we will rally the people, the loyal people, of the whole country. They will pour forth their treasure, their money, their men, without stint, without measure. The most peaceable man in this body may stamp his foot upon this Senate Chamber floor, as of old a warrior and a Senator did, and from that single tramp will spring forth armed legions.

Shall one battle determine the fate of empire, or a dozen? The loss of one thousand men or twenty thousand, of one hundred million dollars or five hundred million? In a year's peace, in ten years, at most, of peaceful progress, we can restore them all. There will be some graves reeking with blood, watered by the tears of affection. There will be some privation; there will be some loss of luxury; there will be somewhat more need for labor to procure the necessities of life. When that is said, all is said.

If we have the country, the whole country, the Union, the Constitution, free government—with these there will return all the blessings of well-ordered civilization; the path of the country will be a career of greatness and glory such as, in the olden time, our fathers saw in the dim visions of years yet to come, and such as would have been ours now, today, if it had not been for the treason for which the Senator too often seeks to apologize!

* * *

"IT GRAZES THE EDGE OF TREASON"

Seldom has the accusation of treason been hurled across the floor of the Senate. Not since the Civil War had the word been used by one Senator of another, not until the afternoon of April 4, 1917 when Senator James Alexander Reed of Missouri attacked Senator George W. Norris of Nebraska for the latter's denunciation of the nation's decision to make war on Germany.

Mr. NORRIS. We are taking a step today that is fraught with untold danger. We are going into war upon the command of gold. We are going to run the risk of sacrificing millions of our countrymen's lives in order that other countrymen may coin their lifeblood into money.

By our act we will make millions of our countrymen suffer, and the consequences of it may well be that millions of our brethren must shed their lifeblood, millions of broken-hearted women must weep, millions of children must suffer with cold, and millions of babes must die from hunger, and all because we want to preserve the commercial right of American citizens to deliver munitions of war to belligerent nations.

I know that I am powerless to stop it. I know that this war madness has taken possession of the financial and political powers of our country. I know that nothing I can say will stay the blow that is soon to fall. I feel that we are committing a sin against humanity and against our countrymen. I would like to say to this war god, "You shall not coin into gold the lifeblood of my brethren." I feel that we are about to put the dollar sign upon the American flag.

Mr. REED. Mr. President, it has been no part of my purpose to participate in this debate, but a statement or series of statements made by the Senator from Nebraska (Mr. Norris) seem to me to demand instant repudiation. There are men in this world of high intelligence who become so obsessed by certain ideas that they permit them to color all other objects coming within their mental vision.

The Senator from Nebraska, I fear, is so obsessed with a fear of "money" and of "profits" and of "fortunes" that all that it is necessary to suggest is that some wealthy concern may have an interest, remote, contingent, or direct, in the subject matter under consideration in order to confuse his mental vision. So we find the Senator here today reading a letter which he says comes from some unnamed Wall Street man. Because of that letter the Senator makes the statements which I propose to challenge. He said:

> We are taking a step today that is fraught with untold danger. We are going into war upon the command of gold. We are going to run the risk of sacrificing millions of our countrymen's lives in order that other countrymen may coin their lifeblood into money.

Mr. President, that is an indictment of the President of the United States. That is an indictment of the Congress of the United States. That is an indictment of the American people. That is an indictment of truth, and it is not the truth. The Senator continues:

> By our act we will make millions of our countrymen suffer, and the consequences of it may well be that millions of our brethren must shed their lifeblood, millions of broken-hearted women must weep, millions of children must suffer with cold, and millions of babes must die from hunger, and all because we want to preserve the commercial right of American citizens to deliver munitions of war to belligerent nations.

Mr. President, that is another indictment of the President

of the United States, of the Congress of the United States, of the American people, and of truth and fact. The Senator continues:

> I know that I am powerless to stop it. I know that this war madness has taken possession of the financial and political powers of our country.

And he continues:

> I would like to say to this war god, "You shall not coin into gold the lifeblood of my brethren."

Then he adds:

> I feel we are about to put the dollar sign upon the American flag.

Ah, Mr. President, I am sorry from my heart that such a statement should have been made at this time by an American citizen in the highest body of the American Congress. If that be not giving aid and comfort to the enemy on the very eve of the opening of hostilities, then I do not know what would bring comfort to the heart of a Hapsburg or a Hohenzollern. If that be not treason, it takes on a character and guise that is so near to treason that the enemies of America will gain from it much consolation.

Mr. WILLIAMS. If it be not treason it grazes the edge of treason.

Mr. REED. As the Senator from Mississippi says with his usual terseness, if it be not treason, it grazes the edge of treason.

* * *

"LET THE ASSASSIN FIRE!"

Only once in the history of the Senate was a pistol drawn by one Senator on another, and this occurred on April 17, 1851, during the long-drawn-out debates on Henry Clay's great Compromise Bill. Principals in this fracas were Senators Henry "Hangman" Foote of Mississippi and Thomas Hart Benton of Missouri. Foote was a bald, waspish little fellow who hated Benton cordially; Benton, burly, a slugger in debate, was now the Nestor of the Senate. Both were duelists of renown. Foote had for days tried to provoke Benton into a physical encounter or a duel. Finally Benton forbade Foote ever to mention his name again. On this morning Foote had the floor. He began a severe attack on Benton. The "late illustrious Senator" to whom Foote referred was John C. Calhoun. Instantly Benton started up and made for Foote who, retreating down the centre aisle of the Old Senate Chamber, drew a big pistol and leveled it at Benton. Pandemonium ensued in the chamber.

Mr. FOOTE. We all know the history of the Southern Address, and the world knows its history. It is the history of the action of a band of patriots, worthy of the highest laudation, and who will be held in veneration when their calumniators, no matter who they may be, will be objects of general loathing and contempt. Who is the author of the Southern Address? He is known to the world. The late illustrious Senator from South Carolina, whose decease a nation now mourns, and over whose untimely death every good man in all Christian countries, at the present time, is now lamenting—is the author, and the sole author, of that address. . . . Those who . . . sanctioned that address are charged with being agitators. And by whom? With whom does such an accusation as this originate? I shall not be personal, after the lesson I have already received here. I intend to be, in a parliamentary sense, perfectly decorous in all things. But by whom is this extraordinary denunciation hurled against all those individuals who subscribed this address? By a gentleman long denominated the oldest member of the Senate—the Father of the Senate. By a gentleman who, on a late occasion—

Here Mr. Foote, who occupied a seat on the outer circle, in front of the Vice President's chair, retreated backward down the aisle, toward the chair of the Vice President, with a pistol in his hand. [Mr. Benton had a moment before suddenly risen from his seat and advanced by the aisle, outside the bar, toward the Senator from Mississippi, following him into the aisle down which he had retreated.] In a moment almost every Senator was on his feet, and calls to "order," demands for the Sergeant-at-Arms; requests that Senators would take their seats, from the Chair and from individual Senators, were repeatedly made. Mr. Benton was followed and arrested by Mr. Dodge, of Wisconsin, and, in the confusion and excitement which prevailed, he was heard to exclaim:

Mr. BENTON. I have no pistols! Let him fire! Stand out of the way! I have no pistols! I disdain to carry arms! Stand out of the way, and let the assassin fire!

While making these exclamations, Mr. Benton was brought back to his seat; but, breaking away from Mr. Dodge, of Wisconsin, who sought forcibly to detain him, he advanced again toward Mr. Foote, who stood near the Vice President's chair, on the right-hand side, surrounded by a number of Senators, and others not members of the Senate. Mr. Dickinson took the pistol from the hand of Mr. Foote, and locked it up in his desk, and Mr. Foote, on the advice of Mr. Butler, returned to his seat.

Mr. BENTON. We are not going to get off in this way. A pistol has been brought here to assassinate me. The scoundrel had no reason to think I was armed, for I carry nothing of the kind, sir.

Mr. FOOTE. I brought it here to defend myself.

Mr. BENTON. Nothing of the kind, sir. It is a false imputation. I carry nothing of the kind, and no assassin has a right to draw a pistol on me.

Several SENATORS. Order! Order!

Mr. BENTON. It is a mere pretext of the assassin. Will the Senate take notice of it, or shall I be forced to take notice of it by going and getting a weapon myself? A pistol has been brought here and drawn upon me by an assassin.

The VICE PRESIDENT. Senators will be pleased to suspend their remarks until order is restored. Senators are requested to be seated.

Mr. CLAY. Mr. President–

The VICE PRESIDENT. Business cannot proceed until order is restored. There is too much noise in the galleries. Quiet and order must be restored.

Mr. BENTON. I demand that the Senate shall take immediate cognizance of the fact of this pistol having been brought here to assassinate me, under the villainous pretext that I was armed–the pretext of every assassin who undertakes to constitute a case of self-defense when laying out the death of his victim. Will the Senate notice it, or shall I myself, for it shall not pass. I will not be satisfied here.

Mr. FOOTE. If my presenting a pistol here has been understood as anything except the necessary means of self-defense, after threats of personal chastisement, it is doing me a wrong. I saw him advancing toward me, and I took it for granted he was armed; for had I thought otherwise, I should have stopped to meet him in that narrow alley. But I supposed that he was armed, and therefore I determined to take ground where I could meet him more fairly, and I drew out the pistol and was ready to fire it in self-defense. I have never sought any man's life, nor gone in quest of any man with a view of taking his life. No, sir, never. My life has been a defensive one from my boyhood. I mention it, not from the imputations that have been thrown out here, but that all the Senators present and the American public, who may hear of this thing, may be witnesses of the fact, that whilst I was making a perfectly parliamentary speech, threatening language was used, menacing gestures indulged in, and an advance made toward me, with the view, as I supposed, of putting violent designs into effect. I therefore retreated a few steps, with a view to get elbow room to act in my own defense, and not to shoot him. So help me God, such alone was my intention.

Mr. BENTON. I have done nothing upon God Almighty's earth to authorize any man to charge me with a breach of the peace, and I will rot in jail before I will give a promise admitting that the charge is true. I regret nothing. It is lying and cowardly to undertake to impute to me the bearing of arms here, in order to justify the use of them upon me. I have done nothing, and I will rot in jail before I will give a promise which admits, by implication, that I have been guilty of a breach of the peace.

* * *

"MY SUBSTITUTE WAS A DEMOCRAT"

Senator James G. Blaine of Maine often sparred with Senators from the southern states who took their places in the Democratic ranks of the upper chamber as their reconstructed states rejoined the Union. On this day in 1879 Senator Blaine was expatiating against a book published in the South and slanted, quite naturally, in favor of that region. It quickly involved him in a fracas, humorous for a change, with Senator John S. Williams of Kentucky, veteran of the Mexican War and former Confederate brigadier.

Mr. BLAINE. It is now indeed a most extraordinary thing to find a gentleman from the South who was originally for secession. I do not know who was. I see very pleasant and complimentary biographies of the various Senators on that side, and they were all dragged into secession. They were dragged into it because their states went, and the honorable Senator from Kentucky (Mr. Williams) was dragged into it because his state did not go.

Mr. WILLIAMS. I did not hire a substitute.

Mr. BLAINE. He says he did not hire a substitute. That is a piece of wit which I am glad to notice. The Senators from Kentucky have twice, both of them, taken a turn when I was on the floor to say they did not hire a substitute, as if that was something very pungent. In the conscription law passed by a Congress of which I was a member, for the first time in the history of the government there was no exemption of Senators or Representatives from the draft. I was a younger man then than I am now, and among the very first men drafted in my district I was one. I did not resign my seat in Congress. I did send a substitute. What would the honorable Senator have done?

Mr. WILLIAMS. I should have gone.

Mr. BLAINE. You would have gone!

Mr. WILLIAMS. I would have gone to the fight.

Mr. BLAINE. I am glad you would have gone in any way on the Union side. But the Senator was not drafted, and he went and fought against the government, even when his state did not secede. I consider this reference to a substitute as a first-class sarcasm; and as the Senators from Kentucky have each tried their hands on it only twice, I hope they will repeat it again.

Mr. WILLIAMS. When my country calls for my services in the army, I am ready.

Mr. BLAINE. I am not disputing it. I only say the honorable Senator went into the rebellion because his state did not go.

Mr. WILLIAMS. I should like to ask the Senator did his substitute fight?

Mr. BLAINE. No. I found out afterward that he was a Democrat. (Laughter.) I was inveigled into hiring him without knowing who he was.

Mr. EATON. Did he sell himself for half price?

Mr. BLAINE. I do not know. I paid full price for him, more than an average Democrat was worth in the war.

* * *

"THIRTY LASHES LAID ON HIS BARE BACK"

Statesmen on Capitol Hill were shocked down to their button shoes one day in 1906 when a new, alarming problem suddenly taxed their legislative wisdom. The Superintendent of Washington Police had just disclosed that, in the last two years, 508 citizens had been arrested for the ancient and honorable (?) sin of wife-beating. The House blazed with wrath. Rushed to the floor was a bill to punish "any male person in the District of Columbia who shall beat, bruise or mutilate his wife, with thirty lashes laid on his bare back." In the van of the statesmen avengers was Robert Adams, Jr., of Pennsylvania, who apparently had made a study of this particular indoor sport. The bill was ridiculed to death.

Mr. ADAMS. Why, Mr. Speaker, the disgrace to this capital is that the Chief of Police reports five hundred and eight wife-beatings in the last two years; and, I take it, it will be to the honor of this capital if this body, responsible for the conduct of the inhabitants of the capital of our country, will institute a course of punishment which will cause it to go out to the world that the American people will not tolerate five hundred brutes in the capital of the country who beat their wives.

Mr. Speaker, I wish to state that the result of this legislation where it exists has been most efficacious. In Maryland this crime has been very much reduced. In Delaware, where they have a whipping post, it has been reduced.

Mr. WACHTER of Maryland. I want to say to the gentleman, for his information, that we have a whipping post in the Baltimore city jail that we would like to sell to the District of Columbia. (Laughter.) Our law is still in existence, but there have been only two men whipped. We have the whipping post for sale. The women do not want it used.

Mr. ADAMS. Where do you get your information?

Mr. WACHTER. Right at home. (Great laughter.)—I mean in Baltimore. (Renewed laughter.)

Mr. JAMES of Kentucky. In Kentucky we had a whipping-post law for petty larceny. That whipping was in public. This bill provides that it shall be in private. Now, if the gentleman wants to stop wife-beating, wouldn't it be a good thing to have it out where everybody could see how well the whipping was done?

Mr. SIMS of Tennessee. In other words, whether we would whip them all alike, and not give thirty lashes lightly to one and thirty lashes heavily to another.

Mr. JAMES. My point is that if this is a good law it ought to be administered where everybody can see how it is administered.

Mr. SIMS. I do not think it is good enough to administer just anywhere. If there isn't room enough elsewhere, we should build a platform on the top of the Washington Monument so that people in the city may see and those from afar may also see (laughter), and will see that at least in whipping wife-beaters we give them a square, open deal. (Laughter.)

Mr. STANLEY of Kentucky. I am surprised that this unusual measure should originate with the distinguished gentleman from Pennsylvania. Of all the men in the House, the last man to shed great big tears as big as buttermilk biscuits over a suffering wife is the gentleman from Pennsylvania. If it had come from some distinguished Representative from Utah, I might have listened with more patience.

Mr. CLAYTON of Alabama. Some of us from the far South over on this side wish to know why the gentleman from Kentucky wants to make us hungry by mentioning buttermilk biscuits.

Mr. CLARK of Missouri. Force of habit.

Mr. STANLEY. As the gentleman from Missouri says, force of habit and time of day. Now, if the gentleman wants to take in all the suffering women of this country, I think he ought to accept an amendment. There are more of them that are in pain because they are unmarried than are in pain because they are married and beaten. (Laughter.) The gentleman from Pennsylvania belongs to a class who really inflict more torture than the wife-beater. Mental anguish is more terrible than physical pain, and if he would only think of the great number whom he has left alone lamenting and upon whom he should have mercy, he would not inflict such agony on the fair sex. If this bill is to go through, I want to offer an amendment that a like punishment shall be inflicted not only on those who are guilty of wife-beating, but those who feloniously refuse to take one.

Mr. BARTHOLDT of Missouri. Mr. Speaker, the man who lays hands on a woman in the manner described in this bill is a brute. In my judgment, Mr. Speaker, it would be a thousand times more merciful to kill the offender outright. Will it have a deterring effect? Not any more than the gallows will deter a man from committing a murder, and all will admit that the gallows in this respect has proved an absolute failure. The American woman enjoys the reputation of occupying a higher position socially than the woman of any country, and as American men we are justly proud of that fact. (Applause.) The whipping post is sure to rob us of this proud distinction. And why? Because it involves the humiliating confession before all the world that in the United States such a contemptible institution is necessary to protect woman against the brutality of man; that the inviolability of the American woman cannot be safeguarded otherwise. Are members of this House willing to destroy, by heralding this fatal admission abroad, the fair reputation of our country in the eyes of the civilized nations?

Mr. HEPBURN of Iowa. Mr. Speaker, I know that nothing I can say will save this bill. It ought to pass, but I am satisfied that it will not. It is a bill to prevent the crime of wife-beating in the capital of this nation, and gentlemen all over the House are laughing at the idea of trying to prevent this crime in the capital of this nation. Five hundred and eight wives have been beaten by their husbands in the last two years, and gentlemen make merry over a law that seeks simply to bring proper punishment to the man who whips his wife. And chivalric gentlemen from Kentucky—chivalric Kentucky—they make merry at the expense of those who want to take away from them the privilege of whipping their wives in the capital of the nation. (Laughter and applause.)

Mr. Speaker, in my judgment this is a serious matter and ought to receive serious attention. The bowels of compassion of the gentleman from Missouri yearn toward the wife-beater. He thinks that it would result in the ruin and degradation of such a man to whip him. Can you ruin a beast like that? Will whipping make him more of a beast?

We boast that the home, the American home, is the unit of our civilization. How can you have homes, American homes, where even in the capital of the nation men may whip their wives? It is proposed to do something to check that destruction of the home. Why, gentlemen say, there is ample provision now. There is no necessity for radical means. Why, our civilization has labored upon these men. That has failed.

The teachings of the church have failed to influence them, a complete, woeful, dismal failure—as shown by the record, this horrible record of five hundred and eight cases in two years of time.

Ah, but the gentlemen say, we will advertise to the capitals of the world that we must go backward centuries to the brutalities of medieval times in order to protect our women. How much better to advertise to the capitals of the world and to all mankind that we are making a manly effort to suppress and exterminate this wrong rather than allow it to go on in the capital of the nation and under the flag that means so much.

* * *

THE NATIONAL EMBLEM—WHAT FLOWER?

The Senate was divided on this issue as usual, though, strange to say, not politically. The carnation, the rose, and even grass had their special champions, while the members from the corn belt of the West stood foursquare for the "golden corn tassel." This was 1959, and the great issue is yet unsettled.

Mr. ALLOTT of Colorado. Mr. President, in this hallowed chamber, we are approaching a somewhat weedy situation. Various proposals for designation of our national flower are springing forth like shoots after a wet spring. They threaten to overrun other even more vital issues.

Therefore, I propose as our national flower, a true flower, one which is the most widely grown cut flower in the United States, one which is perpetually flowering and knows no season. I present it in the spirit of Webster, Clay, and Calhoun, the spirit of amicable compromise. I offer for your consideration, Mr. President: The carnation.

Mr. KEATING of New York. Mr. President, I wish to express my personal gratitude to the distinguished Senator from Colorado for sending to me today a carnation to wear.

However, I invite his attention to a fact with respect to which he may not be informed, regarding the proudest, oldest, and loveliest flower—the rose. I invite his attention to the fact that fossils of the genus *Rosa*, establishing the existence of the rose on this continent for more than thirty-three million years—considerably longer than this body has been in existence—were found in his own native state of Colorado. It is possible that this horticultural fact has escaped the attention of the Senator from Colorado, and that upon realization of that fact he may feel that Colorado should join the state of New York, which has made the rose its state flower. I sincerely hope that that will be the effect of my remarks today.

Mr. ALLOTT. I agree that the rose is a very beautiful, fragile flower. It looks beautiful in a vase.

However, I invite the attention of my distinguished colleague, who is one of my fine personal friends, to the fact that while the rose looks better upon the gown of a woman, the carnation is a flower which both men and women—and particularly men—may wear, with confidence in its ruggedness, its fertility, its virility, its courage, and all the other attributes that go with it.

Mr. KEATING. I think any flower looks better when worn by a woman than in any other surroundings.

I appreciate the remarks of the Senator from Colorado, but it seems to me that he has added an argument for the adoption of the rose, because of all things we are seeking to accomplish in this world, one of the foremost is a closer relationship with our friends and allies. Perhaps the adoption of the rose as the national flower would tend to affect closer relationships.

Mr. DIRKSEN of Illinois. Of course, English history records the War of the Roses, between the House of York and the House of Lancaster. I hope, after this long interlude, that the War of the Roses will not be resumed.

Mr. HICKENLOOPER of Iowa. Mr. President, I am distressed to hear what I consider to be the misguided arguments being advanced here today.

The idea of a national flower or a national floral emblem is highly desirable, but I invite attention to the fact that some of us have introduced a bill proposing that the corn tassel be the national flower. The corn tassel is a very beautiful flower. It represents food, among other things. It represents the strength of our country. It represents the hope of our agricultural regions—and all states are agricultural.

It seems to me that it is not only decorative, but it has great utility, which should appeal. While the rose is beautiful, and is grown in all states, and while the carnation is a wonderful flower, and has great sentimental value, being seen in profusion at funerals, and while I would not discredit the beauty of those flowers, I importune my colleagues to think about the stability and utility of corn, as represented by the corn tassel.

Mr. NEUBERGER of Oregon. Mr. President, I should like to point out to my colleagues on the other side of the aisle that more roses grow in Oregon than in any other state, and that, unlike the corn tassel, the rose does not need price supports to enable it to flourish. (Laughter.)

Mr. MORTON of Kentucky. Mr. President, I wear a carnation. I might add it was given to me, free. I bear the carnation no malice. It is a beautiful flower. From the esthetic standpoint, it serves as a thing of beauty. I have not been able to find that it makes any great contribution to the welfare of our nation or that it is essential to our economic survival in this troubled world.

May I point out that the corn tassel is not a full flower. It is merely the male flower. The ear of the corn is the female flower of the corn plant. I do not think we want to get into any controversy that is going to lose us the women's vote because of our adopting a male flower as the national floral emblem.

I might add, incidentally, that corn is converted into various products. Some of this conversion takes place in my native state of Kentucky. I know from experience we do not want to get into a debate, on what should be the national flower, that is going to stir up the Anti-Saloon League.

At the appropriate time I shall introduce the proper resolution. It is that grass be our national flower.

There are those who say grass is not a flower, but I point out that grass does flower and seed. I point out that our first important resource is grass, and that our most important resource is the cow. Let us look at the cow, the foster-mother of mankind. Where would the cow be, and, further, where would mankind be, but for grass? We are a meat-eating people. How could we satisfy our national hunger for meat, if it were not for grass, on which feed the animals that supply us with beef and mutton and lamb in such lavish quantities?

It was grass that was mentioned first in the story of creation. It was grass, with its deep, penetrating roots, that gave fertility and protection to the great plains and prairie soils of America. It was grass that sustained the buffalo, whence came our forefathers' food. It is grass that feeds the lowing cattle, the gentle sheep, the patient horse. It is to grass that we turn to heal our fields after they have been eroded and ravished by the plow and the cultivator. Grass is truly the hope of the conservationist and the dream of the naturalist.

Mr. DOUGLAS of Illinois. Mr. President, I was somewhat surprised to come into the chamber and learn that the Senator from Kentucky was eulogizing the grass as the national floral emblem. I think this is an attempted travesty on the very important subject. The Senator from Illinois has introduced a resolution making the golden corn tassel our national floral emblem.

I think the Senator from Kentucky was attempting, in a very subtle fashion, to ridicule the resolution. Let me say this so far as the golden corn tassel is concerned. While I do not intend to reflect upon the chief product of Kentucky, which is grass, and very green grass—not blue, but green—I do want to say the golden corn tassel is the natural American floral emblem.

What I am proposing is the golden corn tassel as a symbol both of the beauty and the bounty of the nation. Nothing could be more beautiful than a field of corn in full flower.

Furthermore, corn is indigenous to the North American hemisphere. We have found minute ears of corn at least five thousand years old among the remains of the Indian tribes of the Southwest. I have in my office a photograph of a Mexican piece of sculpture of approximately 1100 A.D., in which the ears of corn are no longer minute but are almost as large as the normal ears of corn today.

It was corn which kept the Pilgrims alive during the first hard winter at Plymouth. It was corn which kept the Jamestown settlers alive during the first difficult winters. Corn went with the pioneers across this nation and furnished the main source of food for the settlers. Corn is now the chief farm crop of the United States. The center of the corn industry is of course in Iowa and in my own state of Illinois.

I will say to the Senator from Kentucky, a large part of the prosperity of Kentucky has been built upon corn, also—corn put into a liquid form. It is corn which perhaps should not have been imbibed by the people of this country, but nevertheless it is taken in a liquid form.

It ill behooves the Senator from Kentucky to try to upgrade grass and downgrade corn.

Mr. MORTON. I want to make clear I was not trying to ridicule the Senator's resolution. I know the Senator is serious and is perfectly sincere in his objective.

I considered the case of corn, and I pointed out that the corn tassel is the male part of the flower and is not the full flower. The Senator will find Susan B. Anthony rolling over in her grave, should he make the fight for the corn tassel.

With respect to the Senator's remarks regarding the contribution of corn in my own state, the Senator will find the Anti-Saloon League and the WCTU knocking on his door to say, "Down with the corn tassel."

I merely bring out the point that the road before the Senator is a hard and rough road. I wish him well, but I intend to continue the fight for grass.

Mr. DOUGLAS. I merely say we intend to keep up the struggle to have the golden corn tassel adopted as the American floral emblem.

* * *

In a speech in the House in 1914, emaciated, lantern-jawed, brown-mustached Willard D. Vandiver of Missouri once referred to Charles H. Grosvenor of Ohio as "the one who looks like Santa Claus and talks like Satan." Grosvenor, snowy-bearded, snowy-haired, and ruddy-faced, made this reply.

Mr. GROSVENOR. Mr. Speaker, I have never prided myself on my personal appearance, but I am not ashamed of it. The gentleman from Missouri violated the proprieties of debate by referring to it. I may be permitted to say that I thank God when people see me they do not think of the death's head and crossbones on a bottle of prussic acid in a druggist's window, and when they hear my voice they do not instinctively recall that old song, "Hark! From the tombs a doleful sound!"

* * *

While he was making a speech in the House in 1894 Representative John J. O'Neill of Missouri was interrupted repeatedly by a member who was noted for the bitterness of his tongue rather than the amount of his gray matter. After the fifth such interruption O'Neill turned on him savagely with the words, "If the gall which you have in your heart could be poured into your stomach, you'd die instantly of the black vomit."

*   *   *

During the interminable debates on the Missouri Compromise in 1820 John Randolph of Roanoke spoke almost daily in the House. Getting impatient at Mr. Randolph's wearying tirades, Representative Philemon Beecher of Ohio took advantage of several pauses in Randolph's harangue to pop up like a jack-in-the-box and move the "Previous question," to which the Speaker would reply, "The gentleman from Virginia has the floor."

Randolph took no apparent notice of the first, second, or even the third interruption, but when Beecher rose the fourth time to move the "Previous question," Randolph changed pace suddenly and said, "Mr. Speaker, in the Netherlands, a man of small capacity, with bits of wood and leather, will, in a few moments, construct a toy that, with the pressure of the finger and thumb, will cry 'Cuckoo! Cuckoo!' With less ingenuity, and with inferior materials, the people of Ohio have made a toy that will, without much pressure, cry 'Previous Question, Mr. Speaker!' " At the same time he pointed his long, skeletal finger at the interrupter. The House was convulsed with laughter. Beecher never quite recovered from Randolph's sarcasm.

*   *   *

OWEN LOVEJOY GETS HIS COMEUPPANCE

Democrats had hard sledding in Congress during the Civil War years. Charges of disloyalty flew round their heads like angry wasps. Particularly offensive this way was Representative Owen Lovejoy of Illinois, who one day in 1863 loosed his venom on Democrats in general and on Sam "Sunset" Cox of Ohio in particular. Cox's wit came to his rescue in a retort that squelched the bulky Lovejoy.

Mr. COX. Notwithstanding all this, we are, forsooth, to be stigmatized by the gentleman from Illinois as secession sympathizers! A few days ago, in the same strain of vituperation, he took me to task, too, for the speech I made in New York City. For lack of something better, he referred to my small size. Could I have had a chance to respond at the time, I would have furnished this epitaph for the gentleman, which would answer all he can say of the Democracy during his life, and suit his case very appropriately after death:

> Beneath this stone OWEN LOVEJOY lies,
> Little in everything—except in size; (laughter)
> What though his burly body fills this hole,
> Yet through hell's keyhole crept his little soul.

* * *

In 1887 General W. H. F. (Rooney) Lee, son of the Confederate commander-in-chief, was elected to the House from Virginia. Soon after, Lee introduced a bill to reimburse the losses of an Episcopal seminary that was burned during the war. While speaking in behalf of his bill he was interrupted.

VOICE IN THE HOUSE. Will the gentleman from Virginia yield for a question?

Mr. LEE. Why, certainly.

VOICE. Was this school continued during the rebellion?

Mr. LEE. Yes, as far as possible. Most of the professors remained there.

VOICE. For whom did these professors pray, for the Unionists or for the Confederates?

Mr. LEE. I do not know. I never heard them pray, but they

were saintly men and I presume they prayed for all sinners and left the good Lord to say who were the sinners.

* * *

Kansas was once the butt of many a senatorial gibe, but all that ended when John J. Ingalls in 1873 took his seat in the upper chamber. To a Delaware Senator who risked criticism of Kansas, Senator Ingalls flashed back: "Mr. President, the gentleman who has just spoken represents a state which has two counties when the tide is up—and only three when it is down."

* * *

A Pennsylvania Senator made the mistake of drawing a disparaging comparison between "bleak Kansas" and the glorious Keystone State which he represented. Ingalls' reply was instant: "Mr. President, Pennsylvania has produced only two great men—Benjamin Franklin of Massachusetts and Albert Gallatin of Switzerland."

* * *

Representative Alexander Hamilton Stephens of Georgia —"Little Aleck," as Lincoln called him—weighed under a hundred pounds, but he was mentally a man of vast weight. He once worsted a gigantic Western opponent in a debate in the House. The big fellow glowered at Stephens and finally burst out, "You little shrimp! Why I could swallow you whole!"

"If you did," replied Stephens, "you'd have more brains in your belly than you ever had in your head."

* * *

The House was debating fortification of the Philippine Islands this day in 1906 when God suddenly took a hand in the matter.

Mr. JAMES of Kentucky. I believe that you said that the Republican party and God are in partnership; that would be joining light with darkness; corruption with incorruption.

Mr. SIBLEY of Pennsylvania. Whenever you talk about the Republicans and God, and it comes in a slurring way from that side often, if the Republican party has been attempting to act in accordance with the will of God the Democratic party had better reverse its policy and its way, instead of standing against the Lord Almighty and all the facts of history, and survey the marvelous victories that have been accomplished by the Republican party following such leadership—the great good it has accomplished in the elevation of moral sentiment and the higher ideals of national life and national honor. Gentlemen talking about God and the Republican party must not endeavor to get away from the meaning of what they say.

Mr. JAMES. Then you were away from God when you were with the Democratic party?

Mr. SIBLEY. Now, my friend, do you want me to enter a plea of guilty? If I enter a plea of guilty will that suffice?

Mr. JAMES. I want to know whether, during the time you were serving the Democratic party, God was on that side, or whether you discovered God when you found the Republican party?

* * *

One of the wickedest shafts ever shot across the floor of the House sped from the tongue of John Randolph of Roanoke one day in the 1820's. This passage is only hinted at in the Annals of Congress, but vouched for by many sources. Gifted Tristam Burges of Rhode Island, who despised Randolph heartily, seized upon an opening to twit the latter because of his presumed sexual impotence. Randolph received Burges' fire, then rose quickly with his historic retort.

Mr. BURGES. Sir, Divine Providence takes care of his own

universe. Moral monsters cannot propagate. Impotent of everything but malevolence of purpose, they can no otherwise multiply miseries than by blaspheming all that is pure and prosperous and happy. Could demon propagate demon, the universe might become a pandemonium; but I rejoice that the Father of Lies can never become the Father of Liars. One adversary of God and man is enough for one universe.

Mr. RANDOLPH. You pride yourself upon an animal faculty, in respect to which the slave is your equal and the jackass infinitely your superior.

* * *

Once when Thad Stevens of Pennsylvania was propounding an important argument he was interrupted several times by Representative Kellian V. Whaley of West Virginia with, "Will the gentleman yield?" On Whaley's third interruption, Stevens turned on him savagely. "I yield to the gentleman from West Virginia for a few feeble remarks." Whaley was drowned out in the uproar provoked by Stevens' retort.

* * *

Senator Judah P. Benjamin of Louisiana was one of the "brilliants" of the pre-Civil War Senate. He was one day taunted by a carping Senator of German extraction with being a Jew. Politely, Benjamin replied, "The gentleman will please remember that when his half-civilized ancestors were hunting the wild boar in the forests of Silesia, mine were the princes of the earth."

* * *

If the gentleman from Maine (Mr. Blaine) would not interrupt me quite so much he would feel a good deal better. He is somewhat like the little boy down in Memphis who undertook to take a twist of a mule's tail. His father said to him afterward, "You don't look so pretty as you did, my boy, but you have learned something."

Representative Samuel S. "Sunset" Cox to James G. Blaine, 1876

* * *

Interrupting speechmakers in the House is an old parliamentary pastime. Back in the Nineties a chronic interrupter was pesky but able John A. Pickler of South Dakota. One day he kept interrupting Marriott Brosius of Pennsylvania, who was soaring on oratorical wings. In desperation Brosius finally let fly a squelcher that Pickler never forgot.

You love your automatic mouth;
You love its giddy whirl;
You love its fluent flow;
You love to wind your mouth up;
You love to hear it go!

A few years later, in 1901, William B. Shattuc of Ohio, after repeated interruptions by a member, broke off in mid-speech and appealed to the Speaker.

Mr. SHATTUC. Mr. Speaker, I ask unanimous consent that I may have the Clerk read some poetry that I wish to print in the *Record*. It is dedicated to the man who always asks on the floor, "Will you yield?"

The SPEAKER. The gentleman from Ohio asks unanimous consent to have some poetry read.

The Clerk read as follows:

BIG MAN WITH BIG MOUTH

I love the man who knows it all,
From east to west, from north to south;
Who knows all things, both great and small,
And tells it with his tireless mouth;

Who holds a listening world in awe
The while he works his iron jaw.

His good, strong mouth! He wields it well!
He works it just for all it's worth.
Not Samson's jawbone, famed, could tell
Such mighty deeds upon the earth;
He pulls the throttle open wide
And works it hard on either side.

Good Lord, from evils fierce and dire,
Save us each day; from fear and woe,
From wreck and flood, from storm and fire,
From sudden death, from secret foe,
From blighting rain and burning drouth,
And from the man who plays his mouth.

* * *

Ford's Theatre in Washington, where President Lincoln was assassinated, is a cherished national shrine. At the time of this colloquy, 1867, James G. Blaine of Maine was Republican floor leader in the House. The inquiring gentleman, Charles A. Eldredge, Democrat from Wisconsin, was apparently looking for loopholes in the Army Bill then under debate. He picked the wrong one.

Mr. ELDREDGE. I desire to inquire of the gentleman from Maine if there is in this bill any appropriation for the purchase of the museum called the Army Museum. And then I would like to have him inform the House, if he will, by what authority that museum was purchased—how it became the property of the War Department, or of the United States.

Mr. BLAINE. It was by authority of an appropriation made by this House.

Mr. ELDREDGE. I think I did not vote for it. I hope the

gentleman will inform the House by what authority the museum was purchased.

Mr. BLAINE. The Army Medical Museum has nothing to do with the Ford's Theatre Museum to which I suppose the gentleman refers. As to Ford's Theatre, that is a matter of three or four years ago.

Mr. ELDREDGE. I have understood that the Secretary of War took possession of that building without any authorization from Congress or from any other source and made it the property of the United States by force—only he consenting.

Mr. BLAINE. Does the gentleman object to that having been done?

Mr. ELDREDGE. Yes, sir; since the gentleman asks me the question, I object most emphatically.

Mr. BLAINE. I desire to say to the gentleman from Wisconsin, who I think, rather ungraciously brings up this subject, that the Secretary of War acted in a way which the Congress of the United States clearly approved, in rescuing that building, *which was the scene of the greatest sacrifice that has been made in modern times*. It was to prevent the desecration (the use of it as a place of common amusement) that the Secretary of War took possession of the building; and the Congress of the United States afterward gave him the money necessary to vest the title to it in the United States.

Mr. SHANKS of Indiana. I wish to say that the murder of President Lincoln was an act of war, and that it was the duty of the Secretary of War to take such steps as became a nation in a state of war.

Mr. BLAINE. If at this late day the gentleman from Wisconsin desires to criticize acts of Secretary Stanton which he believes to have been outside the Constitution or outside the laws, he makes a very unfortunate selection when he singles out this particular transaction; for among the many deeds that will commend the name of Edwin M. Stanton to the patriotic people of this country, that will not be among the least.

* * *

RETORT-ICAL TOM REED

Beau Brummel of the House when the great Thomas Brackett Reed of Maine was Speaker was J. Hamilton Lewis, a fashion plate from the Pacific Coast. One morning Lewis rushed down to the rostrum waving a newspaper.

"Mr. Speaker, I rise to a question of personal privilege. I have here a copy of this morning's New York *Sun* in which I am referred to as a thing of beauty and a joy forever."

Retorted Reed: "The point is well taken. It should have been a thing of beauty and a jaw forever."

* * *

Once an irate, sputtering Democrat came storming down into the well of the House, shaking his fist at Reed and demanding, "What becomes of the rights of the minority?" Replied Reed, casually, "The right of the minority is to draw its salaries, and its function is to make a quorum."

* * *

Annoyed one day by the insistent chatter of two members, Reed turned to the nearby Sergeant-at-Arms and remarked in a tone so loud that all could hear: "They never open their mouths without subtracting from the sum of human knowledge."

* * *

One day when the House was loafing through a tiresome debate, Representative William M. Springer of Illinois began proclaiming his stand in the matter under debate with a show of force. To emphasize his zeal, Springer drew on Henry Clay's oft-quoted and most famous epigram: "I'm right. I know I'm right so I say, with Henry Clay, sir, I would rather be right than President."

The opening was too tempting for Speaker Reed. In a *sotto voce* drawl heard by everyone, Reed said: "The gentleman need not worry, for he will never be either."

* * *

Once during a furious attack on the Republican party by a member from New York, Reed took the wind out of the gentleman's sails with this: "I cannot hope to equal the volume of voice of the gentleman from New York. This is only equaled by the volume of what he does not know."

* * *

Reed loved to unmask sham. An old chap from the Midwest had a habit of rising every morning and asking what bill or resolution was under consideration. It got his name in the *Congressional Record*, which was what he wanted. He would thereupon vanish until the next day. Not then Speaker of the House, Reed had the floor one day when this ancient member rose to repeat his daily routine. The interruption over, Reed hit back: "Now, Mr. Speaker, having embedded that fly in the liquid amber of my eloquence, I will proceed." It brought an avalanche of laughter which ended the old gentleman's daily interruption of House business. Tom Reed's amber became something to be avoided.

* * *

To Representative Henry Cabot Lodge he gave his famous definition: "A statesman is a successful politician who is dead," which he almost matched by another: "The Senate is a nice, quiet sort of place where good Representatives go when they die."

* * *

A strict disciplinarian, Reed enforced the minor as well as the major rules drastically. He banished smoking from the floor. Shirtsleeves were out of order; members must keep their coats on. One day a member wearing low shoes and white socks leaned back and deposited his pedal extremities on his desk. Reed saw it at once and dispatched a page to the offending member with this message: "The czar commands you to haul down those flags of truce."

THE FILIBUSTERERS

WHAT'S A FILIBUSTER?

Mr. President, something has been said about a filibuster. I do not know that I exactly understand what that word, filibuster, means, but I want to say right now that I would to God I had the power to stand here without eating a bite or taking a drink or sleeping a wink until twelve o'clock on the fourth day of March, 1931, if it would keep this iniquitous infernal machine from being put on the people of Amercica. If you call that a filibuster, then I am guilty, and I am ready for the sentence of the court, whatever it may be.

Senator Coleman L. Blease of South Carolina, in 1931, while filibustering against the World Court Protocol

* * *

In 1939 a group of Western Senators, intent on raising the price of silver, launched a filibuster to block all legislation until the price was raised. Late in the battle eloquent Josh Lee, junior Senator from Oklahoma, took up the relay. The Chamber gaped with empty seats. Inattentive Senators sat listlessly writing letters, daydreaming, gossiping, and indulging in other pursuits concomitant to filibustering.

Mr. LEE. Mr. President, I am not responsible for the seats in the Senate chamber not being filled. I am reminded of the preacher who, after preaching a while, said to one of the ushers, "Wake up Brother Brown," to which the usher replied, "Wake him up yourself; you put him to sleep."

We have just heard an able discussion of gold by the Senator from Colorado, Mr. Adams. We have heard a learned speech on silver from the Senator from Nevada, Mr. Pittman. We have heard a glowing tribute to copper from the Senator from Arizona, Mr. Ashurst. Now I propose to put in my nickel's worth. In spite of the fact that it is said more people go crazy over money than any other subject, I shall venture a few observations on the subject of money.

Mr. SCHWELLENBACH of Washington. I should like to inquire just the implications of the Senator's remark. Does he imply that he has already gone crazy or that he expects us who listen to him to go crazy?

* * *

There are still some Senators who think they are the Senate, but the Senate can teach them better if the Senate will. The only way under the sun to do it is to pass a resolution in this body to stay in permanent and perpetual session until this bill is passed. Do not give the filibustering Senators from eleven at night until eleven o'clock the next morning to hunt up new pegs whereupon to hang verbiage. Let them talk until they drop upon their seats. Let them talk until their mouths are so dry that they cannot utter another word.

Senator John Sharp Williams of
Mississippi on how to wear down
a filibuster

* * *

"NO BRAVE MAN WOULD WEAR"

In a Republican no-holds-barred filibuster in 1879 against the Army Appropriation Bill, imperious, arrogant Senator Roscoe

Conkling of New York collided violently with Senator L. Q. C. Lamar of Mississippi. Lamar's withering rebuke to Conkling still rankles in its category. The Democratic majority was at the moment pressing an amendment prohibiting the expenditure of federal funds to station troops at the polls in the South.

Mr. CONKLING of New York. Now, sir, one other word, and I have done. What is this Army Bill? It is a juggle, a contemptible juggle and subterfuge. It is an attempt, by indirection, by stealth, by trick, by an act which is to operate as a fraud, to do that of which we had high sounding proclamation at the end of the last session. It is to compel the Executive and to compel the minority to pay the Democratic party of this country a price as the condition by which they will make appropriations and allow the government to live. That is what it is.

Mr. President, I have endeavored to show this proud and domineering majority—determined apparently to ride roughshod over the rights of the minority—that they cannot and should not do it. But I am ready to be deemed responsible in advance for the assurance that while I remain a member of this body, and, at all events, until we have a previous question, no minority shall be gagged down or throttled or insulted by such a proceeding as this. I say, Mr. President (and I measure my expression), that it was an act not only insulting, but an act of bad faith. I mean that.

Mr. LAMAR of Mississippi. Mr. President, with reference to the charge of bad faith that the Senator from New York has intimated towards those of us who have engaged in opposing these motions to adjourn, I have only to say that if I am not superior to such attacks from such a source I have lived in vain. It is not my habit to indulge in personalities, but I desire to say here to the Senator that in intimating anything inconsistent, as he has done, with perfect good faith, I pronounce his statement a falsehood, which I repel with all the mitigated contempt I feel for the author of it.

Mr. CONKLING. Mr. President, I was diverted during the commencement of a remark, the culmination of which I heard from the member from Mississippi. If I understand him aright, he intended to impute, and did, in plain and unparliamentary language, impute, to me an intentional misstatement. The Senator does not disclaim that.

Mr. LAMAR. I will state what I intended, so that there may be no mistake . . .

The PRESIDING OFFICER. The Senator from New York has the floor. Does he yield to the Senator from Mississippi?

Mr. CONKLING. And I am willing to respond to the Chair. I shall respond to the Chair in due time. Whether I am willing to respond to the member from Mississippi depends entirely upon what that member intends to say, and what he did say. For the time being, I do not choose to hold any communication with him. The Chair understands me now; I will proceed.

I understood the Senator from Mississippi to state in plain and unparliamentary language that the statement of mine to which he referred was a falsehood, if I caught his word aright. Mr. President, this not being the place to measure with any man the capacity to violate the rules of the Senate, or to commit any of the improprieties of life, I have only to say that if the Senator–the member from Mississippi–did impute or intend to impute to me a falsehood, nothing except the fact that this is the Senate would prevent my denouncing him as a blackguard and a coward. (Applause in the galleries.) Let me be more specific, Mr. President. Should the member from Mississippi, except in the presence of the Senate, charge me, by intimation or otherwise, with falsehood, I would denounce him as a blackguard, as a coward, and a liar; and, understanding what he said as I have, the rules and the proprieties of the Senate are the only restraint upon me.

I do not think I need to say anything else, Mr. President.

Mr. LAMAR. Mr. President, I have only to say that the Senator from New York understood me correctly. I did mean to say just precisely the words, and all that they imported. I beg pardon of the Senate for the unparliamentary language. It was very harsh; it was very severe; it was such as no good man would deserve, and no brave man would wear. (Applause on the floor and in the galleries.)

* * *

When a measure to extend the life of the Radio Commission was pressed in the Senate in the closing days of the Seventieth Congress, 1929, it met a prompt and formidable filibuster led by Senator Coleman L. Blease of South Carolina. Blease was congenitally opposed to radio, and carried on his expostulations for hours. He had ample aid from others on the floor.

Now they want to put a radio back here right behind me so as to broadcast what is going on in the Senate. I do not know anything about radios; I never listened to one of them in my life. I do not know what they might do, and that is what I want to ask Senators. What danger might lurk in such an instrument, for instance, at the time of the inauguration, now only three days distant? They might fill that thing up with gas, some deadly gas, and just about the time the crowd assembled in this chamber, everybody in control of the government of the United States, some fellow might turn on a machine down here and just gas out the whole business.

I do not care very much about the radio bill. I will be honest about it. I am opposed to it. I was the only man who voted against it when it came up. I have rather peculiar ideas, I guess, and perhaps a lot of people think they are fool ideas, but to save my life I can not see what right we have to control the air that God Almighty gave the people.

* * *

DRAW POKER AND FILIBUSTERING

On this June day, 1926, the Senate was discussing the much-mooted parliamentary pastime, filibustering, that is, unlimited debate. Senator Oscar W. Underwood of Alabama was pointing out the rules of the game as he viewed them. To illustrate, he drew a parallel between the rules of the Senate and those of a popular sport—draw poker—that had for a century engaged the off hours of statesmen behind the scenes on Capitol Hill. Significantly, the word "poker" had a magic, revivifying effect on the upper chamber. Ninety Senators were instantly on the qui vive.

Mr. UNDERWOOD. One of the troubles in the Senate has been that we conduct filibusters and deny them. There was no concealed filibuster about this one. I stood where I am standing now and informed the Senate that I intended, under the rules of the Senate, to filibuster that bill; and I made it very apparent by applying the filibuster not to the bill but to the *Journal*, where nobody could get by.

Mr. JOHNSON of California. Mr. President, would the Senator do it under the same circumstances again?

Mr. UNDERWOOD. Certainly, as long as the Senate maintains its archaic rules. I want to illustrate. As I said, I possibly can not illustrate to my friend from Arkansas or my friend from Idaho, because they may not know the game.

Mr. ROBINSON of Arkansas. To what games does the Senator from Alabama refer?

Mr. UNDERWOOD. I am going to explain it right now.

If the Senator will take his seat in my chair, I can explain it to him right here.

Mr. ROBINSON. I think just at this time I should prefer to occupy my own chair. (Laughter.)

Mr. UNDERWOOD. There is a game called draw poker . . .

Mr. SHORTRIDGE of California. One moment, Mr. President. (Laughter.)

Mr. ROBINSON. Mr. President . . .

Mr. OVERMAN of North Carolina. The Senator will have to explain what that means.

Mr. UNDERWOOD. I am going to illustrate, if my friends will allow me.

Mr. SHORTRIDGE and Mr. ROBINSON addressed the Chair.

The VICE PRESIDENT. The Senator from Alabama has the floor. To whom does the Senator yield?

Mr. UNDERWOOD. I yield first to the Senator from California.

Mr. SHORTRIDGE. The Supreme Court of the state of Kentucky has decided that it is not a game of chance, but purely a scientific undertaking.

Mr. UNDERWOOD. It was in this instance. Now, I yield to the Senator from Arkansas.

Mr. ROBINSON. Mr. President, the Senator from Alabama may draw the fire of the Senator from California by a reference to that mysterious amusement which he calls draw poker, but I assure him that most of us have no knowledge whatever of the subject. (Laughter.)

Mr. UNDERWOOD. I was sure of that, and therefore I excluded my friend from Arkansas.

Mr. ROBINSON. May I ask the Senator from Alabama a question?

Mr. UNDERWOOD. Yes.

Mr. ROBINSON. The Senator from Alabama, I assume, is an expert on the subject he is now discussing?

Mr. UNDERWOOD. I always try to be candid with my friends, and I am not afraid to say what I believe. I have played the game of draw poker. I regret to say that I am not an expert. That has been forcibly illustrated to me. (Laughter.)

Mr. COPELAND of New York. Mr. President, I understood that the Senator from Alabama was going to explain this game to the Senate.

Mr. UNDERWOOD. I am, if I may have the floor.

Mr. NORRIS of Nebraska. Mr. President, the Senator would have to have something else besides the floor.

Mr. CARAWAY of Arkansas. Mr. President—

Mr. UNDERWOOD. I yield, but I should be glad if I might be allowed to proceed.

Mr. CARAWAY. I merely wanted to remark that that is the first time the Senator got the interest of the other side of the chamber, when he commenced on that subject. (Laughter.)

Mr. UNDERWOOD. To be sure. I realize fully, I will say to my friend from Arkansas, that I now have the most vivid interest of the Senate that I have ever possessed since I have been a member of this body.

Mr. NORRIS. That only illustrates that the Senators on this side are anxious and willing to learn from those on the other side.

Mr. UNDERWOOD. Yes.

Mr. ROBINSON. And that—

> Where ignorance is bliss
> 'Tis folly to be wise.

Mr. SHORTRIDGE. I would like to ask the Senator from Alabama whether three of a kind would beat two pair. (Laughter.)

Mr. UNDERWOOD. I am going to illustrate that right now.

Mr. REED of Missouri. Mr. President, what astonishes me is the interest the Senator from Nebraska has manifested in this subject. (Laughter.)

Mr. UNDERWOOD. If I may come back to the illustration, I think Senators will understand it, even the gentlemen who do not know the game. The old game of draw poker had certain definite rules and regulations as to what was the highest hand. I believe what was called a straight flush was the highest hand available.

SEVERAL SENATORS. A royal flush! (Laughter.)

Mr. UNDERWOOD. A royal flush. But as times progressed, and we reached the age of modern times and modern ideas, innovations were introduced into the game, such as allowing deuces to run wild; I believe that is the term. If a man got a deuce, he could call it an ace, or a king, or anything else. And there were a number of other innovations. Finally the game got to a point where a man could hold innumerable aces and straight flushes, until the game became so confusing that no man knew what he was playing. I do not believe in that kind of innovations. I believe if people are going to play the game, they ought to play it according to the old rules that are laid down in Hoyle, the demonstrated rules.

Mr. REED. Then why does the Senator want to change the old rules of the Senate? I think we have an illustration here not of deuces running wild but of a very fine ace running wild. (Laughter.)

Mr. UNDERWOOD. I thank the Senator for that; but if he will allow me to make my illustration, if he were playing in a game of poker with deuces running wild, and he held four deuces, I take it he would call them four aces. I do not approve of that. I do not believe it is the way to play the game. But as long as it was understood that that was the game we were playing—allowing deuces to run wild—if I were in the game and got four deuces, they would be four aces in my hand.

In the same way I felt that while the Senate had certain rules, the game should be played according to those rules.

Every Senator who knows me knows that I have been opposed to unlimited debate in the Senate ever since I have been a member of the Senate; that I believe in a reasonable cloture rule. But if the Senate is going to play the game of allowing deuces to run wild, to have unlimited debate, and anybody can engage in a direct or concealed filibuster if he desires to do so, I want to assure my friends that when I thought the occasion was of sufficient importance I would not hesitate for a moment, now or any other time, to use the rules of the body by which we play the game to effect the legislation that I desired. I do not blame any Senator for using those rules as long as they are the rules. I am not critical of the Senator who plays the game according to the rules; and that is the rule.

Every Senator here knows that if I wanted to defeat the most important piece of legislation pending in this body today—and I could secure the hearty cooperation of a dozen men in this body—I could start in the morning hour, object to the unanimous consent for the approval of the *Journal*, start to amend the *Journal*, and ten days from now, even if we had continuous sessions, the same *Journal* would be before the Senate of the United States for approval.

* * *

HUEY "KINGFISH" LONG FILIBUSTERS AGAINST THE NRA

Zaniest of the filibusters that have tortured Senatorial patience up the years was the remarkable off-the-cuff one-man harangue delivered by Senator Huey Long of Louisiana in July 1935. For fifteen and a half hours, with only two quorum calls to respite him, Long arrayed his talents against the proposed extension of the National Recovery Act which the Supreme Court had already wrecked. Opening up shortly before noon, Long chattered on until nearly four o'clock the next morning—a remarkable feat of physical endurance in itself. Holding the floor alone, he ran the gamut of wit, derision, bizarre humor, ridicule, sarcasm, wisecracks, jokes, and whimsical dissertations on men, measures, and the Bible. To kill and consume time he dished out elaborate recipes for frying oysters, making Roquefort cheese dressing, and, most famous of all, potlikker. Long's hourly record has been bettered, but his acting, clowning, and showmanship leave all competitors far behind him. At the time, Long was a potential Presidential candidate in the upcoming 1936 election. Here are a few gems from Long's historic chattering. (The captions are the editor's.)

BLUE BUZZARD!

This is the NRA measure. As everybody knows, the NRA is another form of government—not exactly another form of government, I made a mistake; it is another government. NRA is another government. It is not only another government, it has a President and a Senate and a House of Representatives of its own. It has a high court of its own, and several courts under that court. It has a flag of its own. It has law books of its own, rules of its own, regulations of its own, and God knows what else it has. It has the Blue Eagle. That is the insignia instead of the Stars and Stripes.

Yet we find the NRA coming back here again. We are to have another sample of the blue buzzard, another bite out of this bird. It is to be cooked up again to see if it will not taste better. It reminds of boarding-house hash. One day there is put on the table a lot of victuals which no one can eat, and the next day they are ground up and brought out as hash, and you eat it because you do not know what is in it.

Bringing back this blue buzzard! The Supreme Court says it is unconstitutional.

* * *

A man came in to see me the other day and said to me, "I ask you to consider what good I have done for this country. I am the man who taught two trees to grow where one used to grow before." I said, "You are the worst citizen we have in this state under our system of things. You are the man who ought to be condemned and hung tomorrow morning. The idea of your coming in here and asking for consideration because you taught two trees to grow where one used to grow." We want a man who fixes it so that none can grow. We want a man who can teach the people how none could be raised. That is what we want in this year of our Lord 1935, of Franklin Delano Roosevelt "the little."

* * *

MR. ASTOR MIGHT CATCH A "KINGFISH"

Mr. LONG. I desire the Senators to understand that I am not doing any filibustering. I am speaking on this bill. If every member of the United States Senate had listened to what I said on the NRA bill when it was up here we would not be in this mess we are in now.

I am familiar with this business. I had an uncle who used to lend money. He never wanted to lend me a cent; but if I could just get him to come up to the old country place, ten miles out of town, and induce him to stay with us overnight, and get him off all by himself for a week or two, nine times out of ten I wound up by borrowing something from him; but so long as he stayed in town at the bank and everybody else could get hold of him and whisper to him, there was not much chance of my landing any loan from my uncle. I want to tell you that if I were trying to get money out of the President of the United States, and Vincent Astor and the Rockefellers were trying to get money out of him at the same time, and I were trying to get to him before they got to him, but they got hold of him and took him five hundred miles to sea on a five-million-dollar yacht and left me sitting on the dock in July, with the thermometer at 102 degrees in the shade, they would get the money and I would get the sunshine. (Laughter.) That is the difference.

Mr. LEWIS of Illinois. Does my able friend mean to intimate to the audience in the galleries, to the public, and to the able representatives of the press that the President of the United States, as a guest of Vincent Astor on a yacht, was amenable to the influence of his host to such an extent that he would grant or permit the money of the United States or the favors of the government to be granted to his host as the result of and as compensation for the trip on the yacht?

Mr. LONG. What was the question? Do I intimate Mr. Astor would use it for that purpose? Do I intimate Mr. Astor would use that five-million-dollar yacht to make money out of the government? Yes; just like taking candy away from the baby. Certainly I do!

They said you had Mr. Astor before you as a witness. I did not summon Mr. Astor as a witness. I would have had too much sense to expect Mr. Astor to give any testimony that would have done any good. You called Mr. Astor in there, and you said, "Mr. Astor"—I do not know what the questions and answers were. I did not hear them, and I did not read them, but I will repeat them to you. I never heard him, and I never read his testimony, and I never asked what it was, but I will tell you what his answers were. He was asked about this: "Mr. Astor, did you mention any business of the government to Mr. Roosevelt?"

"Oh, no! Nothing of the kind was mentioned. I never even thought about business. In fact, I forgot that I had a contract drawing a few million dollars out of the government Treasury for carrying a postcard down to Timbuktu. Why, no; I never thought about it! I was only interested in fish. There was a peculiar kind of fish down there, and we were having trouble getting the fish in, and these two little hundred-million-dollar contracts did not make any difference with us. We wanted to see if the President could not go down there and bring in a fish, and, for all we know, he might have been able to catch a 'kingfish' while he was down there on that trip." (Laughter in the galleries.)

* * *

PLOW IT UP, BOYS!

Lo and behold, we came along in the year 1932 with ten or fifteen million out of work, $262,000,000,000 of debts, too much to eat and too much to wear, and, by proclamation of the President of the United States, because we had too much to eat and too much to wear, people were hungry, people were starving, people were naked, and people were homeless, we went out to kill cattle because we had too many cattle to eat. We went out to kill hogs because we had too many hogs to eat. We killed the sows to keep them from breeding more hogs that people could not buy. We plowed up the cotton. We burned the corn. We limited the wheat. We took everything, and we christened the Secretary of the Department of Agriculture Lord Royal Destroyer. Out went his agents, destroying the food, destroying the material for clothing, destroying the homes, destroying the reproductive propensities of plant and animal life, because they had found out that there was more to eat and more to wear in the United States than the people had the money to buy!

"People have not the money to buy clothes!" Plow up the cotton, and shear the sheep, and put the cotton and the wool in the Atlantic Ocean!

"People have not the money to buy the dried fruits of California and Louisiana!" Dump it into the Pacific Ocean and into the Gulf of Mexico!

"People have not the money to buy milk and eggs!" Pour it into Lake Michigan and put it up somewhere around in Maine to keep it from coming into New York.

"People have not the money to buy hogs!" Kill ten million of them, and kill all the sows to keep them from bringing any more hogs, because the people have not any money with which to buy.

* * *

HUEY LONG'S HOW-TO-FRY-OYSTERS RECIPE

Mr. President. . . . I have spent a number of evenings acquainting people with how to prepare oysters. I had a bucket of oysters sent to me from Louisiana the other night, and I was asked by a very fine bunch of my friends if I would not drop around with the New Orleans oysters and fry some of them for them in good Louisiana style and way. So, Mr. President, I bought a frying pan about eight inches deep. I bought the frying pan because I was afraid they would not have a frying pan there in which I could fry the oysters. I bought a frying pan, as I said, eight inches deep and about seventeen inches in diameter.

Mr. TYDINGS of Maryland. When the Senator fries oysters, is potlikker one of the concomitants?

Mr. LONG. No; that does not go in with the oysters. I will come to that later. As I was going to illustrate, Mr. President, about these oysters that I got from New Orleans.

I bought this frying pan eight inches deep and fourteen to sixteen inches or seventeen inches in diameter, and I bought a ten-pound bucket of cottonseed-oil lard, but I forgot to get a strainer, and when I got to the place to fry the oysters I had everything there except the meal and the strainer.

The lady had some meal, but she did not have any salt to salt the meal with, and that was the only bad thing about it. The strainer which they had was not the best strainer in the world, but I could use it all right. However, they had no salt for the meal, but I took the oysters, Mr. President, the way they should be taken, and laid them out on a muslin cloth, about twelve of them, and then you pull the cloth over and you dry the oysters. You dry them, you see, first with a muslin cloth, and then you take the oysters, after they have been dried, and you roll them into a meal which is salted. I did not have it salted this night, but it should have been salted. (Laughter in the galleries.)

Mr. President, you roll these oysters in the dry meal. You do not want to cook the meal or put water in the meal at any time or anything like that. Just salt the meal and roll the oysters in it. Then, let the grease get boiling hot. You want the grease about six inches deep. Then you take the oysters and you place the oysters in the strainer, and you put the strainer in the grease, full depth down to the bottom. Then, you fry those oysters in boiling grease until they turn a gold-copper color and rise to the top, and then, you take them out and let them cool just a little bit before you eat them.

Now, Mr. President, most people cannot tell when an oyster is done. They do not know when it has been fried enough. You have got to have them totally submerged and you wait until they rise to the top, and when they rise to the top, a golden-copper color, then the oyster is cooked just exactly right, and then you take the strainer up out of the grease in the dish and the oysters are there and you let them drip for a little while and allow them to cool a little and then you eat them.

* * *

POTLIKKER

Now, I will give my recipe for potlikker. First let me tell Senators what potlikker is. Potlikker is the residue that remains from the commingling, heating, and evaporation (laughter)—anyway, it is in the bottom of the pot! (Laughter.)

Here is how potlikker is made. First you get some turnip greens. You have to wash turnip greens many times. One of the principal reasons why people do not like turnip greens is that they never do get them clean. "You have to wash them lots of times," said Cato, "lots of times." They always call him "Cato." (Laughter.)

Take the ordinary green, turnip greens or mustard greens, though turnip greens are better than mustard greens. Turnip greens contain more manganese than do mustard greens. The trouble with turnip greens is that most people never get the greens washed clean. Sand is always in them. You have to wash them and wash them and wash them, particularly if you have not any flowing water. If you have good flowing water to shower them with, you can wash them more easily. But you have to wash them plenty of times. In order to get every vestige of dirt and sand and grit out of the greens you have to wash them many, many times.

That is the first thing you do—wash the greens. You wash the turnip with the greens or you can cut the turnips off and peel them and wash them by themselves, and then wash the greens by themselves if you want to do it that way.

All right this far! Then you take the greens and turnips and put them in the pot. Remember this: Do not salt them. Do not put any salt, do not put any pepper, do not put any mustard, do not put any kind of seasoning in the pot with them. Put the greens in the pot. Cut up the turnips. The turnip greens could be cut up a little, too. Put them all in there together.

Then when you get them all in the pot together, put in a sizable quantity of water, I should say about as much water as you have of turnip greens. Then put in there a piece of salted side meat. I would say if you had a pot of turnip greens about two thirds the size of this wastebasket which I hold in my hand, or perhaps three fourths that much, you ought to put about a one-pound hunk of side meat that is sliced, but not clear through, just down to the skin part. Put about a pound of side meat in there. That side meat is just salty enough and has just salt enough in it that it will properly temper the turnip greens when it has been cooked enough. That will be all the seasoning that is needed.

When you have cooked the greens until they are tender and the turnips until they are tender, then you take up the turnips and the greens, and the soup that is left is potlikker. (Laughter.) That brings on the real question of the art of eating potlikker, the matter of consuming potlikker. You draw off the potlikker and you eat it separately from the turnip greens.

* * *

"MY ENEMIES PUT ME IN OFFICE"

Mr. LEWIS. I should like to know whether the solicitude of the able Senator from Louisiana as to the salary of the President of the United States and his privileges and power as Commander-in-chief have been awakened in the Senator in view of his contemplation of being President himself.

Mr. LONG. Not exactly. I would not quarrel over the salary. (Laughter.) I would have no differences. If I were made President of the United States, I would not argue about the salary. I say to my friend from Illinois, who wants to know whether I would accept the job of President of the United States, that if the present President keeps going as he is going I may have to take the office. (Laughter.) One can never tell. If he does not improve and they do not run somebody against him in the other party better than the man they ran at the last election, the chances are that I will be almost unanimously nominated and elected President of the United States.

My enemies have given me nearly every job I ever held, strange to say. I deserve practically no credit for getting any position I ever held, even though I got it honestly, or by rugged ways, or by any other methods. I claim to have gotten every one of my offices honestly.

I do not deserve any credit, even though the job is worth anything—and none of them are worth much. I have held all the jobs that are worth anything up to the one I now hold. I have had every honor that the people could bestow on me. I have had them all.

I have had the people throw roses in my path, and I have had them throw brickbats in my window. (Laughter.) I have had all the experiences that come in politics. I know all about politics. No man has had a wider or more varied experience in politics than have I, for my age. So I know something about politics.

I have had them vote to impeach me one month and banquet me the next month, then vote to impeach me the next month and then give me a hundred million dollars to spend the next month. I know the vicissitudes of public and private life to some extent.

I will say this: Time will tell. The only way I can explain how I got the few jobs I have had in politics is that my enemies have had less sense than I have had. They have made the blunders which made the Huey Longs. They are the men who make the Huey Longs.

* * *

Mr. President, I digress to say that I have just been handed a note which says that some smart newspaper has just wired for my Louisiana oyster recipe. People will know how to fry oysters in the United States by this time tomorrow. (Laughter.) I will educate a million people how to fry oysters between now and tomorrow night, and they will know how to enjoy oysters. They have never known before.

To resume; they started to baptize my uncle out in the old milling bottom, and as they led him out, there floated out of his pocket the ace of spades. (Laughter.) As he turned around and walked a little further the king of spades came out, then the queen of spades, and just as the preacher was ready to baptize him the jack and ten-spot of spades came out.

His wife was standing over on the bank. She became frantic and threw up her arms and she said, "Don't baptize him, parson. My husband is lost. He is lost." But the young son was sitting on the bank, and he said, "Hold on, Ma. Don't get excited. If he can't win with the hand he's got there, he can't win at all."

"CHICKEN! CHICKEN! WHAT MAKES YOU ROOST SO HIGH?"

This delicious, ridiculous dish of nonsense was cooked up by Long in describing the celebrated "Chicken-coop Case" which induced the Supreme Court to invalidate the National Recovery Act. It was the highpoint of Long's filibuster. For his hearers—sleepy Senators and jampacked galleries—it was excruciatingly funny low class vaudeville.

I want to explain what that violation of the Live Poultry

Code of the NRA was, so that Senators will understand in advance. They sent a coop of chickens, I think, from New Jersey to New York. In that coop there were some "dominicker" roosters, a plymouth rock, a buff cochin, white leghorns, and some common chickens that nobody knows by any name except chickens, hill-billy chickens, and various other kinds of chickens. When this coop of chickens got to New York a man opened the coop; the chickens began to flutter around, and he looked into the coop and said to himself, "I believe I like that pullet right over there, that frying-size pullet. I believe I will take that one." The man in charge said, "Hold on there; wait a mintue there; before you pull out that pullet hold on a minute; let us get down the NRA rule book and look through it and see what the rule is before you take a chicken out of the coop, because these chickens come in here in interstate commerce and you have got to follow the rule book." So they got down the rule book, volume 6, or whatever volume it was of the code affecting chickens.

I presume there are about sixteen or twenty volumes; I do not know as to that; there may not be so many; but let us say, for the purpose of the argument, they got down volume 6 and looked on page 631 of section 4, subsection Z, subdivision 2, and it said there that no man could reach into a coop of chickens and pick out any particular chicken; that he had to blindfold himself and reach in and take whichever chicken came to hand. (Laughter.)

The rule book of the code said that a man could not reach into a coop of chickens and take whichever one he wanted. "Well," the chicken purchaser said, we will say for the sake of the argument, "that chicken there has got pin feathers that I do not like," or, "I do not want a hen; I want that rooster," or, "I do not want a rooster; I want a frying-size chicken," or, "I want a yellow-legged chicken; I do not want a buff cochin; I want a white leghorn." People are funny that way;

they think there is some difference in chickens. As a matter of fact, there is not much difference in chickens; chickens are nearly about the same. Take them up and take them down, a chicken is a chicken, and you cannot make anything else out of it. However, this code said the purchaser had to take whatever chicken he found. He would not do that. So he proceeded to get the chicken that he wanted, regardless of the law and the code. He took the chicken home and put it in his pot, made some dumplings–probably, in violation of the law, being made too big. (Laughter.) So they indicted the poor devil and ordered him sent to the penitentiary because he got out of the coop the kind of a chicken he wanted. He made the dumplings. He fried some dumplings and probably boiled the gizzard, when he should have roasted it. Mr. President, a gizzard is better roasted than boiled. I found that out years ago. Always roast a gizzard; never fry a gizzard. When he got through with the chicken the man was ordered to jail. Of course a man does not like to go to jail if he can help himself. I have been there myself. I was there one time because I did not have any other place to go and another time because they did not want me to go any other place. But this man decided that he would not go to jail. So he went to court. He hired a lawyer. The case was tried and he lost the case.

The judge called him up and said, "Sorry, old man; you violated the law." The defendant asked, "What law?–the law that Congress passed?" The judge said, "No; you violated a law that the rule-maker under this chicken-coop case made, which is found in rule book, volume 6, page 641, paragraph Z, subdivision 2, which provides that a purchaser has to take chickens as they come; that he cannot discriminate between chickens." (Laughter.) I remember a poem about that:

Chickens, chickens, what makes you roost so high?
Chickens, chickens, they are going to get you before you die.

This fellow then gets a lawyer, pays him his cash, and gets

convicted. He appeals the case to the circuit court of appeals. That is the next court up. . . .

The Supreme Court finally passed on the case. It is a case of very great importance. It is one of the most far-reaching cases of jurisprudence in the country. It is more important than anything since the days of the Roman Empire.

Who knows what the Supreme Court held in that case? This is what they held, that a man has the right to any kind of a chicken he wants to eat. . . .

> Petitioners were convicted in the District Court of the United States for the Eastern District of New York on eighteen counts.

Imagine that! Eighteen chickens, eighteen counts! In my time, Mr. President, if a man came and got a sack full of chickens they did not try him on more than one count. In this case it is divided up—eighteen chickens, eighteen counts, eighteen sentences in the penitentiary. One Dominique rooster could send a man to the penitentiary.

> Charging violations of what is known as the "Live Poultry Code."

The Live Poultry Code! I wonder if they have another for dead chickens. They must have another rule or another code for chickens after they kill them.

Can you beat that? Do you know that if you bought a chicken from a man and it was taken out of a coop in any way other than as it is provided in the code, that that would be a conspiracy? Mr. President, the law provides that whoever conspires to violate a law of the United States is guilty of a conspiracy and he will go to the federal penitentiary. Any man who bought a chicken out of a chicken coop which was taken out of there in any way except as it was stated in the code that it should be taken out of that chicken coop was guilty of a conspiracy to violate the law. If you took a Dominique rooster and twisted his neck off, when the code said that his head ought to be cut off with a hatchet, you would be violating the law. That would be a conspiracy and it would cause you to be sent to the penitentiary.

Talk about law! Where had we finally gotten to when the Supreme Court of the United States finally said, "Hold on"? They said, "Hold on. All the crazy people are not in the insane asylum," they said. "Hold on. Stop a minute; just a minute," said the nine judges. "Just a minute here, you 21-year-old-men. Think a while before you finally get down to where you make this government the laughing stock of the animals of the woods and the fowls of the air. Stop a while."

There never was a polecat conference that had in it any such thing as was before the Supreme Court of the United States in the poultry case. Eighteen counts, eighteen convictions, and the nineteenth conviction on the ground that they wrung the chicken's neck off instead of cutting its head off with a battleax.

* * *

HOW SENATORS GET TOO SMART FOR THEIR PEOPLE

There are a whole lot smarter men in the Senate than I am, but I am a liver man than they are. A dumb live man is a whole lot better than a dead smart man. Long years ago I found out that it was not going to do any good to get wise and not be here to give my wisdom any chance to live; so I saved my eyes. I saved all the various and sundry necessary functions that give me sight and give me hearing. I commend to the ninety-four learned members of this body that if they will just move around among the people, and not get too far above them in learning and skill, they will do well.

For instance, a man stays here in the United States Senate. He learns so much that when he goes back home and begins to talk to a meeting of the country people, they do not know anything about what he is talking about. He has forgotten the kind of language to which those people are accustomed. That is the trouble. Then some old hillbilly comes out of the woods who understands their language, and licks the Senator to a queen's taste, because he got so smart that nobody understood anything about his smartness. It does not make any difference how smart you are; if the people cannot understand it, that is not going to do you any good. So I never get so smart but that the people know that I am pretty well acquainted with these matters, and thereby I save my eyesight.

* * *

"NUTS RUNNING AMERICA"

So we are here now. Why? Why are we here now? We are here now to try to put the NRA through, and the big boys are in the galleries. They are afraid there will be an antitrust law tomorrow. Monday morning will catch them, and they will not have it wiped off the books; so "Hurry, hurry, hurry, and put the NRA back on the books!"

What is the NRA? The national racketeers' arrangement. (Laughter.) That is what they are talking about putting back on the books. NRA–Nuts Running America. (Laughter.) NRA–Never Roosevelt Again. (Laughter.) Put it back on the books! That is what they are trying to do, to put the antitrust laws off the books and put NRA on the books.

* * *

THE DEMOCRATIC PARTY AND THE OLD HEN

Never did I think the time would come, when I followed the Democratic banner and held the Democratic precepts, when I should ever have to argue with Democrats about keeping the antitrust laws on the books. I used to think the party amounted to something. Somebody wanted to know if I am a Democrat. Yes; I am a Democrat. I am still a Democrat. I have not quit the Democratic party, and I have not quit the Democratic principles. I have not quit the Constitution of the United States. I am still a Democrat. I am a genuine Democrat. I am a Democrat who has remained a Democrat, even though the "brain trust" wants me to do something else. It makes me feel like reading a little from Scripture on this matter, from Ecclesiastes, in which reference is made to such things. I will read something from that book. Ecclesiastes comes in after Leviticus and Deuteronomy and Proverbs. It comes right after Proverbs. In this volume I have it is on page 862. Ecclesiastes was supposed to have been written by King Solomon. Many people have indicated that they are rather confused as to who wrote Ecclesiastes. Now what is the party name? Here is what the party name ought to have been: A good name is better than precious ointment.

A good name—that is all the Democratic party had the last time; it had only a good name, the good name that old Jefferson and Andy Jackson left; that is all it had; and the good name that William Jennings Bryan gave it. So we went out and used the only capital stock we had. We promised the people certain things we were going to do. We made promises giving them to understand just what we would do and then we paid no attention to the promises. If I had the ability to do it, I should like to convince every Democrat in the Senate that the quicker we return to the ancient principles and do justice to the common element, the more surely will we get ourselves out of the morass of calamity and of all kinds of confusion, complications, difficulties, and complexities, messed up in every kind of disaster charged against the party everywhere, moping in the wilderness of confusion and nobody knowing what to do, everybody wondering what is going to be the next move and whether it is going to be possible to move, wondering just like a hen sitting on a nest and not knowing how many eggs she has under her, not knowing even what is there. Mr. President, a hen can count but one. That is something many people do not know. You can rob a hen's nest of a dozen eggs and leave one there and the hen will still go back and lay in the same nest. She does not know that the nest has ever been robbed. She can count but one. That is the way the hen operates.

The guinea fowl, however, cannot even count one, but the guinea has the sense of smell, and you have got to take the eggs out of guinea's nest with a long-handled spoon so that the guinea cannot tell that some human hand has been there, or else the guinea will not go back to that nest and lay any more eggs. So long as you will take the eggs from the guinea's nest with a long-handled spoon the guinea will come back and lay eggs all the year; and so long as the prerogatives are taken from under United States Senators with a long-handled spoon they still think everything is all right. (Laughter.) Those desiring to deprive the Senate of its prerogatives have reached the long-handled spoon into the United States Senate and they have taken out every egg the Senate has got any right to hatch out. There is nothing left for the Senate to hatch; but they took the eggs from the Senate with a long-handled spoon, and Senators still think they have got some business being here. . . .

* * *

ROLL OUT THE PORK BARREL! "NO!" CRIED SENATOR CARTER

In the dying hours of the Fifty-sixth Congress, March 3, 1900, Senator Thomas H. Carter of Montana launched a one-man filibuster that scuttled the then-enormous $60,000,000 "Pork Barrel" River and Harbor Bill that contained a little "pork" for improving almost every creek and coastal inlet in America. Denouncing the bill as a vicious raid on the Treasury, he ridiculed it to death, fought off Senators whose creeks would share in the "pork," and mounted his parliamentary blockade to the very last moments before adjournment. These flashes from Senator Carter's money-saving remarks are quite revealing.

Mr. CARTER. Mr. President, I have no hesitation in saying in the presence of the Senate that the basis upon which this bill and all harbor and river bills for a dozen years have been constructed is vicious. I feel now that a public service will be performed in preventing this bill from becoming a law. It is based, framed, constructed and completed upon the despicable principle of division and silence. The bill is surcharged with items repugnant to the judgment of every Senator.

The first forty-seven pages of the bill relate to harbors. These items carry large sums of money. They go to a great extent to swell the aggregate of sixty-odd million dollars carried by this bill. Then follow the rivers. Before taking up the rivers let me call your attention briefly to the harbors.

For instance, we have the sum of $5,000 appropriated to take care of Mattituck Harbor, New York. Who ever heard of Mattituck Harbor before tonight. Where is Mattituck Harbor? If you will turn to page forty of the committee report you will find where Mattituck Harbor is:

> This harbor is a tidal inlet extending about two miles south

from Long Island Sound to the village of Mattituck, on Long Island, about seventy miles east of New York City.

Now mark this unheard-of basis for an appropriation—an astonishing revelation:

> The natural depth of water at the entrance is from one to two feet!
>
> (Laughter.)

We are to start in with from one to two feet of water to dig out a harbor to get up to the village of Mattituck, unknown to anybody outside the postal authorities of the United States and persons living in the vicinity.

Mr. CHANDLER of New Hampshire. What is the depth of the water we are to get?

Mr. CARTER. They want thirty feet of water at Mattituck Harbor. The Senator from West Virginia very aptly suggests to me that turkeys are required as towboats to tow the catfish out of this place when the water gets low. The Senator from Maryland says to me that we had better sink a well up there and pump the water out in order to get a harbor. This sounds ridiculous, but the naked cold truth remains that out of the toiling millions whom we are empowered to tax we are to take $5,000 for this purpose. That takes the opera-bouffe aspects from this case and makes it something of a tragedy.

Mr. WELLINGTON of Maryland. Now I believe that the river and harbor bill should not be passed by the Senate of the United States. It is one of those iniquitous measures that is attempted to be passed upon each and every occasion by interesting this, that, and the other Senator in this, that, and the other state. It is the old flag and an appropriation. I believe it to be an iniquitous measure—to use the vulgar term, a steal.

Mr. CARTER. I am glad to have a recruit who is so enthusiastic as my friend from Maryland. But, Mr. President, I will not delay the Senate with any further reference to New

York, save to refer briefly to two or three items. We have here, for instance, the improvement of Oak Orchard Harbor, $2,000. In the immediate vicinity of Oak Orchard Harbor the schoolchildren know of the harbor, but there is not anybody in the Senate who ever heard of it before. There is not anybody in my state who ever heard of it; and the population of Montana is a traveling population. (Laughter.) I find with reference to Oak Orchard Harbor, New York, for which we are to contribute the sum of $2,000:

The harbor is Oak Orchard Creek.

Not a river, but a creek! (Laughter.)

I recall a survey demanded by a member from Texas, during my brief service in the House of Representatives, of a river in that state, with a view to having some improvements made upon the river in the interest of navigation. When the engineer of the United States Army went down there to examine the river, with a view to having deep water for a hundred miles up through the channel, the member met him at the mouth of the river and said: "Do you think we would be more comfortable going up the river in a buckboard than on horseback?" (Laughter.)

But, Mr. President, I do not wish to go over these small harbors any further. You might follow around the line to Mississippi, Louisiana, Texas, leap across the continent to California, Oregon, Washington, and every point of the United States that gives a vote in either House of Congress, and you will find that the whim of the member, the demand of a constituency in a locality, rather than the serious engineering aspects of the case, has constituted the rule of action.

But when we get to the rivers—and we must get to the rivers, Mr. President—we find in pursuing this bill that, beginning with Vermont, New York, Ohio, Pennsylvania, Michigan, Illinois, Wisconsin, Minnesota, the Great Lakes, every little stream that can by any possibility be tortured into a basis for an appropriation is named in the bill. Not content with this, we go down the Mississippi River. Not content with going down the Mississippi River, we stop at every little creek and inlet that pours water into that majestic stream, and follow that creek or stream up to its source.

Mr. President, Senators will find little instruction, but much of amusement in reading over the names of the various rivers provided for in the state of Virginia. The interest will increase when you pass Virginia, down to the coast of North Carolina. I would at this point like to have the aid of the Senator from that state who is present (Mr. Butler), in the vain attempt, which I shall make to properly pronounce the names of some of the rivers which are provided for in a most bountiful manner here. First is:

> Improving Scuppernong River, North Carolina, $14,000.

I desire to know from the Senator whether my pronunciation of that name is correct?

Mr. BUTLER of North Carolina. The Senator's pronunciation is eminently correct and very euphonious; but the Senator unfortunately is attached to a locality in a part of the earth so far West that he has never yet become acquainted with that luscious grape that is indigenous to North Carolina known as the Scuppernong.

Mr. CARTER. Oh, that furnishes ample justification for the proposed appropriation. I did not connect the grape with the river. (Laughter.) I was thinking of water and not of wine. (Laughter.)

Passing the Grape River, letting $14,000 pass down the stream, we come next to the Pamlico River. I have heard of that river; but the Tar River, never. And yet I suppose the Tar River is well known—in the locality through which it runs. (Laughter.)

Mr. BUTLER. If the Senator did not know that, if he had been in the Union Army in the late war, he would have learned something about tar, because during that war the saying became famous that a soldier from North Carolina had so much tar about him that he would stick and never run.

Mr. CARTER. Judging by the names in this bill, there are more rivers in the state of North Carolina than in any equal portion of the earth's surface anywhere to be found. (Laughter.)

We pass then to South Carolina, and we have the Santee River, $20,000. Then the Wateree River. Here we are getting down to the genuine article—"water." (Laughter.)

Mr. TILLMAN of South Carolina. The Senator from South Carolina is responsible for but two items in the bill. If the Senator from Montana will permit me, I will say for his benefit and information that Almighty God blessed our country with sufficient rain to give us a stock of water in the soil that will cause rivers to flow, and we do not have to dam up the melting snow in order to get reservoirs to endeavor to irrigate. I sympathize with the Senator, for I have been out through this country, and I never could see what it was made for except to hold the world together. (Laughter.) I hope the Senator will be able to get some water in his eloquent effort tonight; but he had better let South Carolina alone, because there is nothing in this bill for South Carolina that is not honest and decent.

Mr. CARTER. Mr. President, I am very glad to have the Senator sustain his well-known reputation for good conscience and rectitude by disclaiming responsibility for these items. (Laughter.) The great abundance of water in South Carolina evidently led the Senator when charged with the destinies of that state to undertake to regulate the whiskey traffic through the state authorities.

Now, we have for the Congaree, $5,000—

Mr. TILLMAN. I will say, if the Senator will permit me, that we do not have to import water to mix with our whiskey. We can always get enough water; but the Senator would have in some portions of his state to carry it along with him.

Mr. CARTER. We do not drink at all. (Laughter.)

Mr. TILLMAN. The Senator means that they do not drink any water at all. (Laughter.)

Mr. WELLINGTON. The idea of expending vast sums of money for the improvement of insignificant streams, such as those cited and noted, one after the other, by the Senator from Montana, makes the scheme laughable and ridiculous. Sir, the time for it has passed by, because instead of benefiting the country by such attempts, the system has become a stench in the nostrils of honest people. The bill before us is a bill of jobs.

It is a bill of big and little steals, in which one man helps the other in looting the Treasury. . . .

Mr. CARTER. A Senator told me an hour ago that there were items in this bill so much more ridiculous than those referred to that they would be entitled to a place in a comic almanac—items not referred to by me at all—as, for instance, as to one item said to be in this report. The engineer who inspected the proposed improvement is alleged to have stated that the only way to improve the stream was to cut down all the brush along its banks, pull out the snags, and when the river went dry to pick up the logs in the bottom, pile them, and burn them, and having done that to just put a dam at the lower end of the river, sink an artesian well, and fill the place with water. (Laughter.)

As a sample of some of the things that were not read this evening, I will call attention to Trinity River in Texas, and let us see what the Trinity River is. There is quite a handsome appropriation for Trinity River—$12,500 being provided for that stream.

> This stream discharges into Galveston Bay through several mouths or passes.

I suppose, a sort of delta at the mouth of the river—

> Opposite each of these a bar existed, over which there was a depth of but 3.5 feet at mean low tide, which was not sufficient for purposes of navigation, at least five feet of water being required.

Now, let us see about the matter. We start there with three feet. We had one place this afternoon with only one foot to start with, but this has three feet and five inches! . . .

Mr. WELLINGTON. Swamp navigation.

Mr. CARTER. Swamp navigation. Then strange, startling, you have not water to run in the river until you dig artesian wells at the head of it. I will stay here until this time tomorrow night, if need be, to prevent that item from going on the statute books of the United States, and I think it is the duty of every Senator in this chamber, measured by my view, to join me in the effort. . . .

How does it find its way here, then? By the way so many items get into this bill—by a system of swapping and trading and the exercising of all such influences as follow swapping, trading, and bartering. No one intends to do wrong in this connection. Nobody feels that he is injuring the government, because the abuse is so old that the custom has gained some degree of respectability by the passage of time.

The bill has grown steadily from a few million dollars not many years ago until now $60,000,000 passes this year without challenging an item. The next bill will come up boldly and brazenly with $75,000,000 to be taken from the public Treasury. The next bill will be $100,000,000.

The rivers are not increasing in number; the harbors are not increasing; but, Mr. President, we are starting out to make rivers where rivers do not exist. (Laughter.) Each and every piece of work that is done involves the necessity of continual maintenance. So this bill, speaking of little creeks down in the country, provides for maintenance of what? Not navigable water—nay, not so; because, as some Senator aptly said last night, the little boats that skip up and down many of these alleged rivers would pass over the country on a fresh field of dew without any river at all—would skate along.

Think of it, Mr. President! This bill carries, as I say, $60,-000,000. It is accompanied by a report of over four hundred pages, passed through the Senate with a couple of dozen members present, about as quickly as the clerks could read it. I feel quite confident it passed in less than four hours; I think in less than three hours.

I have from the beginning attempted to show that this collection of matter known as the river and harbor bill emanated from a system inherently vicious and destined always to lead to an evil result.

It is the system of swapping—not in a wrongful sense—but in the sense of good fellowship in part, and through a desire to get legislation worked along and made successful. Thus it is that the larger items are diminished below the proper degree, that the smaller items may be provided with something. Where you can not do anything better for a district, throw a thousand dollars up there to try to improve a stream that never can be of any value for commerce.

There has not been an attempt on the floor of the Senate to defend any one of the items assailed. Around about me in this chamber I have observed Senators, whose hands are tied by the iniquitous system of construction which obtained in the bill, compelled to stand mute because cooperating, unconsciously it is true, in the execution of this scheme of legislation that carries into effect certain laws unnecessarily squandering the public money.

I am perfectly willing to occupy the remainder of the time, but if any of the ceremonies of the Senate require the attention of the body, I am willing at this moment to surrender the floor.

Mr. WELLINGTON. Perhaps the Senator from Montana, before he sits down, would like to call attention to a few more items in this bill, and will do so on account of the euphonious names. I want to call his attention to Murder Kill River, in New Jersey, and Raccoon Creek, in one of the other states, both of which are to have some three or four hundred thousand dollars expended upon them.

Mr. CARTER. Raccoon Creek is in the list. Raccoon Creek has not been overlooked. Compared with most of the items to which I have alluded, it is a very meritorious item, and that is largely due to the modesty of the Senators from New Jersey.

Mr. President, in conclusion I thank the Senate for the considerate attention given to me in the course of these observations. I have endeavored to do my plain, simple duty. I realize that certain Senators, to whom this bill is very dear, indeed, earnestly wish I had yielded the floor at an earlier hour. I think upon mature reflection, however, any semblance of ill feeling incident to the disappointment of that kind will fade away. I recall many instances of contests on this floor where Senators indulged in very earnest and long-continued discussion, the effect of which was at the time to create some feeling, but it has been the general rule that the plain path of duty dictated by each man's conscience is a safe rule to follow.

JEFFERSON AND LINCOLN

THOMAS JEFFERSON TO THE RESCUE!

Thomas Jefferson has been the unfailing oracle of the "faithful" ever since he died in 1826. The great statesman would probably wake from his sleep at Monticello could he hear some of the absurdities ascribed to him by crossroads and even topflight politicians. His wraith is ever present in the Senate and House ready to back up the "devout." This summoning of Jefferson's apparition to the Senate one day in the 1890's invoked Senator William V. Allen of Nebraska to offer this pungent comment.

Mr. President, the Senator from Wisconsin says I likened him to Thomas Jefferson. I said that if Mr. Jefferson could be taken from his coffin and placed in the Senate chamber and listen to the speech of the Senator from Wisconsin and the warm words of centralism and tyranny embraced in that speech he would be utterly amazed and utterly astonished that the Democracy of this age could have so degenerated from the Democracy of his age. And yet Jefferson has been made to do duty here more frequently than any other statesman of whom I have ever heard or read. Whenever it is essential to entertain these galleries or to entertain the Senate, Thomas Jefferson is trotted out in the Senate chamber like a trick mule at a circus and made to perform all kinds of tricks for the entertainment of those present.

I have heard him charged in this chamber (and I want in my feeble words to defend his memory) with over one hundred inconsistencies on public questions. Yet I do not suppose there is a schoolboy who has read a common school history of this country who does not know that Thomas Jefferson was the great Democrat of this country in his age, that he was thoroughly in accord with the principles of a democratic or republican form of government, that he believed then and taught the doctrine that the power of this country should rest in the people and be diffused as far as possible among all classes of people. However, the Senator from Wisconsin, undertaking to square himself with Jefferson and make himself a Jeffersonian Democrat, says that really Mr. Jefferson was the first great civil service reformer in this country. Mr. Jefferson not only preached, but he practiced the doctrine that to the victor belong the spoils. Mr. President, no person taught in plainer language than Thomas Jefferson the doctrine of rotation in office.

* * *

"NOT ONE TENTH AS MUCH INFLUENCE ON MANKIND AS JOHN ADAMS"

There are many who will differ with Representative Champ Clark of Missouri in this avowal. Clark's admission—and he was a Democrat—occurred in 1894 while he was speaking in favor of establishing a public library for the District of Columbia.

Mr. Speaker, since the world began, no country ever sent to any legislative body such a set of brilliant, philosophical, finely educated, well-equipped men as the South sent to the American Congress before the Civil War. In all the records of mental, political and psychological achievements they have no equal. Yet New England has five hundred times as much influence upon the drift of things in America, upon public opinion in America, as all that brilliant crowd of men that came here from the South before the war.

Take Thomas Jefferson, the greatest philosopher that ever lived, the profoundest thinker that ever devoted himself to the science of politics. Thomas Jefferson, Democrat, statesman, and friend of the human race, had not one tenth the influence on mankind finally that John Adams had, though John Adams, if he had lived a thousand years, never would have as much sense as Jefferson had in fifteen minutes. The reason for the difference is—and I want to state it to the House in a way that they will never forget it—the reason for the difference is that New England turned to the business of writing books.

While Thomas Jefferson was creating states; while Calhoun, Hayne, and Lowndes were expounding the Constitution; while George Rogers Clark was taking possession of a continent; while Taylor and Cass and Scott were fighting for a hemisphere; while Clay and Crittenden and Felix Grundy were electrifying the world with their eloquence; while John Sevier, Sam Houston, and their brethren in arms were taking an empire; while Thomas Hart Benton was battling for possession of the Great Northwest; while Frank Blair was saving the nation; while John J. Crittenden was proposing compromises; while John C. Breckinridge and Judah P. Benjamin and the remainder of those distinguished and brilliant statesmen of the South were uttering polished sentences here that will never die—the schoolmasters up in New England were writing books about America, and, as far as they were concerned, America is New England and New England is America.

By a sort of literary legerdemain every skirmish that took place in New England during the Revolution has been magnified into a great battle and every one of them has its monument. Every molehill is magnified into a mountain. I am not blaming the New Englander. He has been industrious in his day and generation. Every love scrape that happened among the New England hills has been developed into a novel. In reading New England novels I sometimes wonder if any man south of Mason and Dixon's line ever courted a woman. I know he never courted one as courting is represented as being done in a New England novel. I think I know how courting is done down there. Every horse trade or transaction that has taken place up there for years has been made the subject of an essay. The people of New England wrote books. They formed opinions of the people. I do not blame them; but what makes me sick is the fact that the great men who lived and died south of Mason and Dixon's line, who fooled away their lives in politics, have gone down to their graves and are forgotten.

The greatest race of people that ever lived on the face of the earth is composed of the Virginians, the Kentuckians, and the Missourians. Emigration moves on lines of parallel. Virginia peopled Kentucky; Kentucky peopled Missouri; Missouri has peopled the gorgeous and "omnivorous" West. But if Madison and Jefferson and George Mason and Patrick Henry, Nathaniel Macon, John Randolph of Roanoke and that crowd of great men had devoted themselves to commerce instead of politics, Norfolk, instead of New York, would today be the great commercial metropolis of the world. But they did not do it.

* * *

WAS JEFFERSON RIGHT?
NO, SAID SENATOR JAMES REED

In a ringing speech, in June 1926 Senator James A. Reed of Missouri challenged the basic principle of his party's founder:

that lex majoris partis *is the fundamental law of rights. Moreover, Reed went on to prove it—almost.*

Majority rule! Where is the logic or the reason to be found back of majority rule except in the mere necessity to dispatch business? The fact that a majority of one or ten vote for a bill in the Senate is not a certification that the action is right. The majority has been wrong oftener than it has been right in all the course of time. The majority crucified Jesus Christ. The majority burned the Christians at the stake. The majority drove the Jews into exile and the ghetto. The majority established slavery. The majority set up innumerable gibbets. The majority chained to stakes and surrounded with circles of flame martyrs through all the ages of the world's history. The majority in China believe in a doctrine and follow a code of ethics different from ours. Either they are wrong or we are wrong. The majority in India follow a different code of ethics and have a different set of ideas than we, and they far outnumber us. Either they are wrong or we are wrong. The majority went down the pathway of the ages wearing gyves, which they voluntarily forged and fastened upon their arms, and when a minority arose headed by some brave soul they hanged him upon a gibbet, they crucified him upon a cross, they pulled his limbs apart with horrible instruments of torture, and the majority stood there leering and gibing at the man who was the apostle of a better day.

Majority rule without any limitation or curb upon the particular set of fools who happen to be placed for the moment in charge of the machinery of a government! The majority grinned and jeered when Columbus said the world was round. The majority threw him into a dungeon for having discovered a new world. The majority said that Galileo must recant or that Galileo must go to prison. The majority cut off the ears of John Pym because he dared advocate the liberty of the press. The majority to the south of the Mason and Dixon line established the horrible thing called slavery, and the majority north of it did likewise, and only turned reformer when slavery ceased to be profitable to them.

Majority rule! Now, of course, there are times and occasions when it becomes necessary to settle propositions, and we set up a rule that if one man more votes for it than votes against it, we follow and accept that majority mandate. On many questions we have adopted that rule in this body and in the House of Representatives, but not always. Let us see: A treaty is made with a foreign country. The advice and consent of the Senate is necessary. Can a majority give that advice and consent? It can not. There must be a two-thirds majority under the Constitution of the United States. Thank God we have the Constitution, or another like unto the Senator from Alabama would be here tomorrow asking that treaties should be ratified by a majority vote. There are some things so important that they require more than a majority. An official can not be impeached by the Senate by a majority vote, because the framers of the Constitution wisely concluded that if one third of the body doubted the fitness of a man, that man should not occupy a responsible position.

* * *

In the closing hours of the Special War Session of Congress, 1861, Senator Timothy O. Howe of Wisconsin struck a resounding keynote when he rose to cast his vote for a joint resolution approving and confirming all the "extraordinary acts, proclamations and orders" exercised by President Lincoln in meeting the emergency created by the outbreak of the Civil War.

Mr. President, I vote for this measure; and I approve it, as I said at the outset, all the more because the taking of them involved the President in some personal hazard. Why, sir, I have heard that when a chasm opened in the Forum of Rome, it was said by the oracles that whatever was most precious in Rome must go into it to close it; and a soldier, with his armor on, mounted his horse, and spurred him into the chasm; and I am told that the conscious earth closed over him. Sir, while your flag floats from yonder dome, let no man who loves the Republic ever forget that, in the year 1861, the President of the United States saw a horrid chasm opening in the Union of the States, and he did not hesitate a moment, clothed with all that was precious to him in the way of name, or fame, to plunge himself into the chasm. There may be those who, thinking that a post of personal danger, prefer to stand on the brink of the chasm, and throw their shafts at him. As for me, I prefer to do as I have told you today, go down into the gulf with him, and share whatever peril there is there. I avow my approval of his acts—every one of them!

* * *

One day in 1959 when charges of national insecurity and weakened American defenses were flying across the Senate chamber, Senator Everett M. Dirksen of Illinois rose to speak in rebuttal—and at the same time tell another Lincoln story.

Mr. DIRKSEN. Mr. President, the distinguished Senator from Missouri (Mr. Symington) stated as follows:

> Mr. President, the American people are being enticed down the trail of insecurity by the issuance of misinformation about our deterrent power; and specifically about the missile gap.
>
> The intelligence books have been juggled so the budget books may be balanced.
>
> This is a serious accusation, which I make with all gravity.

Mr. President, as I take thought of the unending comment in this security field, I think of an old Missourian in the Civil War days who was passionately devoted to the candidacy of John C. Fremont. This old citizen of Missouri was quoted by the Chicago *Times* of that day in a comment which he made about Abraham Lincoln, the Commander-in-Chief. In that comment he said that Abraham Lincoln's head was "too light for the weight of his feet." Then he made a comment on conducting the war, and he said that running the war reminded him a good deal of the manner of a man who was climbing trees to catch woodpeckers. Some friend said, "You will never catch any woodpeckers that way." "Well," he said, "maybe not, but if I don't catch 'em I'll worry 'em like hell."

I apologize for the term, but it is an exact quote and I got it from the writings of Carl Sandburg.

It seems to me that in this security field all the comments which are being made are nibbling comments on the sniping side, and disparaging, it seems to me, of the defense effort of this administration.

When I think of all the comments by persons who seem to think they are better able to do this job in the defense field than is the President of the United States, I think of the Committee on the Conduct of the War which was established away back in the Civil War days. I make no exceptions. I have in mind Republicans as well as Democrats. On that committee there was a man named Benjamin Wade, from Ohio. He started out as a canal driver and as a mule skinner. Then he became a teacher, as I recall, and then a lawyer. That qualified him to conduct a war. He marched down to the White House, shook his finger at Lincoln, and said, "You have to fire General McClellan." Lincoln said, "Well, whom shall I use to replace him?" And Wade said, "Anybody." Lincoln, out of his majestic concepts, said, "I cannot fight a war with anybody; I must have somebody."

Away back in those days we had a little of the same attitude which is now apparent.

* * *

Blame for the federal defeat at Bull Run in 1861 fell hardest on President Lincoln, who ordered a green army out to do battle, and on superannuated General in Chief Winfield Scott. These two were the whipping boys in the House and Senate. Came the day later in the year when General Scott's physical fitness to command an army was up for consideration. It brought out, in the House, this question of his having been forced to fight against his better judgment.

Mr. RICHARDSON of Illinois. I believe the gentleman from Missouri (Mr. Blair) has taken issue with me upon the fact that General Scott was forced to fight the battle of Bull Run. I will tell the gentleman what occurred yesterday morning in the presence of my friends [Representatives] McClernand, Logan, and Washburne, of Illinois, and also in the presence of the President of the United States and the Secretary of War. I will try and repeat what was said. General Scott said: "Sir, I am the greatest coward in America." I rose from my seat immediately. "Stop, sir," said he. "I will prove it. I have fought this battle, sir, against my judgment. I think the President of the United States ought to remove me today for doing it. As God is my judge, after my superiors had determined to fight it, I did all in my power to make the Army efficient. I deserve removal because I did not stand up, when my army was not in condition for fighting, and resist it to the last."

Mr. WASHBURNE of Illinois. As my colleague has referred to that conversation, I hope he will state to the House what President Lincoln said to General Scott.

Mr. RICHARDSON. I will state it. The President said, "Your conversation seems to imply that I forced you to fight this battle." General Scott then said, "I have never served a President who has been kinder to me than you have been." But, sir, he did not relieve the Cabinet from the imputation of having forced him to fight this battle. He paid a compliment to President Lincoln personally; and, Mr. Speaker, standing here in my place, I desire to say of Abraham Lincoln—and I have known him from boyhood's hour till now—if you let him alone, he is an honest man; but I am afraid he has not the will to stand up against the wily politicians who surround him and knead him to their purposes.

* * *

"MR. LINCOLN—A WEAK AND IMBECILE MAN"

Before the Senate this January 29, 1863, was a measure to indemnify President Lincoln for any flarebacks resulting from his suspension of the writ of habeas corpus. The administration considered the bill imperative to the prosecution of the war. It brought on an explosive scene from Senators fearing arbitrary arrests by government executives. In a fury of aspersions Democratic Senator Willard Saulsbury of Delaware touched a new low in personal vituperation of President Lincoln. Two days later, Saulsbury, threatened with expulsion by the Senate, apologized for his intemperate remarks, but denied that he carried a concealed pistol when he launched his assault on the President.

Mr. SAULSBURY of Delaware. Sir, I think the great fault of the times, and the great fault of the public men in this country, is not speaking out just what they feel and how they feel and how they think. It seems now that a man to be in good odor with what they call the northern confederacy, to which I do not belong, to which I never wish to belong—

Mr. WILSON of Massachusetts. Nobody calls it a northern confederacy.

Mr. SAULSBURY. Sir, it may be in bad odor to utter such sentiments as these in such a presence; but whether in good or bad odor, they are my honest sentiments, and no consideration other than that of the discharge of my honest duty shall keep me from their utterance. I do not want any northern confederacy or any southern confederacy. I should like to see the Union restored as it was, the people living under a common Constitution, obeying a common law, united, happy, prosperous, and free. We do not intend to be drawn at your chariot wheels wherever you choose to carry us. . . . If that be treason, everybody who chooses so to consider it may make the most of it.

Gentlemen on the other side seem to think that some of us on this side of the chamber, who are uttering our honest sentiments, are getting wild. Are they not now going wild? Is it not time to reverse your insane policy? Why attempt to thwart the designs of Providence and make an equality between the white and black races? Is it not a time to stop such an insane policy? What will be gained by it? You have had your five hundred thousand and your million of men in arms; you have had bloody battles; how much nearer are you to preserving the Union, and especially, let me ask, how much nearer are you to preserving the constitutional rights of the people than you were when you started? You have met disasters, defeat everywhere; and why? Because Sambo has been put up as the idol of your worship, and while you keep him as your god you will fail.

Mr. HALE of New Hampshire. Order! sir; order!

Mr. SAULSBURY. Reduce your point of order to writing.

Mr. HALE. I will do it in a minute.

The VICE PRESIDENT. The Senator from New Hampshire will state his point of order.

Mr. HALE. The point of order is that the Senator accuses the Administration, or the dominant party of the country, of making a god of Sambo. (Laughter.)

Mr. SAULSBURY. Reduce it to writing. I am ready to meet the issue. I believe it is true.

The VICE PRESIDENT. In the impression of the Chair, the Senator has a right to make that allegation.

Mr. SAULSBURY. Sir, I will say now that, although I have in this body characterized the acts of the Administration as most oppressive and tyrannical, I never for a moment dreamed that, in so characterizing those acts, I was striking at Abraham Lincoln personally. I meant to characterize the governing motive, the mental power, if you please, of the Administration as thus acting tyrannically and oppressively; and I say here, in the presence of the American Senate, I would not visit pecuniary damages upon Abraham Lincoln. I do not suppose that man so debased, so utterly devoid of all character, that he would do these lawless acts without consultation. I suppose he called around him men in whose judgment and advice he had great confidence; and I suppose he did these acts after consultation with the friends of his administration. I think the acts were clearly and palpably unconstitutional, and every man who has engaged in the execution of them is guilty of a trespass, and liable to punishment. Would I visit that punishment upon Mr. Lincoln? Not at all. But I would visit it upon those guilty agents of executive power who have advised a course of this kind, who have said to him that these things are right.

Mr. President, you know how true it is that when a man is exalted in a high place, he seldom hears anything except the voice of flattery. The solemn words of truth never enter his ears; he is generally told beforehand, "If A, B, or C approaches you, and whispers in your ear so and so, regard him as an enemy of your administration, and an enemy of the country." Thus has it been with Mr. Lincoln—a weak and imbecile man; the weakest man that I ever knew in a high place; for I have seen him and conversed with him, and I say here, in my place in the Senate of the United States, that I never did see or converse with so weak and imbecile a man as Abraham Lincoln, President of the United States.

Mr. GRIMES of Iowa. Mr. President, I desire to know whether this line of remark is in order.

Mr. SAULSBURY. Let the gentleman reduce his point of order to writing.

Mr. GRIMES. I do not know, I am not familiar enough with the rules of this body to know in what terms a man is permitted to characterize a coordinate branch of the legislative authority of the country.

The VICE PRESIDENT. The Chair was not listening to what the Senator from Delaware was saying, and did not hear the words.

Mr. SAULSBURY. That is the fault of the Chair, and not of the Senator who was addressing the Chair. (Laughter.)

The VICE PRESIDENT. The Senator has no right to allude to the other House.

Mr. SAULSBURY. Will the Senator from Iowa reduce his objection to writing?

Mr. SHERMAN of Ohio. I heard the remarks made by the Senator, and I think they are clearly a violation of the rules of the Senate.

Mr. SAULSBURY. Reduce the point to writing.

Mr. SHERMAN. I will state the words. He called the President of the United States an imbecile. It seems to me that is a clear violation of the rules of order.

Mr. SAULSBURY. Reduce the point to writing, that we may have the judgment of the Senate on it.

Mr. SHERMAN. I have stated it to the President of the Senate.

Mr. SAULSBURY. The rule of the Senate is that when a remark is objected to it must be reduced to writing.

The VICE PRESIDENT. It must be reduced to writing.

Mr. SHERMAN. I will reduce it to writing.

Mr. DOOLITTLE of Wisconsin. I believe that that rule only applies to a certain class of cases when a Senator is out of order. It is a matter personal to him.

Mr. SHERMAN. Well, I do not make the point of order; I withdraw it.

Mr. BAYARD of Delaware. I would suggest to my colleague what is my view of what is becoming to the body, and I hope he will adhere to it. I do not think the President of the United States ought ever to be mentioned by name in this body. He may be called by the style of his office, the President of the United States. A member here has a right to arraign his measures, and to arraign his course. That is all perfectly justifiable; but the individual man ought not to be named in the Senate.

Mr. SAULSBURY. I have great respect for the judgment of my colleague, because I was brought up in a state where his name was potential on all questions of law; but I do not choose now to yield my individual judgment either to him or to his ancestry in this regard. I am my own man, and I represent my own state as I think I ought to do, and I do not ask my colleague or anybody else whether I do it properly or not. I choose to put myself upon my right as a Senator. But, sir, we are not now engaged in the great controversies of the past; we are engaged in the momentous issues of the present, and in the great absorbent issues of the future, which force themselves upon our consideration whether we will or not; and I choose–I assume the personal responsibility, the political responsibility, and every other character of responsibility that attaches to my action–to arraign Mr. Lincoln and his administration, or anybody else and his administration, and I do not intend to be deterred from the expression of my opinion by any blackguardism that can be uttered on this floor.

The VICE PRESIDENT. The Senator is out of order in attributing such language to members of the body, and he will take his seat.

Mr. SAULSBURY. To whom, sir–

The VICE PRESIDENT. The Senator is out of order, and under the rules of the Senate he will be seated.

Mr. SAULSBURY. I do not know what is to be its fate; a final vote may be taken upon it tonight; and therefore, sir, the pertinacity with which I choose to make my objection. If it was a mere adjournment to tomorrow, I would easily yield, but a vote may be taken tonight; and this bill proposes what? Let the Senator from Wisconsin, let any Senator upon the other side of the chamber rise and say in the utterances of an honest manhood what he thinks of it. It proposes to legalize the most despotic exercise of power that was ever practiced in any government since the institution of human society. Talk not to me about *lettres de cachet;* talk not to me about the espionage of Napoleon; talk not to me about any of the arbitrary exercises of despotic power in this country since the recollection of the reading of the Senator from New Hampshire and myself; they are all buried beneath the wave of oblivion in comparison to what this man of yesterday, this Abraham Lincoln, that neither you nor I ever heard of four years ago, has chosen to exercise. Sir, it is out of order, I am told, so to characterize the act of an administration; but if I wanted to paint a tyrant; if I wanted to paint a despot, a man perfectly regardless of every constitutional right of the people, whose sworn servant, not ruler, he is, I would paint the hideous form of Abraham Lincoln. If that be treason—

The VICE PRESIDENT. The Chair rules that this course of debate is not pertinent to a question of order, and therefore rules the Senator out of order; and he will take his seat.

Mr. SAULSBURY. Of course I will do so.

The VICE PRESIDENT. The question before the Senate is, "Shall the decision of the Chair stand as the judgment of the Senate?"

Mr. SAULSBURY. The voice of freedom is out of order in the councils of the nation!

The VICE PRESIDENT. The Senator is out of order; and the Sergeant-at-Arms will take him in charge unless he observes order.

Mr. SAULSBURY. Let him take me.

The VICE PRESIDENT. The Sergeant-at-Arms will take the Senator in charge.

In accordance with the order of the Vice President, the Assistant Sergeant-at-Arms, Isaac Basset, Esq., approached Mr. Saulsbury, who was seated at his desk. After a brief conversation they went without the bar and left the Senate chamber.

* * *

A STATUE FOR LINCOLN? "IMPOSSIBLE," SAID SENATOR SUMNER

The idea of putting a statue of Abraham Lincoln in the rotunda of the Capitol ran into stone-wall opposition when it was proposed in Congress shortly after his assassination. Radicals in both Houses openly tried to block it. In January 1866 a bill to employ a young sculptress, Vinnie Ream, to carve the statue brought on a storm. Leading the opposers was gifted Senator Charles Sumner of Massachusetts. Vinnie Ream, a talented artist, had applied for the task because Lincoln had given her sittings for a bust of him shortly before his death. The debate ran on for weeks before final approval. Vinnie Ream's statue of Lincoln today adorns the Rotunda of the Capitol. However, the finest example of her genius is the splendid statue of Admiral Farragut in the square that bears his name.

Mr. WADE of Ohio. I move to take up the joint resolution (H.R. No. 197) authorizing a contract with Vinnie Ream for a statue of Abraham Lincoln.

Mr. SUMNER of Massachusetts. I hope that will not be taken up.

SEVERAL SENATORS. Oh, let us vote.

Mr. SUMNER. Senators say, "Oh, let us vote." The question is about giving away ten thousand dollars.

Mr. CONNESS of California. Taking it up is not giving money away, I hope.

Mr. SUMNER. The question is, I say, about giving away ten thousand dollars; that is the proposition involved in this joint resolution.

Mr. CONNESS. For a statue?

Mr. SUMNER. The Senator says "for a statue"—an impossible statue, I say; one which cannot be made.

Mr. McDOUGALL of California. I am somewhat surprised to hear the Senator from Massachusetts, who professes to be not merely an amateur but a connoisseur in art and an admirer of beautiful things and a person understanding them well, object to a proposition of this kind. We are all informed that the person who makes this proposition to us is an artist; she has evinced her skill. . . .

Mr. SUMNER. I am unwilling to utter a word that would bear hard upon any one, least of all upon a youthful artist where sex imposes reserve, if not on her part, at least on mine; but when a proposition like this is brought forward I am bound to meet it frankly. You might as well place her on the staff of General Grant, or put General Grant aside and place her on horseback in his stead. . . .

Therefore, sir, for the sake of economy, that you may not heedlessly lavish the national treasure; for the sake of this Capitol, itself a work of art, that it may not have anything in the way of ornamental which is not a work of art; for the sake of our martyred President, whose statue should be by a finished artist; and for the sake of art throughout the whole country, that we may not set a bad example, I ask you not to pass this resolution.

Mr. NESMITH of Oregon. Sir, the Senator might have raised the same objection to Mr. Lincoln, that he was not qualified for the Presidency because his reading had not been as extensive as that of the Senator, or because he had lived among rude and uncultivated society. I claim for this young lady, sprung from a poor family, struggling with misfortune and adversity, that she has developed such natural genius that her talents in this direction should be fostered and cultivated in preference to our giving this work to any foreigner. The Senator from Massachusetts has pandered so long to European aristocracy that he cannot speak of anything that originates in America with common respect.

If this young lady and the works which she has produced had been brought to his notice by some near-sighted, frog-eating Frenchman, with a pair of green spectacles on his nose, the Senator would have said that she was deserving of commendation. If she could have spoken three or four different languages that nobody else could have understood, or, perhaps, that neither she nor the Senator could understand, he would vote her fifty thousand dollars. (Laughter.) He is a great patron of art, but not a patron of domestic art. He is a patron of foreign art; he is a patron of those who copy and ape European aristocracy, and he does not propose to patronize or encourage the genius which grows up in our own great country, particularly in the wilds of the West. . . .

I challenge the Senator from Massachusetts to produce one of the foreign artists, of whom he boasts so much, who can produce the equal of that bust. I deprecate his panegyrics upon foreign artists in derogation of those raised in our own country, and particularly those of the great West.

Mr. SUMNER. Where have I said anything in praise of a foreign artist in depreciation of the artists of our own country? I have alluded with praise to the artists of our own country.

Mr. NESMITH. I heard nothing of that. I heard the Senator speak with particular reference to that door which was cast in Munich.

Mr. SUMNER. Which is by a western artist, Mr. Rogers,

reared in the West. I give him praise for what he has done.

Mr. NESMITH. I appeal to Senators on this floor, to those who have natural taste, to those who have an eye for beauty, as I admit the Senator from Massachusetts has not, to support this young lady in her efforts to produce what will be a magnificent statue of Mr. Lincoln.

Mr. McDOUGALL. This young lady is undoubtedly a lady of marked genius; and she has proved, so far as the bust is concerned, that she has produced the best likeness of Lincoln of any person that has attempted it. I have the right to say so, because I was perhaps better acquainted with Mr. Lincoln in his lifetime than any gentleman on this floor; he was a companion of mine many years ago, with whom I was long familiar. I have not been satisfied with any attempt to reproduce his features till I saw the bust produced by this lady. She has achieved a success, showing that she has true genius; and if she is young, the better for her. In five years more she will be as great a genius as she ever will be, no matter how long she may live. "Whom the gods love die young."

Mr. YATES of Illinois. Sir, I am here to say that I shall vote for this proposition with the most delightful pleasure. I think I knew Mr. Lincoln as well as any member of the Senate; I remember his features well; and I think that the artist whose claims are now before the Senate has had as fine a conception, and in the bust she has made has given an exact likeness of Mr. Lincoln. . . .

Mr. HOWARD of Michigan. Now, sir, I am willing to vote the sum of ten thousand dollars for the purpose of securing a good statue of Abraham Lincoln; but I am not willing to vote that sum or any other sum to this person and take the risk of an entire failure in the end. If this country in its history has ever produced a statesman, and a great man deserving to be memorialized in its annals, not only upon the pages of history but in the works of art, it is Abraham Lincoln. . . . I would as soon think of a lady writing the *Iliad* of

Homer; I should as soon think of placing at the head of an army a woman for the conduct of a great campaign.

Mr. COWAN of Pennsylvania. They have done both.

Mr. HOWARD. It has not been their general history.

Mr. McDOUGALL. They have done it.

Mr. HOWARD. No, sir. I would as soon expect from the pen of a woman the *Paradise Lost* or any other great work of genius which has honored our race.

Mr. McDOUGALL. Did you ever read the fragments of Sappho?

Mr. HOWARD. I have read the fragments of Sappho.

Mr. McDOUGALL. What do you say about that?

Mr. HOWARD. That certainly does not prove that Sappho was capable of writing Homer's *Iliad*.

Mr. McDOUGALL. She exceeds Homer in many respects.

Mr. HOWARD. In many respects—in erotic expressions she certainly exceeds Homer. Whether the proposed work in the present case would have a similar merit I cannot say.

But, sir, without trifling on the subject, and without meaning to say a word in disparagement of this young lady, whom I suppose to be a young lady of genius, I insist that we are taking a great risk in entrusting the execution of this work to her.

Mr. SUMNER. A statue is one of the highest forms of art. There have been very few artists competent to make a statue. There is as yet but one instance that I can recall of a woman successful in such an undertaking. But the eminent person to whom I refer had shown a peculiar genius early in life, had enjoyed peculiar opportunities of culture, and had vindicated her title as artist before she attempted this difficult task.

. . . .Voltaire was in the habit of exclaiming, in a coarse Italian saying, that "a woman cannot produce a tragedy." You have already seen that. I do not venture on the remark that a woman cannot produce a statue; but I am sure that, in the present case, you ought to take every reasonable precaution.

Mr. COWAN. I shall vote for this resolution, Mr. President, because I understand that this little child of genius has struggled up amid poverty and difficulty to this great result through the medium of her statuary. I must confess I do not know much about statuary myself. Modern statuary, I think, would be about as well made by the tailor and the shoemaker, all except the head, as by anybody else. (Laughter.) Ancient nude statuary required an exact knowledge of anatomy and of the human form in the natural state. How it is proposed to have this statue of Mr. Lincoln I am not advised. Whether it is to be draped with a Roman toga, or with a white jacket and black coat and blue pantaloons, I do not know. (Laughter.)

Mr. WADE. Perhaps with a cannon ball in his hand.

* * *

"THOUGH DEAD HE SPEAKETH"

In 1879 the Democrats, with majorities in both Houses of Congress, were threatening to repeal all federal election laws, to kill off all statutes posting federal troops at the polls throughout the South. Taunted by his opponents, James G. Blaine of Maine rose in the upper chamber to hurl this dramatic challenge at the Southern majority.

A leading Democrat from the South, a man who has courage and frankness and many good qualities, has boasted publicly that the Democrats are in power for the first time in eighteen years, and that they do not intend to stop until they have wiped out every vestige of every war measure. All the war measures of Abraham Lincoln are to be wiped out!

The Bourbons of France busied themselves, I believe, after

the restoration in removing every trace of Napoleon's power and grandeur, even chiseling the 'N' from public monuments raised to perpetuate his glory; but the dead man's hand from Saint Helena reached out and destroyed them in their pride and in their folly. And I tell the Senators on the other side of this chamber–I tell the Democratic party, North and South–South in the lead and North following–that the slow, unmoving finger of scorn from the tomb of the martyred President on the prairies of Illinois will wither and destroy them. "Though dead he speaketh!"

PATRIOTISM, THE CONSTITUTION, STUMP SPEECHES AND SUCH

CONSTITUTIONALITY AND THE GLANDERS

The 1876 Centennial Celebration Bill was under fire in the House from J. Randolph Tucker of Virginia and others who said it was unconstitutional. Up rose Martin I. Townsend of New York with a squelcher.

Mr. Speaker, I understand that if a strict constructionist wants a measure to succeed, it is constitutional; and if he does not want it, it is unconstitutional. I understand, sir, that the legal position was perfectly expressed by an Irishman in my district. He bought a horse, and when a man owns property he thinks it is the best thing in the world. So the Irishman led his horse out and showed it to his neighbors. One neighbor, wishing to worry him, asked whether his horse had the glanders.

"What is it you call the glanders?" asked the Irishman.

"It is not for me to tell you, but I want to know whether your horse has the glanders?"

"Well," said the Irishman, "if he is better for having the glanders, he has the glanders, but if he is worse for the glanders, he hasn't the glanders at all." Now, the gentleman from Virginia must pardon me, but I think this bill has not got the glanders at all.

* * *

IT WAS UNCONSTITUTIONAL

So said Representative James Thompson of Pennsylvania in ridiculing arguments against a census bill in 1849 and the taking of certain statistics therewith.

I am tired of this constitutional controversy. Scruples in certain quarters have no end, and to illustrate to what extent constitutional scruples may lead, I cannot refrain from relating a story which I heard the other day concerning a Virginia gentleman; and Virginians, you know, are never wrong, though sometimes peculiar. This gentleman became very sick, and it was feared that he could not recover. An intimate friend called upon him to know if he had anything to communicate—any last request to make before his departure to another world. "Yes," said the sick man, "there is one thing that I desire—I do not wish to be buried at the public expense. I wish my friends to provide for my burial." "Why," said his friend, "what objection have you to being buried at the public expense? That honor has been conferred upon many. Why not upon you?" "Because," replied the other, "I have reflected upon the subject, and have come to the conclusion that it is unconstitutional." This serves to show the ruling passion of a strict constructionist, strong in death.

* * *

In 1860, with the breakup of the Union imminent, Senator William H. Seward of New York rose in his place to declare that the power had departed from the South, the scepter fallen from her hands, that the great North would henceforth wield the power and scepter of government. In answer to Senator Seward rose a South Carolina Senator, Governor James H. Hammond, who addressed to his Northern associates on the floor these words.

Sir, what the Senator from New York says is true. The power has passed from our hands into yours; but do not forget it, it cannot be forgotten, it is written upon the brightest page of history, that we, the slaveholders of the South, took our country in her infancy, and, after ruling her for near sixty out of the seventy years of her existence, we return her to you without a spot upon her honor, matchless in her splendor, incalculable in her power, the pride and admiration of the world. Time will show what you will do with her, but no time can dim our glory or diminish your responsibility.

* * *

We brag about ourselves, brag more about our government, that "we are so great." God knows we cannot be as great as we think we are, and that is so necessarily, because it is simply impossible, when God Almighty could hardly be that great himself. But there are some consolations in American history. One of them is: The American people have never yet elected a man who was a "plumb born fool" President of the United States. It sometimes seems that it would be so when you consider the way the nominations are made and the elections carried on, but we have never yet done so. And then there is another consolation. If we should accidentally elect a "plumb born fool" President of the United States, they are not likely to elect him again or to succeed him with another. So that these evils cannot last longer than four years, even if that sort of fool is going to be in the White House.

Senator John Sharp Williams of
Mississippi, 1906

* * *

Mr. Speaker, what is patriotism? Is it a narrow affection for the spot where a man was born? Are the very clods where we tread entitled to this ardent preference because they are greener? No, sir; this is not the character of the virtue, and it soars higher for its object. It is an extended self-love, mingling with all the enjoyments of life, and twisting itself with the minutest filaments of the heart. It is thus we obey the laws of society because they are the laws of virtue. In their authority we see, not the array of force and terror, but the venerable image of our country's honor. Every good citizen makes that honor his own and cherishes it not only as precious but as sacred. He is willing to risk his life in its defense, and is conscious that he gains protection while he gives it.

Representative Fisher Ames of Massachusetts, 1796

* * *

In a debate in the House on a naval bill during the 1880's a Northern member opened his vials of wrath on the South. The word "rebel" rolled from his tongue repeatedly. To reply, up rose "Private" John M. Allen of Mississippi, who stated that he had served as a teen-age boy through four years of war, only to lay down his arms when the Confederacy fell.

Mr. ALLEN. It was perhaps a youthful indiscretion in me, still I stuck at it until all was lost. Then a comrade and I started home, and after traveling some days it occurred to us that we were not doing right: that home was not the place for us while there was an armed Confederate force in the field, and we should go to Kirby Smith, west of the Mississippi. Still we had a hankering for home. Leisurely we wended our way, debating what to do. Finally we saw an old countryman just ahead of us, sitting on a log in his shirtsleeves, with one gallus across his left shoulder and an old straw hat partly concealing his auburn locks.

We approached him, submitted our trouble to him, and asked his advice. The old fellow expressed the opinion that the war was over and advised us to go home, get to work, and do the best we could.

He then said, "Boys, this here war has been a awful war. Think of the blood that's been spilt, and the men that's been kilt, and the money that's been spent. It's jist awful. But, boys, do you know what troubles me more'n all them things? It's jist this, that arter a while some d—d fools will be crying rebels at us." Mr. Speaker, I have simply related this circumstance so fixed in my memory. I make no application of it. I have nothing more to say.

* * *

It is not our duty to be the Don Quixote of the earth; and if it were, we are not capable of performing the function. Why, sir, there are people in this country today—not my enthusiastic friends around me here, but there are really old-fashioned people in the country today who really entertain serious doubts as to the ability of what we call the government of the United States—the House, the Senate and the Executive—to successfully run this government of ours. Yet we are absolutely aching to waltz out into the international arena and "lick" all the other nations of the world.

Representative Charles A. Boutelle of Maine

* * *

I will not yield one inch to secession; but there are things that I will yield, and there are things to which I will yield. It is somewhere told that when Harold of England received a messenger from a brother with whom he was at variance, to inquire on what terms reconciliation and peace could be effected between the brothers, he replied in a gallant and generous spirit. "The terms are the affection of a brother and the earldom of Northumberland." "And," said the envoy as he marched up the hall amid the warriors who graced the state of the king, "if Tosti, thy brother, agrees to this, what terms will you allow his ally and friend, Hadrada, the giant?"

"We will allow," said Harold, "to Hadrada, the giant, seven feet of English ground, and if he be as they say, a giant, some few inches more," and as he spake the hall rang with acclamation.

Senator Edward D. Baker of Oregon, 1861

* * *

In olden times the words "I am a Roman citizen" protected any man when he uttered them, whether on the banks of the Euphrates or on those of the storied Rhine, whether on the plains of Persia or in the mountains of Spain. Why, in that ancient day to be a Roman was greater than a king. I want the announcement "I am an American citizen" to be as the Roman cry in the day of the Caesars—a title of nobility, an armor of defense, a sword of protection, a shield for the weak and suffering, the undying glory of this great nation, man's last and best attempt at self-government.

Representative Grove Johnson of California

* * *

John Adams was not ashamed to make Fourth of July orations—orations which, if uttered today, would be sneered at as spread-eagle speeches. Would to God there were more spread-eagleness in the land than there is. Our Fourths of July have become unmeaning holidays, for boys to fire off crackers and throw up Roman candles. Orations in praise of our glorious land are rarely heard. It is to be hoped this centennial year may be the commencement of a new era; that this great jubilee at Philadelphia may cause to be hatched a new brood of American eagles, to be spread in succeeding years.

Representative Carter H. Harrison of Illinois on the Centennial Celebration Bill, 1875

Lacking a better topic, a red-hot patriot in the House rose one day and began heaping objurgation on Benedict Arnold. A backwoods orator, he lacked grammatical finish. He concluded his philippic with a grand flourish: "Mr. Speaker, Benedict Arnold was a traitor who tried to sell his country. It was the everlastin' ruination of him; and for what he done he will be rewarded with the volcanic eruptions of eternal infamy, and go down to the remotest posterity kivered all over with hell's arsenic!"

* * *

BREAK OUT ALL THE FLAGS!

It was Jackson Day, January 8, anniversary of Old Hickory's victory over the British at New Orleans in 1815. One hundred bills were on the docket announcing the arrival of the glorious day. Objection was raised on the cost of printing so many bills all saying the same thing. It brought a member from the backwoods of Missouri to his feet with a ringing retort.

Mr. Speaker, the gentleman is suddenly seized with the retrenchment gripes, and squirms around like a long red worm on a pin-hook. Gentlemen keep continually talking about economy. I myself do not believe in tying the public purse with cobweb strings; but when retrenchment comes in contact with patriotism, it assumes the form of smallness. Such economy is like that of Old Skinflint, who had a pair of boots made for his little boy without soles, that they might last the longer. I reverence the day we celebrate. It is fraught with reminiscences the most stirring. It brings to mind one of the grandest events ever recorded in letters of living fire upon the walls of fame by the strong right arm of the god of war! On such occasions we should rise above party lines and political distinctions.

I never fought under the banner of Old Hickory, but, by the Eternal, I wish I had. If the old war-horse was here now, he would not know his own children from the side of Joseph's coat of many colors—Whigs, Know-nothings, Democrats, hard, soft-boiled, scrambled, and fried—Lincolnites, Douglasites, and blatherskites! I belong to no party; I am free, unbridled, unsaddled, in the political pasture. Like a big bobtailed bull in fly-time, I charge around in the high grass and fight my own flies. Gentlemen, let us show our liberality on patriotic occasions. Why, some men have no more patriotism than you could stuff in the eye of a knitting-needle. Let us not squeeze five cents till the eagle on it squeals like a locomotive or an old maid. Let us print the bills, and inform the country that we are as full of patriotism as Illinois swamps are of tadpoles.

* * *

Because I believed that, having assumed responsibility in the Philippine Islands, William McKinley was right in asking the question, "Who would haul down the flag?" one of my friends suggested that if I entertained such views my place was over on this side of the Chamber instead of on that, and I promptly responded that if it was necessary for one to have a seat upon the Republican side of the Chamber in order to act in accordance with his patriotic convictions of duty he could consider my place over there from that moment. Mr. Speaker, I had to wait to read these speeches of the distinguished presiding officers of the Democratic national convention six years, for them to endorse and ratify those very views for which they banished me from their side over here on to this side of the Chamber.

One of these gentlemen—if I may repeat a private conversation—I won't indicate which one—one of them said, "Why, Sibley, we knew six years ago that free silver was dead just as well as you did, but it was such a lovely corpse that we wanted to keep it with us as long as we could."

Representative Joseph C. Sibley
of Pennsylvania, 1906

* * *

Mr. Speaker, in the course of this debate much has been said about the Constitution of the United States, but no more, perhaps, than is said about that instrument in most of the debates of this body. The Constitution, for mere talking purposes, is a great favorite, not only in the House, but in the Senate. As a rule, whenever a measure of importance is before us we are reminded by some one that the Constitution is in the way of making it a valid law. In construing the fundamental law of the government all lawmakers feel that they are at home. In the country debating societies the same feeling is to be seen. It must be that some debate on the Constitution at a country school house, or it may be in Congress, was in the mind of him who wrote:

> If Webster from his grave
> Could to this place repair
> And hear the Constitution thus explained,
> Great God! how he would swear!

Representative George E. Seney
of Ohio speaking on a direct tax
refunding bill, 1888

* * *

Had Webster lived till 1865 he would have seen his great arguments in reply to Hayne inspiring, guiding, commanding, strengthening. The judge in the court is citing them. The orator in the Senate is repeating them. The soldier by the camp fire is meditating them. The Union cannon is shotted with them. They are flashing from the muzzle of the rifle. They are gleaming in the stroke of the saber. They are heard in the roar of the artillery. They shine on the advancing banner. They mingle with the shouts of victory. They conquer in the surrender of Appomattox.

Senator George F. Hoar of Massachusetts in his oration when dedicating Daniel Webster's statue in Statuary Hall

* * *

"ONE MASS OF LIVING VALOR"

To meet the onslaught of civil war, President Lincoln summoned a Special Session of Congress that convened July 4, 1861. Lincoln's program called for men, munitions, and money in quantities never dreamed of by the lawmakers before. On July 10, 1861 Senator Edward (Ned) Dickinson Baker of Oregon, superb orator and old friend of the President, called for all-out support of the man in the White House. Already Baker had donned a blue uniform with silver eagles on his shoulders, first and only member of the Senate ever to speak while in the uniform of a soldier. His call to arms echoed through the chamber and re-echoed through the Union. Few today ever heard of Ned Baker, who, within three months, was to die by Confederate bullets at Ball's Bluff.

I propose to ratify whatever needs ratification. I propose to render my clear and distinct approval not only of the measure but of the motive which prompted it. I propose to lend the whole power of the country, arms, men, money, and place them in his hands with authority almost unlimited until the conclusion of this struggle.

He has asked for four hundred million dollars. We propose to give him five hundred million dollars. He has asked for four hundred thousand men. We propose to give him half a million; and for my part I would cheerfully add a cipher to either of these figures.

I want sudden, bold, forward, determined war; and I do not think anybody can conduct war of that kind as well as a dictator.

I do know that the determined, aggregated power of the whole people of this country—all its treasure, all its arms, all its blood, all its enthusiasm, kindled, concentrated, poured out in one mass of living valor upon any foe—will conquer!

* * *

I rise simply to recall an historical incident which illustrates the spirit that ought to control the actions and utterances of a representative of the American people at any foreign post. At the outbreak of the Civil War, Mr. Charles Francis Adams represented the United States at the Court of St. James. On one occasion he was in conversation with some English gentlemen in high authority whose sympathies were on the side of the Confederacy. Up to that time success in the field had crowned the Confederate arms, and one of these Englishmen, thinking, possibly, to annoy Mr. Adams, said to him, "Mr. Adams, these Confederates seem to fight well." Mr. Adams' reply was, "Yes, sir, they do. They are my countrymen."

Representative Galusha A. Grow
of Pennsylvania

* * *

Now, Mr. President, I stand here in my place, meaning to be unawed by any threats, whether they come from men living or dead, that arms should be raised against the individuals or from states. But, after all that has occurred, if any one state or a portion of the people of any state, choose to place themselves in military array against the government of the Union, I am for trying the strength of the government. I am for ascertaining whether we have a government or not—practical, efficient, capable of maintaining its authority, and of upholding the powers and interests which belong to a government. Nor, sir, am I to be alarmed or dissuaded from any such course by intimations of the spilling of blood. If blood is to be spilled, by whose fault is it? Upon the supposition I maintain, it will be the fault of those who choose to raise the standard of disunion, and endeavor to prostrate this government; and, sir, when that is done, so long as it pleases God to give me a voice to express my sentiments, or an arm, weak and enfeebled as it may be by age, that voice and that arm will be on the side of my country for the support of the general authority, and for the maintainance of the powers of this Union.

Senator Henry Clay of Kentucky while pressing his great Compromise of 1850 that, he thought, would solve the slavery question forever

* * *

Sir, I intend to stand by that flag of the Union of which it is the emblem. I agree with Mr. Stephens of Georgia "that this government of our fathers, with all its defects, comes nearer the objects of all good governments than any other on the face of the earth." I have been told, and I have heard it repeated, that this Union is gone. It has been said in this chamber that it is in the cold sweat of death; that, in fact, it is merely lying in state waiting for the funeral obsequies to be performed. If this be so, and the war that has been made upon me in consequence of my advocating the Constitution and the Union is to result in my overthrow and in my destruction, and that flag, that glorious flag, the emblem of the Union, which was borne by Washington during the seven years' struggle, shall be struck from the Capitol and trailed in the dust; when this

Union is interred, I want no more honorable winding sheet than that brave old flag, and no more glorious grave than to be interred in the tomb of the Union.

Senator Andrew Johnson of Tennessee, February 1861

* * *

By descent, I am one fourth German, one fourth Irish, one fourth English, and another quarter French. My God! If my ancestors are permitted to look down upon me, they might perhaps upbraid me. But I am also an American!

Representative Joseph G. Cannon of Illinois, April 1917

* * *

I would like to hear some of the members of this House give more credit to Providence and to God Almighty than they do for saving the Union. I recall an anecdote of the War of 1812 that bears on providential interposition. On the evening before the battle of New Orleans, a British and American picket came near enough to hold a colloquy when the Britisher ventured the prediction that a battle would result the next day. Forecasting events, he said, "On our side we have General Keane, General Gibbs and Lord Pakenham, and we will be bound to whip you." The Kentuckian replied, "Well, on our side we have the Lord God Almighty, the Lord Jesus Christ, and Old Hickory Jackson, and if we don't whip you, I'll be damned!"

Representative W. Jasper Talbert of South Carolina, 1900

* * *

Mr. Speaker, there is one spot somewhere in the broad domain of the United States the mention of which always touches a tender spot in my heart. Its mention produces in my bosom a sweet melody like to the music produced by the playful angel hands upon the strings of golden harps. I learned to love it in my earliest childhood and when I read in this bill that three thousand dollars was to be used to improve that river it made me forgive the members of the committee for their sins of omission and commission, and advocate the enrollment of their names among those who love story, song and home. The place is the one indicated in the song:

'Way down upon the Swanee River,
Far, far away;
Dar's where my heart is turning ever,
Dar's where the old folks stay.

Thank God, the Swanee River is to be improved and cared for!

Representative George W. Ray
of New York

* * *

Had the Greek been asked how long his freedom would last, he would have replied with the same infatuation which seems to have seized us, "Forever!" And yet the matrons who raised up sons for the state, and sent them forth commanding them to "return bearing their shields or borne on them," have been succeeded by the groveling tenants of the harem, and slavish degenerate sons have succeeded free and noble sires all over the land of Leonidas and Lycurgus. Let us take warning by their sad fate, and not permit ourselves to be drifted into this focus of centralized despotism and destruction either by congressional mal-legislation or by judicial construction.

Representative Benton McMillin
of Tennessee, 1883

* * *

"WE ARE IN THE HOUSE OF OUR FATHERS"

1876 was a Presidential Year, and Maine's James Gillespie Blaine, Republican leader of the House, was the Man of the Year. Blaine was as brilliant a figure as American politics ever produced. On January 10 he rose in the House to make his bid for the Presidency by waving the bloody shirt, fanning the dying embers of civil strife, and accusing the ex-President of the Confederacy of being the most vicious murderer in history. Blaine's timing was exact. Before the House was a general Amnesty Bill that would restore all ex-Confederates to citizenship. At this moment Blaine took the floor to offer an amendment that would exclude Jefferson Davis from the ameliorating provisions of the bill. For his listeners he proceeded to open the graves and parade the horrors of Andersonville before the House and nation. Thus he began his attack.

Mr. BLAINE. In my amendment, Mr. Speaker, I have excepted Jefferson Davis from its operation. Now, I do not place it on the ground that Mr. Davis was, as he has been commonly called, the head and front of the rebellion, because on that ground I do not think the exception would be tenable.

But I except him on this ground: that he was the author, knowingly, deliberately, guiltily, willfully, of the gigantic murders and crimes at Andersonville.

Libby prison pales into insignificance before Andersonville. Sir, since the gentleman from Pennsylvania introduced this bill I have taken occasion to reread some of the historic cruelties of the world. I have read over the details of those atrocious murders of the Duke of Alva in the Low Countries, which are always mentioned with a thrill of horror throughout Christendom. I have read the details of the massacre of Saint Bartholomew that stands out in history as one of those atrocities beyond imagination. I have read anew the horrors untold and unimaginable of the Spanish Inquisition.

And I here, before God, measuring my words, knowing their full extent and import, declare that neither the deeds of the Duke of Alva in the Low Countries, nor the massacre of Saint Bartholomew, nor the thumb-screws and engines of torture of the Spanish Inquisition begin to compare in atrocity with the hideous crime of Andersonville!

* * *

But Blaine's flamboyant calumnies did not go unanswered, though the Southern Democratic ranks in the House were stunned. Next day Benjamin H. Hill of Georgia, or simply Ben Hill, rose to reply. Great of mind and speaking power was Hill. A former member of the Confederate Senate, he had been confidential adviser to Jefferson Davis during the war. It was his duty, he felt, to the South and to Davis to defend the latter and challenge Blaine's charges. Here is the opening of Hill's speech, but best remembered was his eloquent, moving peroration that wrung from an enemy the words, "That is the best speech made in the House in twenty years." In this Centennial Year of the Civil War Ben Hill's peroration bears repeating for all–North and South, East and West.

Mr. HILL. Mr. Speaker, the House will bear witness that we have not sought this discussion. Nothing could have been farther from the desires and purposes of those who with me represent immediately the section of the country which yesterday was put upon trial, than to reopen the discussion of the events of our unhappy past.

We had well hoped that the country had suffered long enough from feuds, from strife, and from inflamed passions, and we came here, sir, with a patriotic purpose to remember nothing but the country and the whole country, and, turning our back upon all the horrors of the past, to look with all earnestness to find new glories for the future.

The gentleman who is the acknowledged leader of the

Republican party on this floor, who is the aspiring leader of the Republican party of this country, representing most manifestly the wishes of many of his associates—not all—has willed otherwise. They seemed determined that the wounds which were healing shall be reopened; that the passions which were hushing shall be reinflamed.

Sir, he stands before the country with his very fame in peril if he, having made such charges, shall not sustain them. I hope no gentleman imagines that I am here to pass in eulogy upon Mr. Davis. The record upon which his fame must rest has been made up, and he and his friends have transmitted that record to the only judge who will give him an impartial judgment—an honest, impassioned posterity. No eulogy from me can help him, no censure from the gentleman can damage him, and no act or resolution of this House can affect him.

But the charge is that he is a murderer, and a deliberate, willful, scheming murderer of 'thousands of our fellow citizens'!

For ten years he and his have been reviling the people who were not allowed to come here to meet the reviling. Now, sir, we are face to face, and when you make a charge you must bring your proof. The time has passed when the country can accept the impudence of assertion for the force of argument, or recklessness of statement for the truth of history. . . .

I do not doubt that I am the bearer of an unwelcome message to the gentleman from Maine and his party. He says there are Confederates in this body, and that they are going to combine with a few from the North for the purpose of controlling this government.

Oh, Mr. Speaker, why cannot the gentlemen on the other side rise to the height of this great argument of patriotism? Is the bosom of the country always to be torn with this miserable sectional debate whenever a Presidential election is pending? To that great debate of half a century before secession there were left no adjourned questions. The victory of the North was absolute, and God knows the submission of the South was complete.

But, sir, we have recovered from the humiliation of defeat, and we come here among you and we ask you to give us the greetings accorded to brothers by brothers.

We propose to join you in every patriotic aspiration that looks to the benefit, the advancement, the honor of every part of our common country. Let us, gentlemen of all parties, in this Centennial Year, indeed have a jubilee of freedom. We divide with you the glories of the Revolution, and so we shall divide with you the glories of the future.

Brave Union men of the North, you who fought for the Union for the sake of the Union, you who ceased to fight when the battle ended, and the sword was sheathed, we have no quarrel with you, whether Republicans or Democrats. We felt your heavy arm in the carnage of battle; but above the roar of the cannon we heard your voice of kindness, calling "Brothers, come back!" And we bear witness to you this day that the voice of kindness did more to thin the Confederate ranks, and weaken the Confederate army, than did all the artillery employed in the struggle. We are here to cooperate with you; to do whatever we can, in spite of all our sorrows, to rebuild the Union; to restore peace; to be a blessing to the country; and to make the American Union what our fathers intended it to be—the glory of America, and a blessing to humanity.

Sir, my message is this: There are no Confederates in this House; there are now no Confederates anywhere; there are no Confederate schemes, ambitions, hopes, desires, or purposes here. But the South is here, and here she intends to remain.

Go on and pass your qualifying acts, trample upon the Constitution you have sworn to support; abnegate the pledges of your fathers; incite raids upon our people, and multiply your infidelities until they shall be like the stars of heaven or the sands of the seashore, without number; but know this, for all your iniquities the South will never again seek a remedy in the madness of another secession.

We are here; we are in the House of our Fathers; our brothers are our companions, and we are at home to stay, thank God!

We come to gratify no revenges, to retaliate no wrongs, to resent no past insult, to reopen no strife.

We are here to cooperate with you; to do whatever we can, in spite of our sorrows, to rebuild the Union; to restore peace; to be a blessing to the country, and to make the American Union what our Fathers intended it to be—the glory of America and a blessing to humanity.

But to you, gentlemen, who still seek to continue strife, and who are not satisfied with the blood already shed, who insist that we shall be treated as criminals and oppressed as victims—to you we make no concessions. Martyrs owe no apologies to tyrants.

We ask you, gentlemen of the Republican party, to rise above all your animosities. Forget your own sins. Let us unite to repair all the evils that distract and oppress the country. Let us turn our backs upon the past, let it be said in the future that he shall be the greatest patriot, the truest patriot, the noblest patriot, who shall do most to repair the wrongs of the past, and promote the glories of the future.

* * *

PERSONAL EXPLANATION

Mr. [Oscar] TURNER of Kentucky. Mr. Speaker, I rise to a question of personal privilege. My attention was called yesterday to an editorial in the *Daily Memphis Avalanche* of June 28, in which, speaking of myself, it is stated that I recently found it necessary to assure the country that I had not been drunk for three whole days. Every member upon this floor knows that that statement is entirely false and without foundation, and I denounce it as such. Further it is stated in the same article that I am a "conspicuous member of the House–conspicuous for my inability to keep sober." Now it is a fact that I have not drank any spirituous or other intoxicating liquors during this entire session of Congress. (Cries from the floor: Good! Good! Wonderful!)

Mr. [Jay A.] HUBBELL of Michigan. I am sorry the gentleman's good sense did not come to him a little sooner and induce him to keep a little quiet about this whole thing, and then he would not be compelled to rise to a personal explanation in the House to prove that he never was drunk. I do not think he was ever drunk.

* * *

RAISE ME UP, BOYS!

This gem, presumably delivered at a Democratic pole-raising in Ohio in 1868, during the presidential campaign when Horatio Seymour was the Democratic standard-bearer, was later repeated on the floor of the House. It speaks for itself.

Fellow-citizens, I came down from my pleasant home in the country, where I have spent the best part of my life in feeding pigs, hoeing corn, and drinking whiskey. I have found that a little good old corn whiskey is good for you, it is wholesome, it is necessary to keep the Democracy from oozing out at my finger ends–as Marryat says in one of his novels. I am known hereabouts; many good old Democrats that inhabit this darkened spot have oftentimes taken charge of me and tenderly treated me as long as I had money, when I was not in a perpendicular condition–while my Republican friend above here many and many a time kicked me out of his house in the depth of winter, in the heat of summer, early in spring, and late in the autumn. And why, my Democratic fellow-citizens? Because I had been taking a little of the stuff to keep my patriotism alive. You took me in, fellow Democrats —you fed me with that feed that is good for me—you nursed me tenderly, and I paid the bills for all of us, and on that account I am at this pole-raising, to tell you how much I love you. (Cheers.)

I am a Democrat, fellow citizens. I don't know who Seymour is. Marryat in his novels don't mention him, and the works on shipwrecks don't say anything about him, and I don't care who he is, whether old or young, drunk or sober, good or bad, black or white—he is on the Democratic ticket and I will vote for him. (Great cheering.) My Democratic fellow citizens, I am getting dry. I could tell you all about the shipwrecks from Noah's first expedition to the present, but I know you are dry and I will not consume your time. I will say that the old ship is not going steady; something is wrong, the rudder is unshipped, breakers are ahead, and we will run aground unless we elect Seymour or Jeff Davis, or some other good man. (Vociferous cheering.) The White House is in mourning for the good old Democrats of yore. I am an Irishman, and being an Irishman, I am ready to swallow Seymour, boots and all, if we have the good old Democratic times we had from 1856 to 1860. My fellow Democrats, the pole is up, I helped to raise her, and now all I ask of you is to raise me up if ever you should see me in need of raising. Now, let us all drink.

THE GREAT AMERICAN INFANT

FOOLISH FREE-TRADE IDEAS

Where is the best market in the world? Where the people have the most money to spend. Where have the people the most money to spend? Right here in the United States of America after twenty-seven years of protectionist rule. And you are asked to give up such a market for the markets of the world! Why, the history of such a transaction was told twenty-four hundred years ago. It is a classic. You will find it in the works of Æsop, the fabulist. Once there was a dog. He was a nice little dog. Nothing the matter with him except a few foolish free-trade ideas in his head. He was trotting along happy as the day, for he had in his mouth a nice shoulder of succulent mutton. By and by he came to a stream bridged by a plank. He trotted along, and looking over the side of the plank, he saw the markets of the world and dived for them. A minute after he was crawling up the bank the wettest, the sickest, the nastiest, the most muttonless dog that ever swam ashore!

Representative Thomas B. Reed
of Maine on the tariff, 1888

* * *

Down in my district a boy went to mill for the first time, and did not understand the *modus operandi.* So when the miller took out the toll the boy thought he had stolen it; but as it was a small matter he said nothing about it. When the miller took up the sack, poured all the rest of the corn into the hopper, and threw the sack on the floor, the little chap thought he had stolen that, too, and he thought, furthermore, that it was high time for him to take his departure. Consequently he grabbed the empty sack and started home as fast as his legs could carry him. The miller, deeming the boy crazy, pursued him. The boy beat him in the race home, and fell down in the yard, out of breath.

His father ran out and said, "My son, what is the matter?"

Whereupon the boy replied, "That old, fat rascal up at the mill stole all my corn, and gave me an awful race for the sack!"

Now that illustrates the working of the high protective tariff precisely. The tariff barons have been skinning the farmer for lo! these many years. They've gotten all our corn, and now they are after the sack!

Representative W. Jasper Talbert of South Carolina

* * *

I voted for it [the Wilson Tariff Bill] because the men who claimed to be the leaders of the Republican party said it was right; for I am one of that unfortunate class called new members. I am simply kneeling at the feet of the political Gamaliels who run and control the Republican party. I am simply swallowing the drippings from the sanctuary, not the sweets of the inner table. I admire the courage and revere the ability of these men and yesterday I voted for that bill because they said it was right; but I was in the condition of the Irishman who had never seen any peaches before and was given some of them. He ate them ravenously, and then he was asked how they tasted. Said he, "Sure, sir, they tasted very good, but the seeds sure scratched my throat going down." And so my throat was scratched yesterday in voting for a Democratic tariff bill for revenue only.

Representative Grove L. Johnson of California, 1896

A constituent has supplied the following poetic contribution as reflective of the current taxpayer's sentiment, which I think we will do well to keep in mind.

> There's a tax when I phone and a tax when I wire,
> There's a tax on my heat and my fireplace fire.
> There's a tax on my lights and a tax on my books
> And if I would fish there's a tax on my hooks.
> There's a tax on my hat and a tax on each shoe,
> There's a tax on my shirt and other things too.
>
> There's a tax on the oil I rub on my hair
> And a tax on the toothpaste I use with such care.
> I'm taxed if I gargle, and if I get ill
> I'm taxed if I swallow a capsule or pill.
> I'm taxed when I plan and taxed when I talk
> And a tax on my sex makes me taxed when I walk.
> They tax all the money I earn, beg or win,
> Then tax me a-plenty for blowing it in.

Representative Thomas L. Ashley of Ohio, 1960

* * *

The Payne tariff bill has also shown that the Republicans are expert mathemeticians. They can add, subtract, multiply, and divide all in one operation. They can add to the wealth of the rich, subtract from the substance of the poor, multiply millionaires, and divide themselves—all in one bill.

Representative Jack Beall of Texas, 1910

* * *

The greatest robber tariff this country can ever have is one that robs American labor of its employment by permitting the products of the poverty-stricken labor of the world to supply our home market. That robbery brings want and misery to the fireside of the sons of toil, fills the land with the saddest of all sights in this world's pilgrimage—that of an honest man begging in vain for employment that he may earn his daily bread by his daily toil.

Representative Galusha A. Grow of Pennsylvania

* * *

Now I wish to say that the precise logic which is used to show that there is money enough in the Treasury of the United States, that its receipts and expenditures are in accord—the very same logic that is used to show that could be fairly employed to demonstrate that the Prodigal Son was an itinerant capitalist in search of a livestock investment and eating husks for his health under the advice of his physician. The exact logic that has been brought in here to show that the national income needs no addition could be properly used to show that Lazarus, luxuriating among the rich man's dogs, was in reality engaged in organizing a loan and trust company and collecting bread crumbs for his personal amusement.

Senator Jonathan P. Dolliver of Iowa

* * *

Lobbying reached a zenith in 1932, when the tariff suddenly became involved in a tax measure to raise imperative revenue. Lobbies worked round the clock. Members of the House and Senate literally stampeded the favored list of imports on which excise duties would be levied. It was brought to a sudden stop by Senator Millard E. Tydings of Maryland, who ironically introduced an amendment containing 504 tariff changes that would benefit Maryland industries. Fervently he shouted across the chamber.

Have we gone mad? Have we no idea that if we carry this period of unrest from one week to another a panic will break loose which all the tariffs under heaven will not stem? Yet we sit here to take care of some little interest for this state or that, instead of rising above petty sectionalism and acting for the nation. "My state! My state!" My God! Let's hear "My country!" What good is your state if your country sinks into the quagmire of ruin?

* * *

"WHAT INDUSTRIES SHOULD BE DESTROYED?"

Way back in 1888 a Democratic fire-eater in a Fourth of July patriotic blast, remarked that the Great American Infant, though one hundred years old, was "yet muling and puking in its nurse's arms." The GAI he referred to was, and still is, the tariff, over which more words have gushed out in Congress than even on the nation's wars. On this eternal issue—with, historically, the Democrats against tariffs and the Republicans for them—Senators Taft of Ohio and Fulbright of Arkansas had a considerable discussion in February 1953.

Mr. FULBRIGHT. He (Secretary of Agriculture Benson) lays down a generalized philosophy in these words: "Inefficiency should not be subsidized in agriculture nor any other segment of our economy."

The assumption here is that the American farmer is inefficient. The fact is that the American farmer is a miracle of efficiency. Last year only five and a half million farmers were responsible for our prodigious outpouring of food and fiber crops.

If, however, Mr. Benson is to apply the philosophy that inefficiency should not be subsidized, then he will find himself in sharp conflict with ancient Republican party doctrine.

Dozens of highly inefficient industries are protected and

subsidized by the United States government at the expense of all the people through protective tariffs. The very fact that these industries have to have high tariffs is proof that they are inefficient. For, when an industry is highly efficient—as the automobile industry is—it not only does not demand high tariffs but is able to export in competition with like industries throughout the world.

Mr. TAFT. I wonder if the Senator would like to list the one hundred inefficient industries in the United States which he thinks ought to be destroyed.

Mr. FULBRIGHT. I think a good example is the briar-pipe industry—not that it should be destroyed . . .

Mr. TAFT. That is a small industry which involves an investment of only a few million dollars. What main industries would the Senator like to destroy by reducing the tariffs?

Mr. FULBRIGHT. My point is—and I shall pursue it a little further—that if the point Mr. Benson was making was that agriculture is inefficient and therefore should not be subsidized, as would appear from the statement which I have just quoted . . .

Mr. TAFT. As I understand the Senator's position, hundreds of inefficient industries which are protected by the Republicans ought to be destroyed. I should like to know what industries the Senator wishes to destroy.

Mr. FULBRIGHT. The Senator is attempting to put words in my mouth. I did not say they should be destroyed. This is the point with respect to what the Secretary said: "Inefficiency should not be subsidized in agriculture nor any other segment of our economy."

There is an assumption that agriculture is inefficient. I deny that. But if that is his philosophy, I should say that it is not in accord with the ancient protective tariff policy of the Republicans, because the very purpose of the tariff is to protect from competition industries which necessarily must be inefficient relative to products which might be imported.

Mr. TAFT. Hundreds of thousands of workmen in Ohio are engaged in the pottery industry, which probably would be wiped out in the event the protection was removed. I have concern for those workmen. They have labored all their lives in that industry, and I do not think they should be deprived of work and forced to try to find jobs in other industries, when they have reached ages at which probably they could not find other jobs.

The bicycle industry is in a similar situation, perhaps. It is not a large industry, but the total amount of dollars involved is not small to the probably three or four hundred thousand men who are engaged in that industry.

Mr. FULBRIGHT. I do not criticize what the Senator from Ohio is doing, because I think this matter constitutes perhaps the most fundamental difference between the two political parties, a difference which goes back to the days of Calhoun. I have always thought that if any one thing could be selected as the cause of the Civil War, this is it. This matter takes on a somewhat different aspect at this particular time, of course.

In the case of pottery I would say that if it be true that the American pottery makers cannot compete under any circumstances with foreign producers of pottery, then the American pottery industry perhaps is uneconomic and inefficient, and a procedure for its gradual elimination possibly should be provided.

On the other hand, Mr. President, I say that our system of enterprise can compete. I am never willing to accept the idea that, upon balance, and for most of our people, the great majority of them cannot compete with the people of other countries.

Mr. TAFT. Mr. President, let me say that the threat to the American pottery industry does not help solve the European problem, because the threat to that industry comes almost entirely from Japan, where the wages paid in the pottery industry are approximately one tenth of those paid in the pottery industry of the United States. Of course, wages constitute a substantial part of the total cost in the pottery industry. There is nothing inefficient about the Ohio pottery industry. The simple point is that the American pottery industry workmen must be paid approximately ten times what the Japanese pottery industry workmen are paid. As a result, if all tariffs are removed, the Japanese will take over the pottery industry.

Then the Japanese will find another industry in which they can be equally efficient, as compared to American workmen, but in which the wages paid Japanese labor are also perhaps only one tenth of the wages paid American labor. In that way the Japanese can put that American industry out of business.

Mr. FULBRIGHT. Of course, Mr. President, what the Senator from Ohio is saying is that the foreign workmen know more about these matters than our workmen do, and thus can outproduce our workmen. I do not believe that is so.

I do not know much about pottery; but in the five-and-ten-cent stores I see large amounts of pottery that do not appear to be hand painted; it seems to be mass produced. I do not wish to go into the details of that subject, for I do not have enough knowledge about that specific industry to be able to discuss it.

However, I have assumed that the pottery industry is one in which the Europeans have excelled. On the other hand, I realize that importations from Japan constitute a very grave problem in this field, which we have to meet. If we do not make some provision to enable Japan to trade with the free world, Japan will have no alternative but to trade with Russia; there is no use in deceiving ourselves about that.

* * *

GREAT SNAKES AND HIGH WAGES

With his ever-ready wit, Representative "Sunset" Cox of New York many a time ridiculed the tariff arguments adduced by its proponents. This time it had to do with the idea advanced in 1884 by the pro-tariff men that high tariffs produced high wages.

The usual thing is an elaborately constructed table—figures arranged in symmetric columns; for do they not carry an air of authority? Are they not wonderfully effective even with those who do not read them? The usual thing, I observe, is an elaborate table, professedly comparing wages in England and the United States. It exhibits a low scale of wages for England and a high scale for the United States. And thus run the wonderful syllogisms:

1. Major premise: England has free trade. Minor premise: England has low wages. Conclusion: Free trade produces low wages.

2. Major premise: The United States has protection. Minor premise: The United States has high wages. Conclusion: Protection produces high wages.

Really, Mr. Speaker, this sort of logic is very easy. There is no end to the propositions we might prove. Thus:

3. Major: England has a queen. Minor: England has low wages. Conclusion: Queens make wages low.

4. Major: The United States is infested with snakes. Minor: The United States has high wages. Conclusion: Snakes make wages high.

* * *

BY-PLAY ON THE McKINLEY TARIFF BILL

Mr. PICKLER of South Dakota. I shall vote for it because I believe it will place multiplied thousands of sheep upon our Western prairies, from whose wool will be manufactured, and manufactured in the towns and cities of these prairies, around about which these flocks feed and thrive, sixty million dollars' worth of woolen fabrics, now yearly imported into this country.

Mr. HAYES of Iowa. Will they not freeze to death in the winter?

Mr. McADOO of New Jersey. They will be "protected" so that they cannot freeze.

* * *

Mr. Speaker, I thought that the grasp of the tax gatherer stopped at the edge of the grave; that when we passed to another land it was to a world "where the wicked cease from troubling and the weary are at rest." But, sir, they pursue a man even beyond the tomb. Notwithstanding that they have taxed the shroud in which the corpse is clad, notwithstanding they have taxed the coffin in which he is placed, they now come along to tax the gravestone that is erected o'er him. My God! Where is it to end? I trust that in the great hereafter, when we stand before the judgment seat of God, we shall at least find that salvation is free.

Representative Asher G. Caruth of Kentucky opposing an increase in the tariff on granite

* * *

In depicting how the 1892 tariff on wool hurt the farmer, Representative Luther F. McKinney of New Hampshire related a chat he had with a farmer in his state on the subject of sheep-raising.

I said to him, "You used to raise lots of sheep here. Now you have not any sheep in your county." "Well," the farmer replied, "they are rapidly going out. We used to raise a pretty big lot of sheep on this farm when I was a boy, but we have gone down and down until we have only one old sheep on the place." I said to him, "I suppose you keep it as a memento." He said, "We have got a hydraulic ram down in the meadow that supplies the house and barn with water. That is the only sheep we have got; and today, under this tariff, if the McKinley bill continues to raise the tariff, we will not be able to support a hydraulic ram in the state of New Hampshire."

* * *

I have accepted the principle laid down as to borax by the Senator from Arkansas, that the principle upon which borax was to be made dutiable was the principle that just enough duty should be put upon an article to enable the industry to survive, and I pictured to myself the great thankfulness which would come over the producers of borax when they realized that they were to be allowed to exist. I felt that when the duty should be fixed and the industry allowed to survive, the Senator from Nevada and the Senator from California and other producers of borax might well gather around a borax pit in the sands of the Humboldt River and proceed to sing in devout thankfulness the good old Psalm:

> And are we wretches still alive,
> And dare we yet rebel?
> 'Tis wondrous, 'tis amazing grace
> That keeps us out of hell.

Senator William E. Chandler of New Hampshire during the Tariff Debate, 1894

* * *

Are you going to take every dollar there is in the United States out of the pockets of the people every six months? The day is coming, and it is not going to be long in coming at the rate we are traveling, when you will milk the incomes of the United States dry. Do you suppose any man wants to go out and engage in manufacturing enterprises or in farming operations, or in milling or mining, to make an income, for no other purpose than to have some dreary-eyed politician suggest it be spent to uplift mankind?

Representative Martin Dies of Texas

* * *

In the campaign of 1892 the tariff was made the issue, and Mr. Cleveland was elected on the free trade side of that issue, and just as soon as he was settled in the White House he turned in and called Congress together in extra session for the purpose of repealing the purchasing clause of the Sherman Silver Act. Elected on the tariff issue he turned in to reform finance. In 1896, the campaign in which Mr. McKinley was elected President, the financial question was the great issue, and now just as soon as he is inaugurated we find Congress convened together in another extra session to deal with the tariff. Whenever we elect a President on the tariff issue he sets in to reform finance, and when we elect one on the financial issue he sets in to reform the tariff.

Representative W. Jasper Talbert of South Carolina, 1897

ELOQUENCE,
EULOGY AND EPITAPHS

"ZENITH CITY OF THE UNSALTED SEAS"

The most remarkable burlesque ever staged in Congress was J. Proctor Knott's travesty known as his "Duluth Speech." In this display of wit, Knott christened Duluth "Zenith City of the Unsalted Seas." On January 27, 1871 the House was considering a bill to grant a subsidy for building a railroad from the St. Croix River to Lake Superior. It involved giving away some of the public domain. Knott, a freshman in the House, was given ten minutes to voice his opposition. It led him to remark that his facilities for getting time to speak were so poor that if he were standing on the brink of perdition and the sands crumbling under his feet he could not get time enough from the House to say the Lord's Prayer. Yet, as his stream of intriguing exaggeration gathered momentum, his ten minutes ran out. Cries of "Keep it up! Don't stop!" rang through the House. And keep it up he did—in a beguiling gush of impromptu wit that consigned him to lasting fame and the governorship of Kentucky, plus, in later years, a banquet by the city of Duluth.

Years ago, when I first heard that there was, somewhere in the vast *terra incognita*, somewhere in the bleak regions of the great Northwest, a stream of water known to the nomadic inhabitants of the neighborhood as the river St. Croix, I became satisfied that the construction of a railroad from that raging torrent to some point in the civilized world was essential to the happiness and prosperity of the American people, if not absolutely indispensable to the perpetuity of republican institutions on this continent. (Great laughter.)

I felt instinctively that the boundless resources of that prolific region of sand and pine-shrubbery would never be fully developed without a railroad constructed and equipped at the expense of the government, and perhaps not then. (Laughter.) I had an abiding presentiment that, some day or other, the people of this whole country, irrespective of party affiliations, regardless of sectional prejudices, and "without distinction of race, color, or previous condition of servitude," would rise in their majesty and demand an outlet for the enormous agricultural productions of those vast and fertile pine-barrens, drained in the rainy season by the surging waters of the turbid St. Croix. (Great laughter.)

And now, Mr. Speaker, in the middle of these teeming pine-barrens at the mouth of the St. Croix, is Duluth–Duluth, Zenith City of the Unsalted Seas. (Laughter.) Duluth! The word fell upon my ear with peculiar and indescribable charm, like the gentle murmur of a low fountain stealing forth in the midst of roses, or the soft, sweet accents of an angel's whisper in the bright, joyous dream of sleeping innocence. Duluth! 'Twas the name for which my soul had panted for years, as the hart panteth for the water-brooks. (Renewed laughter.) But where was Duluth? Never in all my limited reading had my vision been gladdened by seeing the celestial word in print. (Laughter.) And I felt a profounder humiliation in my ignorance that its dulcet syllables had never before ravished my delighted ear. (Roars of laughter.) I asked my friends about it, but they knew nothing of it. I rushed to the library and examined all the maps I could find. (Laughter.) I discovered in one of them a delicate, hair-like line, diverging from the Mississippi near a place marked Prescott, which I supposed was intended to represent the river St. Croix, but I could nowhere find Duluth.

Nevertheless, I was confident it existed somewhere, and that its discovery would constitute the crowning glory of the present century, if not of all modern times. (Laughter.) I knew it was bound to exist, in the very nature of things; that the symmetry and perfection of our planetary system would be incomplete without it (renewed laughter); that the elements of material nature would long since have resolved themselves back into original chaos if there had been such a hiatus in creation as would have resulted from leaving out Duluth. (Roars of laughter.) In fact, sir, I was overwhelmed with the conviction that Duluth not only existed somewhere, but that, wherever it was, it was a great and glorious place.

I was convinced that the greatest calamity that ever befell the benighted nations of the ancient world was in their having passed away without a knowledge of the actual existence of Duluth; that their fabled Atlantis, never seen save by the hallowed vision of inspired poesy, was, in fact, but another name for Duluth; that the golden orchard of the Hesperides was but a poetical synonym for the beer-gardens in the vicinity of Duluth. (Great laughter.) I was certain that Herodotus had died a miserable death because in all his travels and with all his geographical research he had never heard of Duluth. (Laughter.) I knew that if the immortal spirit of Homer could look down from another heaven than that created by his own celestial genius upon the long lines of pilgrims from every nation of the earth to the gushing fountain of poesy opened by the touch of his magic wand; if he could be permitted to behold the vast assemblage of grand and glorious productions of the lyric art called into being by his own inspired strains, he would weep tears of bitter anguish that, instead of lavishing all the stores of his mighty genius upon the fall of Ilion, it had not been his more blessed lot to crystallize in deathless song the rising glories of Duluth. (Great and continued laughter.)

Yet, sir, had it not been for this map, kindly furnished me by the legislature of Minnesota, I might have gone down to my obscure and humble grave in an agony of despair because I could nowhere find Duluth. (Renewed laughter.) Had such been my melancholy fate, I have no doubt that with the last feeble pulsation of my breaking heart, with the faint exhalation of my fleeting breath, I should have whispered, "Where is Duluth?" (Roars of laughter.)

But, thanks to the beneficence of that band of ministering angels who have their bright abodes in the far-off capital of Minnesota, just as the agony of my anxiety was about to culminate in the frenzy of despair, this blessed map was placed in my hands; and as I unfolded it a resplendent scene of ineffable glory opened before me, such as I imagine burst upon the enraptured vision of the wandering peri through the opening gates of Paradise. (Renewed laughter.) There, there for the first time, my enchanted eye rested upon the ravishing word, "Duluth."

If gentlemen will examine it they will find Duluth not only in the center of the map, but represented in the center of a series of concentric circles one hundred miles apart, and some of them as much as four thousand miles in diameter, embracing alike in their tremendous sweep the fragrant savannas of the sunlit South and the eternal solitudes of snow that mantle the ice-bound North. (Laughter.) How these circles were produced is perhaps one of those primordial mysteries that the most skillful paleologist [sic] will never be able to explain. (Renewed laughter.) But the fact is, sir, Duluth is preeminently a central place, for I am told by gentlemen who have been so reckless of their own personal safety as to venture away into those awful regions where Duluth is supposed to be, that it is so exactly in the center of the visible universe that the sky comes down at precisely the same distance all around it. (Roars of laughter.)

Then, sir, there is the climate of Duluth, unquestionably the most salubrious and delightful to be found anywhere on the Lord's earth. Now, I have always been under the impression, as I presume other gentlemen have, that in the region around Lake Superior it was cold enough for at least nine months in the year to freeze the smokestack off a locomotive. (Great laughter.) But I see it represented on this map that Duluth is situated exactly halfway between the latitudes of Paris and Venice, so that gentlemen who have inhaled the exhilarating airs of the one or basked in the golden sunlight of the other may see at a glance that Duluth must be a place of untold delights (laughter), a terrestrial paradise, fanned by the balmy zephyrs of an eternal spring, clothed in the gorgeous sheen of ever-blooming flowers, and vocal with the silvery melody of nature's choicest songsters. (Laughter.) In fact, sir, since I have seen this map I have no doubt that Byron was vainly endeavoring to convey some faint conception of the delicious charms of Duluth when his poetic soul gushed forth in the rippling strains of that beautiful rhapsody,

> Know ye the land of the cedar and vine,
> Where the flowers ever blossom, the beams ever shine?

As to the commercial resources of Duluth, sir, they are simply illimitable and inexhaustible, as is shown by this map. I see it stated here that there is a vast scope of territory, embracing an area of over two million square miles, rich in every element of material wealth and commercial prosperity, all tributary to Duluth. Look at it, sir (pointing to the map). Here are inexhaustible mines of gold, immeasurable veins of silver, impenetrable depths of boundless forest, vast coal-measures, wide, extended plains of richest pasturage, all, all embraced in this vast territory, which must, in the very nature of things, empty the untold treasures of its commerce into the lap of Duluth. (Laughter.)

Look at it, sir (pointing to the map), do not you see from these broad, brown lines drawn around this immense territory that the enterprising inhabitants of Duluth intend some day to enclose it all in one vast corral, so that its commerce will be bound to go there whether it would or not? (Great laughter.) And here, sir (still pointing to the map), I find within a convenient distance the Piegan Indians, which, of all the many accessories to the glory of Duluth, I consider by far the most inestimable.

And here, sir, recurring to this map, I find in the immediate vicinity of the Piegans "vast herds of buffalo" and "immense fields of rich wheat lands."

(Here the hammer fell.)

(Many cries: "Go on!" "Go on!")

The SPEAKER. Is there objection to the gentleman from Kentucky continuing his remarks? The Chair hears none. The gentleman will proceed.

Mr. KNOTT. I was remarking, sir, upon these vast "wheat fields" represented on this map in the immediate neighborhood of the buffaloes and the Piegans, and was about to say that the idea of there being these immense wheat fields in the very heart of a wilderness, hundreds and hundreds of miles beyond the utmost verge of civilization, may appear to some gentlemen as rather incongruous, as rather too great a strain on the "blankets" of veracity. But to my mind there is no difficulty in the matter whatever. The phenomenon is very easily accounted for. It is evident, sir, that the Piegans sowed that wheat there and plowed it in with buffalo bulls. (Great laughter.) Now, sir, this fortunate combination of buffaloes and Piegans, considering their relative positions to each other and to Duluth, as they are arranged on this map, satisfies me that Duluth is destined to be the beef market of the world.

Here, you will observe (pointing to the map), are the buffaloes, directly between the Piegans and Duluth, and here, right on the road to Duluth, are the Creeks. Now, sir, when the buffaloes are sufficiently fat from grazing on those immense wheat fields, you see it will be the easiest thing in the world for the Piegans to drive them on down, stay all night with their friends, the Creeks, and go into Duluth in the morning. (Great laughter.) I think I see them now, sir, a vast herd of buffaloes, with their heads down, their eyes glaring, their nostrils dilated, their tongues out, and their tails curled over their backs, tearing along toward Duluth, with about a thousand Piegans on their grass-bellied ponies, yelling at their heels! (Great laughter.) On they come! And as they sweep past the Creeks they join in the chase, and away they all go, yelling, bellowing, ripping, and tearing along, amid clouds of dust, until the last buffalo is safely penned in the stock-yards of Duluth! (Shouts of laughter.)

Sir, I might stand here for hours and hours, and expatiate with rapture upon the gorgeous prospects of Duluth, as depicted upon this map. But human life is too short and the time of this House far too valuable to allow me to linger longer upon the delightful theme. (Laughter.) I think every gentleman on this floor is as well satisfied as I am that Duluth is destined to become the commercial metropolis of the universe, and that this road should be built at once. I am fully persuaded that no patriotic Representative of the American people, who has a proper appreciation of the associated glories of Duluth and the St. Croix, will hesitate a moment to say that every able-bodied female in the land between the ages of eighteen and forty-five who is in favor of "a woman's rights" should be drafted and set to work upon this great work without delay. (Roars of laughter.) Nevertheless, sir, it grieves my very soul to be compelled to say that I cannot vote for the grant of lands provided for in this bill.

Ah! sir, you can have no conception of the poignancy of my anguish that I am deprived of that blessed privilege!

(Laughter.) There are two insuperable obstacles in the way. In the first place, my constituents, for whom I am acting here, have no more interest in this road than they have in the great question of culinary taste now perhaps agitating the public mind of Dominica, as to whether the illustrious commissioners who recently left this capital for that free and enlightened republic would be better fricasseed, boiled, or roasted (great laughter); and in the second place these lands, which I am asked to give away, alas, are not mine to bestow! My relation to them is simply that of trustee to an express trust. And shall I ever betray that trust? Never, sir! Rather perish Duluth! (Shouts of laughter.) Perish the paragon of cities! Rather let the freezing cyclones of the bleak Northwest bury it forever beneath the eddying sands of the raging St. Croix! (Great laughter.)

* * *

"HAYSEED JOE" CANNON GETS HIS NICKNAME

In his maiden speech in the House, February 18, 1874, Representative Joseph Gurney Cannon of Illinois earned his nickname, "Hayseed Joe." He made his debut as champion of free seeds for the farmer. His eloquence led Representative William Walter Phelps of New Jersey to interrupt with, "The gentleman from Illinois must have oats in his pocket." Ready with his wit as always, Cannon went into his famous peroration.

Mr. CANNON. I understand the gentleman. Yes, I have oats in my pocket and hayseed in my hair, and the Western people generally are affected in the same way; and we expect that the seed, being good, will yield a good crop. I trust, twofold; and the sooner legislation is had, not only as proposed in this bill, but in all other respects as the people desire and equity and justice will dictate, the better it will be in the long run for all the people in this country, whatever may be their calling or wherever they may reside.

Mr. PHELPS [next day]. That hayseed glowed around his head like a halo of the martyrs, and when he spoke of the oats in his pocket it was with such force and such eloquence that I knew he felt them.

* * *

Mr. Chairman, it seems to me this is a very singular case. According to the report, the "full board of surgeons" who examined this man's case "reported that he was four eighteenths disabled by disease of the digestive system, four eighteenths by rheumatism, six eighteenths by disease of the heart, and ten eighteenths by eczema, making an aggregate of twenty-four eighteenths." Certainly, as these figures show more than a total disability, the man must be dead; he must have gone clear over. I think the bill ought to be passed so as to help pay his funeral expenses.

Representative W. Jasper Talbert of South Carolina on a pension bill

* * *

July 25, 1916. Before the Senate was a resolution appealing to Great Britain to commute the death sentence against Sir Roger Casement, the Irish revolutionary. In depicting Ireland's tribulations and glories Senator Ashurst of Arizona quoted Tennessee's former Senator "Bob" Taylor's beautiful tribute to Ireland a decade before.

If I were a sculptor I would chisel from the marble my ideal of a hero. I would make it the figure of an Irishman sacrificing his hope and his life on the altar of his country;

and I would carve on its pedestal the name of ROBERT EMMET.

If I were a painter I would make my canvas eloquent with the deeds of the bravest people that ever lived, whose proud spirit no power can ever conquer and whose loyalty and devotion to the hopes of free government no tyrant can ever crush. And I would write under the picture, IRELAND.

If I were a poet I would melt the world to tears with the pathos of my song. I would touch the heart of humanity with the mournful melody of Ireland's wrongs and Erin's woes. I would weave the shamrock into garlands of glory for the Emerald Isle, the land of heroes, the nursery of liberty. Tortured in dungeons and murdered on scaffolds, robbed of the fruits of their sweat and toil, scourged by famine and plundered by the avarice of heartless power, driven like the leaves of autumn before the keen winter winds, this sturdy race of Erin's sons and daughters have scattered over the face of the earth, homeless only in the land of their nativity, but princes and lords in every other land where merit is the measure of men.

* * *

In all the literature of eulogy you will find no finer passage than that uttered by James G. Blaine of Maine at the close of his oration before the Joint Congress at the memorial ceremonies for martyred President James A. Garfield on February 2, 1882. Blaine wrote and rewrote his oration eleven times.

As the end drew near, his early craving for the sea returned. The stately mansion of power had been to him a wearisome hospital of pain, and he begged to be taken from its prison walls, from its oppressive stifling air, from its homelessness and hopelessness. Gently, silently, the love of a great people bore the pale sufferer to the longed-for healing of the sea, to live or die, as God should will, within sight of its healing billows, within sound of its manifold voices. With wan, fevered face tenderly lifted to the coming breeze, he looked out wistfully upon the ocean's changing wonders; on its far sails whitening in the morning light; on its restless waves rolling shoreward to break and die beneath the noonday sun; on the red clouds of evening arching low to the horizon; on the serene and shining pathway of the stars. Let us think that his dying eyes read a mystic meaning which only the rapt and parting soul may know. Let us believe that in the silence of the receding world he heard the great waves breaking on a farther shore, and already felt upon his wasted brow the breath of the eternal morning.

* * *

Punctual to every duty, death found him at the post of duty, and where else could it have found him, at any stage of his career, for the fifty years of his illustrious public life? From the time of his first appointment to his last election by the people of his native town, where could death have found him but at the post of duty? At that post, in the fullness of age, in the ripeness of renown, crowned with honors, surrounded by his family, his friends, and admirers, in the very presence of the national representation, he has been gathered to his fathers, leaving behind him the memory of public services which are the history of his country for half a century, and the example of a life, public and private, which should be the study and the model of the generations of his countrymen.

Peroration of Senator Thomas Hart Benton's Eulogium over John Quincy Adams on February 24, 1848

* * *

"WHEN ALL OTHER FRIENDS DESERT"

The fame of Senator George Graham Vest of Missouri rests not so much on his eloquence in the Senate and on the stump as on his beautiful Eulogy on the Dog, which he delivered before a Missouri jury in a lawsuit involving a dog. Once, in the 1890's, Senator Vest, by unanimous request, repeated this gem of oratory on the Senate floor.

Gentlemen of the jury. The best friend a man has in this world may turn against him and become his enemy. His son and daughter that he has reared with loving care may become ungrateful. Those who are nearest and dearest to us, those whom we trust with our happiness and our good name, may become traitors to their faith. The money that a man has he may lose. It flies away from him when he may need it most. Man's reputation may be sacrificed in a moment of ill-considered action. The people who are prone to fall on their knees and do us honor when success is with us may be the first to throw the stone of malice when failure settles its cloud upon our heads. The one absolutely unselfish friend a man may have in this selfish world, the one that never deserts him, the one that never proves ungrateful or treacherous, is the dog.

Gentlemen of the jury, a man's dog stands by him in prosperity and poverty, in health and in sickness. He will sleep on the cold ground when the wintry winds blow and the snow drives fiercely, if only he may be near his master's side. He will kiss the hand that has no food to offer, he will lick the wounds and sores that come in encounter with the roughness of the world. He guards the sleep of his pauper master as if he were a prince.

When all other friends desert, he remains. When riches take wings and reputation falls to pieces, he is as constant in his love as the sun in its journey through the heavens. If fortune drives the master forth an outcast into the world, friendless and homeless, the faithful dog asks no higher privilege than that of accompanying him, to guard him against danger, to fight against his enemies, and when the last scene of all comes, and death takes his master in its embrace and his body is laid away in the cold ground, no matter if all other friends pursue their way, there by his graveside will the noble dog be found, his head between his paws and his eyes sad, but open, in alert watchfulness faithful and true, even unto death.

* * *

"THE WARWHOOP SHALL WAKE THE SLEEP OF THE CRADLE!"

Senator Carter Glass once observed that he never knew a speech in Congress to change a vote. He should have excepted Representative Fisher Ames of Massachusetts, from whose lips, on April 28, 1796, at Philadelphia, flowed the words that dazzled his audience, changed votes, and saved the Jay Treaty with Great Britain. At stake was a measure to provide funds to implement the treaty. Federalists and anti-Federalists locked horns. James Madison reckoned his anti's had a twenty-vote margin to defeat the treaty. Under the treaty Britain agreed to abandon the Western forts she had occupied since the Revolution. Ames seized this as his weapon, fear of what might happen if the treaty were rejected. Leave the forts in British hands and you unleash Indian savagery on the frontiers. Verbally waving aloft the scalping knife and tomahawk, Ames swept the House, changing votes right and left. Here was his peroration.

On this theme my emotions are unutterable. If I could find words for them, if my powers bore any proportion to my zeal, I would swell my voice to such a note of remonstrance, it should reach every log house beyond the mountains. I would say to the inhabitants, "Wake from your false security! Your cruel dangers, your more cruel apprehensions, are soon to be renewed! The wounds, yet unhealed, are to be torn open again! In the daytime your path through the woods will be ambushed! The darkness of midnight will glitter with the blaze of your dwellings! You are a father—the blood of your sons shall fatten your cornfield! You are a mother—the war-whoop shall wake the sleep of the cradle!"

On this subject you need not suspect any deception of your feelings. It is a spectacle of horror that cannot be over-drawn. If you have nature in your hearts, it will speak a language compared with which all I have said or can say will be poor and frigid.

Will it be whispered that the treaty has made me a new champion for the protection of the frontiers. It is known that my voice as well as my vote have been uniformly given in conformity with the ideas I have expressed. Protection is the right of the frontiers; it is our duty to give it.

By rejecting the posts [forts], we light the savage fires—we bind the victims. This day we undertake to render account to the widows and orphans whom our decision will make, to the wretches that will be roasted at the stake; to our country; and I do not deem it too serious to say, to conscience and to God. We are answerable, and if duty be anything more than a word of imposture, if conscience be not a bugbear, we are preparing to make ourselves as wretched as your country.

There is no mistake in this case. Experience has already been the prophet of events, and the cries of future victims have already reached us. The Western inhabitants are not a silent and uncomplaining sacrifice. The voice of humanity issues from the shade of their wilderness. It exclaims, that while one hand is held up to reject this treaty, the other grasps a tomahawk. It is no great effort of the imagination to conceive that events so near are already begun. I can fancy that I listen to the yells of savage vengeance and the shrieks of torture. Already they seem to sigh in the western wind—already they mingle with every echo from the mountains!

I rose to speak under impressions that I would have resisted if I could. Those who see me will believe that the reduced state of my health has unfitted me, almost equally, for much exertion of body or mind. Yet, when I come to the moment of deciding the vote, I start back with dread from the edge of the pit into which we are plunging. Even the minutes I have spent in expostulation have their value because they protract the crisis, and the short period in which alone we may resolve to escape it. I have thus been led by my feelings to speak more at length than I had intended.

Yet I have as little personal interest in the event as anyone here. There is, I believe, no member who will not think his chance to be a witness of the consequences greater than mine. If, however, the vote should pass to reject, and a spirit should rise, as it will, with the public disorders to confusion worse confounded, even I, slender and almost broken as my hold on life is, may outlive the government and Constitution of my country.

* * *

"BLOODY HANDS TO HOSPITABLE GRAVES"

Thomas Corwin, "Wagon Boy" from Ohio, was endowed with a quality of wit and humor that amounted to positive genius. He was a glory of the Congress in the era of his service. Yet he is best remembered for his greatest mistake, which had neither wit nor humor in it. A Whig, he opposed the Mexican War (as did Abraham Lincoln) and steadfastly pleaded against it. On February 11, 1847 he rose in the Senate to denounce President Polk's Three-million-dollar Bill to finish off the war. His speech was a masterpiece in the wrong direction. It presumably cost him the Presidency. In it he coined the expression "Bloody hands to hospitable graves" so often repeated during the Civil War. Here is a portion of that speech.

The President involves you in war without your consent. Being *in* such a war, it is demanded as a duty that we grant men and money to carry it on. The President tells us he shall prosecute this war till Mexico pays us, or agrees to pay us, all its expenses. I am not willing to scourge Mexico thus; and the only means left me is to say to the Commander in Chief, "Call home your army, I will feed and clothe it no longer. You have whipped Mexico into three pitched battles. This is revenge enough; this is punishment enough."

What is the territory, Mr. President, which you propose to wrest from Mexico? It is consecrated to the heart of the Mexican by many a well-fought battle, with his old Castilian master. His Bunker Hills, and Saratogas, and Yorktowns are there. The Mexican can say, "There I bled for liberty! and shall I surrender that consecrated home of my affections to the Anglo-Saxon invaders? What do they want with it? They have Texas already. They have possessed themselves of the territory between the Nueces and the Rio Grande. What else do they want? To what shall I point my childen as memorials of that independence which I bequeath to them, when those battlefields shall have passed from my possession?"

Sir, had one come and demanded Bunker Hill of the people of Massachusetts, had England's lion ever showed himself there, is there a man over thirteen and under ninety who would not have been ready to meet him? Is there a river on this continent that would not have run red with blood? Is there a field but would have been piled high with the unburied bones of slaughtered Americans before these consecrated battlefields of liberty should have been wrested from us? But this same American goes into a sister republic, and says to poor, weak Mexico, "Give up your territory—you are unworthy to possess it. I have got one half already—all I ask of you is to give up the other!" England might as well, in the circumstances I have described, have come and demanded of us, "Give up the Atlantic slope. Give up this trifling territory from the Alleghany mountains to the sea; it is only from Maine to St. Mary's—only about one third of your Republic, and the least interesting portion of it." What would be the response? They would say, we must give this up to John Bull. Why? "He wants room." The Senator from Michigan says he must have this. Why, my worthy Christian brother, on what principle of justice? "I want room!"

Sir, look at this pretense of want of room. With twenty millions of people, you have about one thousand millions of acres of land, inviting settlement by every conceivable argument—bringing them down to a quarter of a dollar an acre, and allowing every man to squat where he pleases. But the Senator from Michigan says we will be two hundred millions in a few years, and we want room. If I were a Mexican I would tell you, "Have you not room in your own country to bury your dead men? If you come into mine we will greet you with bloody hands, and welcome you to hospitable graves."

But you still say you want room for your people. This has been the plea of every robber-chief from Nimrod to the present hour. I dare say, when Tamerlane descended from his throne built of seventy thousand human skulls, and marched his ferocious battalions to further slaughter, I dare say he said, "I want room."

* * *

CHAMP CLARK SUBMITS HIS OWN FAMOUS EPITAPH

On December 10, 1894 a Republican member of the House began twitting Clark on his defeat for reelection—"You talk like you had been whipped in the last election." Lame-duck Clark rose to the bait at once.

I stand here as one of the men who went down—not to stay down. There is a resurrection and a life, yes, after death. There will be a resurrection and a life; don't you be afraid of that. What was the cause of my defeat? A system of grossest lies, a complete and unlimited use of the boodle of this country, a subsidized press, a lot of conscienceless demagogues that never ought to have even a name, a host of mountebanks and jugglers sent us down.

In 1841 there was a Parliament elected in England of seven-hundred-odd men, only ninety of them in favor of free trade. The Parliament was elected to maintain the Corn Laws. These ninety men, before the seven years of that Parliament expired, had accomplished a wonderful result, and I wish gentlemen to remember it today. Before that seven years expired both the Whig and Tory parties ran races to see which one could be first to violate the principles on which they were elected, and to establish free trade. Popular clamor drove Sir Robert Peel from power. The liars made the laboring people of England believe he would ruin them, and they drove him out. They said he would ruin the country. They lied. The results of his efforts succeeded in making England so great that one philosopher has declared it was equivalent to the discovery of a new force in nature or to the discovery of a new continent.

They took the tariff off every article except seven. They got more revenue out of the seven articles than they had out of seven thousand. Peel died. Business multiplied. Everybody prospered. The laboring men of England, the very men that they said he had ruined, took up a penny subscription. They erected to his memory a magnificent monument on which they inscribed the words, "He gave the people cheap bread." Nobler epitaph than that no man has.

I went down in the late landslide. I walked the plank in the goodliest company that the fickle multitude ever consigned to the black waters of political defeat. I would rather go down with those men than survive with some men that I see sitting around here grinning. The men that sit around here jeering and grinning at men like me, who went down for truth, have no idea of the force of public opinion in America.

When my time comes to die—there's a good deal of life in me yet, and I will be back here to make many entertaining speeches—when my time comes to die, when I am laid away in the cold, cold ground, and poor Yorick has had his jest, I do not want any nobler epitaph than this:

> Here lies Champ Clark, who, in the year of our Lord and Master one thousand eight hundred and ninety-four, stood in the American Congress and did battle for the principle that the great body of the American people should have cheaper clothing, cheaper food, cheaper medicine, cheaper necessaries of life, more luxuries, and be better able to educate their children.

* * *

I do not object if the Easterner believes that the aurora borealis is only the glow in the sky from the factories and furnaces of the East. I do not object if the Westerners believe as they do, that the glow of the setting sun is but a reflection of the grain fields of the West. Then, why should they object if I believe, as I do, that the great Milky Way is but a reflection in the sky of the rice and cotton fields of Dixie?

Senator Robert Taylor of Tennessee

I say: Give the American cow a fair chance. She has been a faithful servant of man. She landed with our ancestors at Plymouth Rock; and, tied behind the old weather-beaten emigrant wagon, she has marched with the household goods of the pioneers who have taken possession of this land from ocean to ocean. She has increased and multiplied and replenished the earth, until today the industries which she has made possible contribute annually to the wealth of the world more money than the great combinations of modern capital—more than iron and steel, more than lumber and coal, more than cotton and wheat, more than all the looms of New England, more than all the mysterious riches of gold and silver. Yet there are men in this House whom I have heard today sneering at this bill who spend most of their time trying to get protection for some insignificant enterprise or "talking through their hats" in the silver debate. I say give the American cow a fair chance! For myself, I am in favor of her monopoly—a monopoly that God gave her—in the production of butter and cheese. And if every man in this House who in the days of his boyhood got up at daylight to feed the cows and stayed up after dark in order to milk them; if every man who has churned actual cream with a reliable upright churn and has watched with a boy's enthusiasm the old-fashioned process of making cheese in the days of its honor and repute, will stand by this bill, we will drive from the American barnyard the horde of counterfeiters and cheats at common law and keep them out "till the cows come home."

Representative Jonathan Dolliver
of Iowa, 1896, speaking against
the "filled cheese" bill

* * *

"FIRST IN WAR, FIRST IN PEACE. . . ."

On December 27, 1799, thirteen days after the death of George Washington at Mount Vernon, Congress assembled for a memorial service in the German Lutheran Church at Philadelphia, then the nation's capital. The eulogy on this sad occasion, written by Representative Henry "Light Horse Harry" Lee of Virginia, was delivered by Representative John Marshall of Virginia because of Lee's unavoidable absence. Here is the exordium of Lee's funeral oration and his peroration, in words that come ringing down the years.

The Founder of our Federal Republic, our Bulwark in war, our Guide in peace, is no more. Oh that this was but questionable! Hope, the comforter of the wretched, would pour into our agonized hearts its balmy dew. But, alas! there is no hope for us; our Washington is removed forever. Possessing the stoutest frame, and purest mind, he had passed nearly to his sixty-eighth year in the enjoyment of high health; when habituated by his care of us to neglect himself, a slight cold, disregarded, became inconvenient on Friday, oppressive on Saturday, and defying every medical interposition, before the morning of Sunday put an end to the best of men.

An end did I say? His fame survives! bounded only by the limits of earth, and by the extent of the human mind. He survives in our hearts, in the growing knowledge of our children, in the affection of the good throughout the world; and when our monuments shall be done away, when nations now existing shall be no more, when even our young and far-spreading empire shall have perished, still will our Washington's glory unfaded shine, and die not, until love of virtue cease on earth, or earth itself sink into chaos.

* * *

How, my fellow citizens, shall I single to your grateful

hearts his preeminent worth? Where shall I begin in opening to your view a character throughout sublime? Shall I speak of his warlike achievements, all springing in obedience to his country's will—all directed to his country's good?

First in war—first in peace—and first in the hearts of his countrymen, he was second to none in the humble and endearing scenes of private life; pious, just, humane, temperate, and sincere; uniform, dignified, and commanding; his example was as edifying to all around him as were the effects of that example lasting.

To his equals he was condescending, to his inferiors kind, and to the dear object of his affections exemplarily tender; correct throughout, vice shuddered in his presence, and virtue always felt his fostering hand; the purity of his private character gave effulgence to his private virtues.

His last scene comported with the whole tenor of his life. Although in extreme pain, not a sigh, not a groan escaped him; and with undisturbed serenity he closed his well-spent life. Such was the man America has lost; such was the man for whom our nation mourns.

* * *

MORT SUR LE CHAMPS D'HONNEUR

Silver-tongued Senator (and Colonel) Ned Baker of Oregon was gone. On October 20, 1861 he fell pierced by Confederate bullets at Ball's Bluff, barely twenty-five miles up the Potomac from Washington. On this December day, 1861, as Congress reassembled, Senator James A. McDougall of California rose to pronounce a moving eulogy of Baker, closing with this passage.

A poet of the middle ages, speaking of Carthage as then a dead city, the grave of which was scarcely discernible, says:

> For cities die, kingdoms die; a little sand and grass cover all that was once lofty in them, and glorious; and yet man, forsooth, disdains that he is mortal! Oh, mind of ours, inordinate and proud!

It is true that cities and kingdoms die, but the eternal thought lives on. Great thought, incorporate with great action, does not die, but lives a universal life, and its power is felt vibrating through all spirit and throughout the ages.

I doubt whether or not we should mourn for any of the dead. I am confident there should be no mourning for those who render themselves up as sacrifices in any great, just, and holy cause. It better becomes us to praise and dignify them.

It was the faith of an ancient people that the souls of heroes did not rest until their great deeds had been hymned by bards, to the sounds of martial music.

Bards worthy of the ancient time have hymned the praise of the great citizen, Senator, and soldier who has left us. They have showered on his memory

> Those leaves, which for the eternal few,
> Who wander o'er the paradise of fame,
> In sacred dedication ever grew.

I would that I were able to add a single leaf to the eternal amaranth. In long years, when our night of horror shall have passed, and there shall have come again

> The welcome morning with its rays of peace

young seekers after fame and young lovers of freedom, throughout all this land, yea, and other and distant lands, will recognize, honor and imitate our late associate as one of the undying dead.

* * *

On February 15, 1878 the Bland Silver Bill for remonitizing the white metal reached a vote in the Senate. Without fanfare,

Senator L. Q. C. Lamar of Mississippi rose to speak. Confronting him—indeed, in his hand—was a copy of the resolutions passed by the legislature of his state instructing him to vote for the bill. His courageous explanation of his intended vote is one of the best short classics in American oratory.

Mr. President, between these resolutions and my convictions there is a great gulf. I cannot pass it. Of my love to the state of Mississippi I will not speak; my life alone can tell it. My gratitude for all the honor her people have done me no words can express. I am best proving it by doing today what I think their true interests and their character require me to do. During my life in the state it has been my privilege to assist in the education of more than one generation of her youth, to have given the impulse to wave after wave of the young manhood that has passed into the troubled seas of her social and political life. Upon them I have always endeavored to impress the belief that truth was better than falsehood, honesty better than policy, courage better than cowardice. Today my lessons confront me. Today I must be true or false, honest or cunning, faithful or unfaithful to my people. Even in this hour of their legislative displeasure and disapprobation I cannot vote as these resolutions direct. I cannot and will not shirk the responsibility which my position imposes. My duty, as I see it, I will do; and I will vote against this bill.

When that is done my responsibility is ended. My reasons for my vote shall be given to my people. Then it will be for them to determine if adherence to my honest convictions has disqualified me from representing them; whether a difference of opinion upon a difficult and complicated subject to which I have given patient, long-continued, conscientious study, to which I have brought entire honesty and singleness of purpose, and upon which I have spent whatever ability God has given me, is now to separate us; whether this difference is to override that complete union of thought, sympathy, and hope which on all other and, as I believe, even more important subjects, binds us together. Before them I must stand or fall; but be their present decision what it may, I know that the time is not far distant when they will recognize my action to-day as wise and just; and, armed with honest convictions of my duty, I shall calmly await results, believing in the utterances of a great American who never trusted his country in vain, that "truth is omnipotent, and public justice certain."

* * *

REQUIESCAT IN PACE

Picking the bones of the dead Confederacy went on in Congress for thirty years after Appomattox. In 1888 the Senate faced the question of what to do with Confederate property still left in England. It brought Senator Randall Gibson of Louisiana to his feet with something in the nature of a requiem.

Sir, the Confederate States died a manly and noble death on the field of battle many long years ago, and all that was left of them was that sentiment of honor which the men who carried the muskets in the ranks and the officers who wore wreaths on their collars inherited from a proud ancestry, and which I believe will be transmitted to and abide with the people of the Southern states so long as our mountains shall lift their summits to the skies and our rivers flow to the sea.

I would inscribe upon its memorial tablet the epitaph penned by one of the greatest race for his own:

> Good friend, for Jesus' sake, forbear
> To dig the dust inclosed here:
> Blest be the man that spares these stones
> And curst be he that moves my bones.

* * *

WHAT? NEVER HEARD OF TUPELO?

Speaker of the House Champ Clark once rated "Private" John Mills Allen of Mississippi as one of the six greatest wits ever to sit in Congress. Best known of Allen's classics was his "Tupelo Speech," which was sparked by a proposal to establish a fish hatchery at Tupelo, Mississippi. The date was February 20, 1901.

Mr. Speaker, I do not deem it necessary to take up twenty minutes' time to pass this amendment, but as this fish hatchery is to be established at Tupelo, and I find among some people in the country—even some newspaper men, who are supposed to impart information to others, and some gentlemen who have been elected to Congress, and who tell me that they have not only been to school, but gone through college—so much ignorance about Tupelo that I think I ought—in justice to them, not to Tupelo—to enlighten them some on this subject. (Laughter.)

If I were willing to avail myself of all the traditions and many well-authenticated but not absolutely accurate historical suspicions, I might invest this subject with much more historical and romantic interest. But I propose to confine my remarks to well-authenticated facts, ignoring such traditions, believed by many of our people to be true, as that when Christopher Columbus had his interview with Ferdinand and Isabella of Spain, that in his efforts to persuade them to back him in his expedition that led to the discovery of America, he assured them that an all-wise Creator, creating a world like this, was bound to have made somewhere near its center such a place as Tupelo. (Laughter.)

. . . . In 1513 the knightly Ponce de Leon landed upon the coast of Florida, and perverted history has it that he started out to look for the fountain of youth and limitless gold fields, when in truth and in fact he really started to look for Tupelo.

(Laughter.) You are all familiar with the disaster that overtook his expedition. Later, in 1540, the great and adventurous discoverer, Hernando de Soto, landed his expedition on the coast of Florida, and finally succeeded in reaching and discovering, for the first time by a white man, Tupelo. To come down to a later period, those of you who know anything of the history of your country will remember the contentions and contest that lasted for many years between the French, English, and Spanish governments for the ownership of the Mississippi territory. I am informed by those familiar with the real designs of those great nations at that time that the real motive of all of them was the ownership of Tupelo. (Great laughter.)

Finally, the United States, appreciating the importance of the position, took advantage of their dissensions and acquired Tupelo. (Renewed laughter.)

Everything went on very well until about 1861, when the South concluded to secede from the Union. I am reliably informed that when Horace Greeley and others sought Mr. Lincoln and asked him to "let the wayward sisters depart in peace," he shook his head and said, "No; this secession takes from the United States Tupelo (laughter), and we will not submit to it." And it was to rescue to the Union this town that brought on the war. (Renewed laughter.)

The armies of the Union were first directed against the capital of the Confederacy at Richmond, Virginia, but some obstructions were thrown in the way of that army at Bull Run, and they were persuaded to return to Washington. Another great army was then marshaled under the command of General Grant, who landed at Pittsburg Landing, on the Tennessee River, and began his operations against Tupelo. (Laughter.)

General Albert Sidney Johnston and myself met General Grant's army at Shiloh (laughter), and for most of the first day we had a real good time with them, and but for General

Johnston being killed and me being scattered on the evening of that day there is no knowing what might have happened or how the history of this country might have been changed. (Great laughter.)

Suffice it to say, I retired on Corinth, and when we were there, sorely pressed, President Davis ordered General Beauregard to fall back to Tupelo, and there make a great and desperate stand for the life of the Confederacy. And it seems that Generals Grant and Halleck were so much impressed with the dogged determination of the Confederate army to defend Tupelo to the death of the last man that they turned away in other directions. . . .

But Mr. Lincoln seemed never to have lost sight of the importance of Tupelo to the Union, and he marshaled another army under that able commander, General A. J. Smith, and started them to capture Tupelo. General Stephen D. Lee and General Forrest, with their commands, were sent to intercept him, but in maneuvering for positions General Smith got between Forrest and Lee and Tupelo and succeeded in capturing the town; and in an effort to dislodge him from there the desperate and bloody battle of Harrisburg, which is in the suburbs of Tupelo, was fought, in which nobody had any decided advantage, but General Smith evacuated the town and went back to Memphis. But the very fact that Tupelo had fallen seems to have broken the spirit of the Confederates, and we never did much good after that. (Great laughter.)

Many of you gentlemen have never been to Tupelo. I hope none of you entertain any idea of dying without going there. I should hate to have to have it said of any member of this Congress—for all of whom I have such a kindly feeling—that they did not aspire to visit Tupelo before they died. (Laughter.) I extend you all an invitation to come, and promise you a royal welcome. Come and go with me on College Hill some evening and see one of our Tupelo sunsets. (Laughter.)

Come and see one of our Southern, silvery, Tupelo moons!

I think it is the only place in the South where we have the same beautiful moons we had before the war. (Laughter.) I have often been asked about the size of Tupelo. I confess I have not been able to get the exact figures from the last census. The tabulating machines do not seem to have been able to work it out yet; but I can say, Mr. Chairman, that by sufficiently extending the corporate limits of our town we can accommodate a population larger than the city of London. (Laughter.) The truth is that our lands about Tupelo have been so valuable for agricultural purposes that we have not yielded them up for building a city as rapidly as we should have done. (Laughter.)

I can say, Mr. Speaker, that while there are larger places than Tupelo, I do not think there is any other place just exactly like it. Tupelo is very near, if not exactly, in the center of the world. The horizon seems about the same distance in every direction. (Laughter.) The sun, when doing business on regular schedule, comes right over the town, and sometimes gives us a hot time in the old town. It is a great place for the investment of capital, where it will be welcomed and protected. Come early, gentlemen, and avoid the rush!

This, Mr. Speaker, is a proposition to establish there a fish hatchery. We have the ideal place for a fish hatchery. Why, sir, fish will travel over land for miles to get into the water we have at Tupelo. Thousands and millions of unborn fish are clamoring to this Congress today for an opportunity to be hatched at the Tupelo hatchery. (Loud laughter.)

Now, Mr. Speaker, I only wish to say in conclusion that if there is a member here who wishes to have his name connected by future generations with that of Judas Iscariot and Benedict Arnold, if he wishes to have himself and his posterity pointed at with scorn, if he desires to be despised by men and shunned by women, let him vote against this amendment and he will secure all this infamous notoriety. (Loud laughter and applause.)

DEMOCRATS vs. REPUBLICANS

POLITICIANS' INFERNO

Mr. President, it is the laborer you always talk about. That reminds me of a story I heard in Texas of a man who said he had fallen asleep. He had a dream and he dreamed he went to hell. He was telling about what he saw when he got down there, and some fellow, who was a politician, asked him, "Did you see any Democrats down there?" He said, "Oh, yes; there were a few, not many, but there were a few around." "What were they doing?" "They were talking about reducing taxation and things of that sort, trying to do something for the public good." "Did you see any Populists down there?" "Yes, there were a few Populists." "What were they talking about?" "They were talking about having a good time in hell by issuing greenback money, $150 for every individual in hell." "Did you see any Republicans down there?" "Oh, yes." "What were they doing?" "Every one of them was holding a Negro between him and the fire."

Senator Roger Q. Mills of Texas
during a tariff debate, 1894

*   *   *

Mr. Speaker, I have no doubt that when our Democratic friends shall have uttered their last shout on earth against Republicanism and progress and protection of American citizens, and shall appear at the great judgment seat, and when Satan shall close up his bill of sale on these Democratic disloyal politicians who offered no prayer during the war for our success, but clogged up the wheels of progress, they will, when he calls them home to himself, say to him, "Satan, this is clearly unconstitutional."

Representative William Williams of Indiana, 1873

* * *

An Ohio Congressman once quoted this speech by an old-time Democratic politician: "Fellow citizens! In accordance with time-honored custom I come to declare my political sentiments. You know I am a Democrat, rocked in the cradle of Democracy, and was never anything else and never will be. There are three topics that now agitate the state: the United States Bank, the tariff, and the penitentiary. I shall pass over the first two very briefly, as my sentiments are well known, and come to the penitentiary, where I shall dwell for some time."

* * *

The doom of Cannonism and czarism, of Aldrichism and bossism has been sounded. The Republican party has been dismembered. Like Gaul of old, it is now divided into three parts—regular Republicans, insurgent Republicans, and chameleon Republicans. The regular Republicans ride the elephant all the time; the insurgent Republicans ride some and walk some, occasionally giving the poor old beast a savage kick, but always taking care to hold on to the tail as an evidence of their allegiance. The chameleon Republicans walk with the insurgents when it is popular and ride with the regulars when it is profitable.

Representative Jack Beall of Texas, 1910

* * *

Speaker Thomas B. Reed of Maine once described the Democratic party as "a man riding backwards in a railroad car: he never sees anything until he gets past it." On a speaking tour through his state during a presidential campaign, he was unduly heckled by a Democrat in his audience. At last the Democrat shouted out, "Aw, go to hell!" Reed pinned the gentleman's ears back with, "I have traveled in many parts of the state and have spoken at many meetings, but this is the first time I have ever received an invitation to the Democratic headquarters."

* * *

Told on the floor of the House was the story of a crowd of Democrats sitting one day on the porch of a hotel in northern New Hampshire during the Grant-Seymour campaign of 1868. An old traveler, ragged, dirty, rusty, unshaven and unshorn, ambled up and stared vacantly at the crowd that began to ply him with questions. Finally, someone asked him, "You're a Seymour man, aren't you, old fellow?" Straightening up he answered, "From my present appearance you would probably take me for a Democrat, but I ain't. I learned my politics before I took to drink."

* * *

Recently, when standing on the platform of a car the porter came to me and gently tapped me on the shoulder and said, "Mister, you must not stand upon this platform." I said, "Sir, what is the platform for?" and he replied, "Mister, it is to get in on." I never understood the full meaning and purport of that definition of a platform or what a platform was really intended for until I reread the plank in the Republican platform against trusts, and then I discovered for the first time the full purport and meaning of a political platform, especially a Republican platform—that they are not made to stand on, but to "get in on."

Representative William Williams of Illinois, 1901

* * *

Much has been said by our Democratic friends about their platform of 1892. I am reminded of a lady acquaintance of mine, who in war times went to the provost marshal at Little Rock with another lady friend to take the oath of allegiance. Her friend took the oath first, but the other lady, who was a good Southern woman, hesitated. Said she, "I can't take that oath. You know how I feel." Her friend said to her, "Oh, go on, Mrs. Smith, and take it. God will know you don't mean it." And in the same spirit the Democratic party adopted the platform at Chicago.

Representative John F. Lacey of Iowa

* * *

Great Guns and Little Fishes! You slid into office on a platform every plank of which has been demolished, but have patched it up, oiled and veneered it, and are going to try to slide in again—but you will be disappointed. It will be a case of "Slide, Kelly, slide!" but you will not reach homeplate again. You reached home on an error in 1912, but the people will fool you in 1916.

Representative Edwin E. Roberts of Nevada, 1914

* * *

IT'S A HELL OF A PLACE, SAID THE GENTLEMAN FROM MISSOURI

Speaker Champ Clark of Missouri entered the House in 1893. Even as a freshman he was razor-sharp in the eternal wrangling between Democrats and Republicans. But the day he compared the Republican side of the House to hell he stuck his tongue into a hornet's nest.

Mr. RAY of New York. I am sorry, indeed, Mr. Speaker, that our Democratic brethren think so ill of the Republican party. The distinguished gentleman from Pike County, Missouri, the Honorable Champ Clark, who represents the "true inwardness" of the Democratic party in all its sweetness, and loveliness, and beauty, declared the other day, with many a shake of his head, and with many a violent gesture, that if any man desired to visit Hades he had but to walk down the broad center aisle of this chamber and turn to the right, that is, the Republican side, and he would immediately find himself in hell.

Mr. CLARK. Does not the gentleman know that I simply adopted the simile of a distinguished protectionist Democrat on this side of the House?

Mr. RAY. I did not know whether you were adopting somebody else's language or were expressing your own views. I had supposed that the gentleman from Pike County, Missouri, was so original in his ideas that he could make a speech without adopting the ideas of anyone. The gentleman depicted the Democratic side as the happy land of eternal bliss, the heaven on earth and the hope of eternity; and he invited the American people to come over there and join them. Inasmuch as the Republican party is a unit on the great questions now agitating the public mind, harmonious in counsel, united in action, gentlemanly in deportment and language, and ever watchful of the interests of the people in all sections of our country. . .

Mr. LIVINGSTON of Georgia. Is that a compliment to the leaders or the masses of the Republican party?

Mr. RAY. It is a compliment to the leaders of the Republican party. It is also a compliment to the masses of the Republican party, and some of the remarks are intended as a rebuke to any gentleman who on the floor of this House shall denounce the Republican side as a hell upon earth. As unity and a desire for prosperity is the attitude of the Republican party on all these questions, while the Democratic party is constantly engaged in petty quarrels and bickerings, we can but conclude that the Democratic warhorse from Pike County is utterly perverted in his tastes, lost to moral sense and perception, and that to him hell is heaven and heaven is hell; and to him, judging from his utterances, the wail of the damned would be the sweetest music.

* * *

It was 1896 and four members of the House—all Democrats—were discussing the coming convention at Chicago to nominate their candidate for the Presidency. Apparently, they were dispirited over the outlook. Suggestions for the platform were going the rounds, as was the decanter.

Declared one of them, if the convention adopted a free-silver plank the party would divide and collapse. The second predicted a similar catastrophe if the convention put in a sound-money plank. The third was noncommittal, though predicting that a straddle plank would butter no Democratic biscuits. The fourth man had said nothing, but, tossing off his liquor, he volunteered a story that would indicate about where he stood.

"Gentlemen, a poor woman entered a store one day and asked to see some wrappers. The salesman spread out a varied assortment before her and poured praise on them. Beautiful wrappers, plain wrappers, rainbowed wrappers; all sorts and colors and conditions of wrappers. The woman looked them all over but seemed unable to make a choice. The salesman put on more steam, brought down even more wrappers off the shelves and expatiated on their merits and beauties. He couldn't understand it.

"These are all you have?" inquired the woman.

"Yes, madam, those are all we have, and we think we have the best stock in town and the most beautiful."

"Well," remarked the woman with some hesitation after another inspection, "I don't know as it matters so much. It's for a corpse."

* * *

WHY BEAT A DEAD SKUNK?

This little colloquy occurred in the Senate in the 1870's, after Senator Willard Saulsbury of Delaware had spent some minutes belaboring his Republican opposites.

Mr. SAULSBURY. And now, before I leave you, I will only express for you the same kind feeling which the judge always expresses for the murderer when he has concluded the sentence of execution against him, "May God Almighty have mercy on your souls, ye murderers of my country's Constitution."

Mr. NYE of Nevada. That is generally the last that is said, is it not?

Mr. SAULSBURY. Mr. President, I will reply to the Senator's question by relating one of his own anecdotes—he is full of them. He stated that on one occasion someone saw a man beating a dead skunk with a club. The man beating it was a Universalist. His neighbor remonstrated with him for beating the skunk after it was dead. Said he, "You are a Universalist; you do not believe in a state of future rewards and punishments; you ought, therefore, not to beat the skunk after he is dead." "Well," said the man who was beating it, "that is my faith in general, but in reference to this particular skunk I think it deserves punishment after death." So in reference to this political party. Although sentence may have been passed and prayer offered, it is not dead yet, but if it was dead, it is a political skunk that needs punishment after death.

* * *

After Cleveland's election in 1884 Charles H. Winfield of New Jersey informed the House:

For twenty-four years the Republicans have periodically predicted the death of the Democratic party, but it has proven a very tough corpse. It seems eternally young. It is younger and more vigorous today than when its opponents began making their predictions, and it will soon be called on to mingle with the mourners at the obsequies of those political prophets, which will be very much like the funeral occasion when a good old deacon was carried out and the choir and the congregation sang,

> Believing, we rejoice
> To see the "cuss" removed.

* * *

Related in the Senate was the story of an open political meeting back in Andrew Jackson's time. Suddenly an Old Hickory enthusiast bellowed out "Hurrah for Jackson!" to which a bystander retorted "Hurrah for a jackass!" "All right," shouted back the Jacksonian, "you can hurrah for your favorite candidate and I'll do the same for mine."

* * *

Mr. Speaker, I say the courage of these Democrats is amazing. They get up here day after day and admit that the country after a year of their rule is in a condition of bankruptcy, that it is borrowing money, that it is paying interest on bonds, that it is increasing the public debt. Death and devastation mark their track everywhere, and yet they have the courage to get up here and charge it all upon us, who are in a minority of one hundred in this House, and in a minority in the Senate, and who are rather in a minority in the Executive also. Now, what is the foundation for this? Why do they do it? How do they have the courage? It is because they can rely upon the invincible want of knowledge of their constituents. It is because they represent a class of people who can easily be deceived, who do not understand the facts of history or the facts of the hour. A gentleman said to me not long ago that the Democratic party would last forever; that it would be here at the end of a hundred years. That is so. There always has got to be a hind end of things.

Representative Thomas B. Reed of Maine

* * *

As a Mississippi friend once told me, "When a good Democrat comes in to register we ask him to read some easy section of the Constitution, as, for example, Article I, Section 4, Clause 1, which goes, "The Congress shall assemble at least once in every year." But when a Republican comes in to register we require him to read and explain some such clause as this: "No bill of attainer or *ex post facto* shall be passed." And then he added, "It works beautifully."

Representative James T. McCleary of Minnesota

* * *

HOW CAP'N CROSS GOT OUT OF THE MUD

Sharpshooting between Democrats and Republicans is as old as the parties themselves. Volleys of anecdote and wit, much of it loaded, besprinkle the records. This story, with its Lincolnesque flavor, was told during a crossfire in 1882 by Rep-

resentative Albert S. Willis of Kentucky. Under debate was so-called Civil Service Reform and—so the Democrats charged—the Republican failure to do something about it while in power.

Mr. WILLIS. This course of conduct on the part of the Republican party, this quadrennial outburst for reform when a Presidential election is in progress, brings me in the most natural way to my story, which is about a mariner. I refer to old Captain Cross, who lived down on the raging Ohio, and was the gallant commander of a first-class mud-scow. Even among the boatmen of the Ohio River, where sanctity is the exception rather than the rule, he was regarded as the most profane man that ever walked the deck of a boat. His profanity was notorious.

Upon one occasion he landed at the town of Owensborough and his boat got stuck fast in the mud. Here was a crisis. How could he get out of it? He called his first mate and told him to go up into the town and ring a bell and tell the people that Captain Cross was converted, that he had got religion, that he intended to reform, to change his life, to quit cussing, to lay aside his evil ways and become a pious and devoted Christian. His mate went up in town and rung the bell and made proclamation according to orders.

Moved by curiosity, piety, and sympathy, a vast crowd of men, women, and children poured down to the river bank, where the Captain's craft was in danger. He said to them, "A prayer-meeting will be held in the rear of this boat." They all went on the boat and back to the stern, and as soon as they got there the bow of the boat rose out of the mud, and he told them that the prayer-meeting was ended, that he had no further use for them, and they could go home, ashore, or to hell. (Laughter.)

Mr. ROBESON of New Jersey. Is that the attitude of the Democratic party?

Mr. WILLIS. That is the attitude of the gentleman who interrupted me, and the party to which he belongs. Every four years the Republican ship gets stuck in the mud. A Presidential election is coming on, and they make a great many professions of reform; they tell the good people of the country they intend to change their evil ways. But when they get them, when they have induced the good people of the United States to come on board their political craft and join in the great prayer-meeting for reform, when through their aid and prayers and votes the Republican ship is out of the mud, they tell them, in language probably not so profane as that of the captain on the Ohio, but equally as emphatic, that the prayer-meeting is ended, they have no further use for them; they are put ashore or are thrown overboard like Jonah was, and the ship moves on its way.

* * *

The other Democratic Senators keep an unwonted silence. They prudently avoid a discussion with the Senators from Vermont and Ohio and Iowa and Rhode Island. They have shown marvelous wisdom. Aelian, an ancient author, in his book entitled *Varia Historia*, says that, when the geese fly over Mount Taurus, nature has taught them, for fear of the eagles, to carry stones in their mouths that they may keep silence till the danger is past. Our Democratic friends on the other side show great sagacity in this debate in observing the customs of their ancestors.

Senator George Hoar of Massachusetts

* * *

My colleague says, "I firmly believe that the Republican party does contain the elements of a healthy regeneration." He also says, "The only way to preserve the vitality of the Republican party is to make it the party of the progressive reforms; in other words, the new party which is bound to come in one form or another." He further says, "I think, therefore, the Republican party has the stuff in it to become the new party." From these expressions I gather this threefold proposition; first, that a new party must come; second, that the Republican party needs to be born anew; and thirdly, that, on the whole, may be, it contains the proper ingredients out of which to make the coming new party. Sir, I deny my colleague's claim to originality in this proposition. I hold him up as a plagiarist. It is identically the proposition of a certain county tribunal, which, having determined to build a new jail, passed three resolutions on the subject: first, that they would build a new jail; second, they would build a new jail out of the materials composing the old one; and third, that the old one should stand until the new one was built.

Senator Charles Drake of Missouri, in reply to Senator Carl Schurz, of the same state

* * *

The proof you Democrats present for the people's consideration reminds me of the tramp who knocked at a farmer's door and asked for something to eat. The good-hearted old farmer looked at him and asked, "Are you a Christian?" "Why, can't you tell?" answered the tramp. "Look at the holes worn in the knees of my pants. Don't they prove it?" The farmer's wife promptly brought him a handout, and the tramp turned to go. "Well," asked the farmer, "what made the holes in the seat of your pants?" "Backsliding," replied the tramp as he hurried off. Now, my friends, that's what's the matter with you and your party. You have all worn holes in the seats of your breeches by backsliding. You are genuine backsliders, but some of you will have to offer a different reason for the porosity of the posterior part of your trousers after the people register their kicks at the coming election.

Representative Edwin E. Roberts of Nevada, 1914

* * *

Now, Mr. Speaker, is the Democratic party as we see it represented here in the Congress run by the horse or the jackass? Or is it a composite of the horse and jackass, a sterile coalition for power?

Representative Thomas B. Curtis of Missouri, 1957

* * *

A number of college boys who were studying "bugology" concluded they would play a joke on their old professor, and set about the preparation of a new specimen which they proposed to take to him for classification. So they took the legs of a spider, the antennae of a moth, the wings of a grasshopper, the thorax of a bee, the abdomen of a beetle and the head of another insect and fastened them together in such a manner as to present to all appearances an insect theretofore unclassified and unknown. They took their newly created insect to the class and laid it on the professor's table. They sheepishly gathered around and asked him to what class of insects the newly discovered insect belonged. The old man was familiar with all kinds of insects, for he had been professor of entomology for, lo, these many years. He put on his glasses, looked it over carefully and smilingly told the boys that in his opinion it was a "humbug." Now that is what is the matter with this omnibus revenue measure you have just passed. The people, when they put on their glasses, will readily classify it as a Democratic "humbug."

Representative Edwin E. Roberts of Nevada, 1916

The Senator who reported this bill at times takes upon his lips the name of Thomas Jefferson, and at other times declares himself a disciple of Andrew Jackson. Thomas Jefferson, the great lover of human liberty, the hater of slavery, would have surrounded the American manufacturer with protection by almost a Chinese wall. What have these sages in common with the Senator from Indiana? "It is not every one who saith: 'Lord! Lord!' who shall enter into the Kingdom of Heaven." And it is not every man who crieth "Democrat! Democrat!" that Thomas Jefferson or Andrew Jackson would admit to his company. When the men who reported this bill to the Senate say to Thomas Jefferson or Andrew Jackson, "Lord! Lord! have we not prophesied in thy name?" they will be likely to get the answer "I never knew you. Depart from me ye that work iniquity."

Senator George Hoar of Massachusetts

* * *

Mr. ENLOE of Tennessee. I would like to ask the gentlemen: Who made the laws under which this idleness that is at present existing came about? (Groans from the Republican side.) You gentlemen on that side *ought* to groan when such a question is asked, because it is bound to hurt.

Mr. HEPBURN of Iowa. When you are fully "grown," you will not ask such questions.

Mr. MILLIKEN of Maine. I will try to answer the gentleman from Tennessee respectfully because my friends on the other side are a good deal like the old lawyer's jury. When he interviewed them (before the trial) individually they all agreed with him, but pretty soon they brought in a verdict against his client, and he said, "Gentlemen, personally you are first-rate fellows, but as a compact mass you are a set of scamps."

* * *

"TO THE VICTOR BELONG THE SPOILS OF THE ENEMY"

To Democratic Senator William L. Marcy of New York belongs the distinction (or otherwise) of first enunciating this political credo. It was an American rendering of the ancient Brennic cry "Vae Victis." *In a virulent debate in the Senate in 1832 Henry Clay, John Calhoun, and Daniel Webster ganged up to block confirmation of their common enemy, Martin Van Buren, as Minister to Great Britain. They assailed Van Buren as inventor of political proscription in the federal government. In reply to this accusation Senator Marcy made the bland admission that has ever since attached Jackson's administration to the spoils system.*

I know, sir, that it is the habit of some gentlemen to talk with censure or reproach of the politics of New York. Like other states, we have contests, and, as a necessary consequence, triumphs and defeats.

It may be, sir, that the politicians of the United States are not so fastidious as some gentlemen are, as to disclosing the principles on which they act. They boldly preach what they practice. When they are contending for victory they avow their intention of enjoying the fruits of it. If they are defeated, they expect to retire from office. If they are successful, they claim, as a matter of right, the advantages of success. They see nothing wrong in the rule that to the victor belong the spoils of the enemy.

* * *

Fifty-odd years later Senator Zebulon Vance of North Carolina reaffirmed Marcy's bitter dictum. He took an even tougher line. It was 1888, fourth year of Cleveland's first term. Cleveland had not thrown out enough Republican of-

fice-holders to suit Vance. Here's how he expressed this delightful political pastime of cutting the losers' official throats.

After four years, or almost four years of trial, instead of the general ruin which was prophesied, what do we find? There has been some ruin, I admit it; but not enough to suit me. There has come ruin to many a Republican office-holder. There is where I say there has not been enough to suit me. When I fight a man and whip him, his scalp is mine. If I had the power, if our honored President had listened to me, there would not be a single, solitary rose left to mark where the garden had been. My sentiments toward these people who have so long abused the powers of the government, and used it in every conceivable shape to their enrichment and to the fattening of corporations, and to the unjust taxation of the people, and to the corruption of their fellow-citizens—my sentiments toward them are the same as those which animated the green countryman who visited the menagerie. He went in with a hickory stick under his arm, and in prowling around and looking at the animals he came across a live snake. Immediately he grasped his stick, and, before he could be arrested, had killed it. The owner ran up to him in great indignation. "What do you mean, you rascal, by killing that snake? That was a show snake, and it cost me a thousand dollars." "It don't make any difference," said the countryman. "Damn 'em! I kills 'em wherever I find 'em!"

* * *

His (Ambassador Bayard's) predecessor, Mr. Lowell—a famous personality always and everywhere honored, but who when ambassador was treated with still greater respect and the profoundest regard—when he was speaking to an English audience one day, and reference was made to American politics, said, "It is a rule with us, recognized as most fit, that family affairs should not be discussed before strangers." That same Lowell once delivered an address in England with a title which could be perverted by a narrow-minded man into a partisan word. The subject of the address was "Democracy." But he treated it in a higher sense, with a loftier spirit. It contained no partisan railing; and when he concluded an Englishman would have vainly asked of his neighbor, "Is he a Democrat or a Republican?" No; he was an American, and only an American. He conducted himself in accordance with the duty of an ambassador in his action and his utterances.

Representative Robert R. Hitt
of Illinois

* * *

The Republicans are a unit against this measure, but their arguments are not valid. Mr. Johnson of Indiana made a long, labored speech against it, but his speech reminds me of the story of an old Negro who, after twenty years of freedom, went back to see his old master. Sitting on the porch steps, the old master asked what had become of the old Negro's boy John. "Well, suh, John was riding on the railway cars and got killed in a wreck." "Well, Jim, don't ever get on the cars any more. And what about your boy Dick?" "Well, suh, he was lost in a steamboat explosion." Advised the white man, "Well, Jim, don't you ever get on a boat any more. And what about Tom?" "Well, suh, he was riding a horse and the horse ran away and killed him." Advised the white man, "Jim, don't you ever get on a horse any more." The old Negro promised he never would and said, "Now, Mister Tom, I want to know what's become of your boys, Bill, Dave, and Jack?" "Well, my boys all died a natural death in bed." "Then, Mister Tom, let me give you a piece of advice. Don't you never go to bed any more."

Representative W. Jasper Talbert of South Carolina

* * *

SPEAKER TOM REED HOG-TIES THE DEMOCRATIC NO-QUORUM BLOC

Speaker Thomas B. Reed, the "Great White Czar," won his niche in the parliamentary hall of fame by smashing the Democratic no-quorum roadblock in the House, January 1890. Of the 330 members the Republicans mustered 166, a slim margin of control. In voting on all Republican legislation the Democrats were physically present but constructively absent when their names were called, making it virtually impossible to marshal a quorum. No quorum, no business. It was an ancient prerogative. Reed staged a one-man revolution to end this for once and all. He would get a quorum by counting enough Democrats present but not voting to make a quorum. On January 29 the first order of business was a contested election. Rollcall showed 161 yeas, 2 nays and 163 (all Democrats) not voting, simply sitting silent. There was no quorum. Standing like a giant on the rostrum (he weighed 350 pounds and stood six feet, three inches tall) Reed summoned the Clerk to his side and ordered him to record the non-voting Democrats he could see and call by name from his perch. The moment he called the first name bedlam broke out. The Democrats rose en masse and surged down against the rostrum, hurling "Tyrant," "Usurper" and "Dictator" at Reed, who was imperturbable, placid, and utterly polite. In a pitched battle Reed ruled that every member should be counted in determining a quorum instead of those who merely answered the rollcall. But Reed's insistence on making a quorum made him master of the House, and the famous Reed Rules just about hog-tied Democrats and Republicans alike. This is the way it began on a quiet morning in 1890.

The SPEAKER. On this question the yeas are 161, the nays 2.

Mr. CRISP of Georgia. No quorum.

The SPEAKER. (Rising.) The Chair directs the Clerk to record the following names of members present and refusing to vote. (Applause on the Republican side.)

Mr. CRISP. I appeal. (Applause on the Democratic side.) I appeal from the decision of the Chair.

The SPEAKER. Mr. Blanchard, Mr. Bland, Mr. Blount, Mr. Breckinridge of Arkansas, Mr. Breckinridge of Kentucky . . .

Mr. BRECKINRIDGE. I deny the power of the Speaker and denounce it as revolutionary.

The SPEAKER. (With a slight rap of his gavel.) The House will be in order.

Mr. BLAND of Missouri. Mr. Speaker, I am responsible to my constituents for the way in which I vote and not the Speaker of the House.

Paying no attention, Speaker Reed resumed his maddening count of the Democrats present.

The SPEAKER. Mr. Brookshire, Mr. Bullock, Mr. Bynum, Mr. Carlisle, Mr. Chipman, Mr. Clements, Mr. Clunie, Mr. Compton . . .

Mr. COMPTON of Maryland. I protest against the conduct of the Chair in calling my name.

The SPEAKER. Mr. Covert, Mr. Crisp, Mr. Culberson of Texas, Mr. Cummings, Mr. Edmunds, Mr. Enlow, Mr. Fithian, Mr. Goodnight, Mr. Hare, Mr. Hatch, Mr. Hayes . . .

Mr. HAYES of Iowa. I appeal from any decision so far as I am concerned.

The SPEAKER. Mr. Holman, Mr. Lawler, Mr. Lee, Mr. McAdoo, Mr. McCreary . . .

Mr. McCREARY of Kentucky. I deny your right, Mr. Speaker, to count me as present, and I desire to read from parliamentary law on that subject.

The SPEAKER. The Chair is making a statement of the

fact that the gentleman from Kentucky is present. Does he deny it?

Mr. Montgomery, Mr. Moore of Texas, Mr. Morgan . . .

Mr. MORGAN of Mississippi. I protest against this as unconstitutional and revolutionary.

The SPEAKER. The gentlemen will be in order. The Chair is proceeding in an orderly manner.

Mr. Outhwaite . . .

Mr. OUTHWAITE of Ohio. I wish to state to the House that I was not present in this House when my name was called. The Chair is therefore stating what is not true. It is not for the Chair to say whether I shall vote or not or whether I shall answer my name when it is called.

The SPEAKER. Mr. Owens of Ohio, Mr. O'Ferrall . . .

Mr. O'FERRALL of Virginia. I protest against this assumption of power by the Speaker.

Mr. COOPER of Indiana. I ask by what right or by what parliamentary law the Speaker of this House declares men present and voting who have not voted?

The SPEAKER. The Chair does not declare men present and voting who have not voted.

Mr. BRECKINRIDGE of Kentucky. It is disorderly. It is a disorderly proceeding on the part of the Speaker.

The SPEAKER. Mr. Stewart of Texas, Mr. Tillman, Mr. Turner of Georgia.

Mr. COOPER. I demand an answer to the parliamentary inquiry. By what rule of parliamentary law or by what right does the Chair undertake to direct that men shall be recorded as present and voting?

Mr. WHEELER of Alabama. Must the representatives of the people remain silent in their seats and see the Speaker of the House inaugurate a revolution?

The SPEAKER. The Chair will state the question: The question of quorum was raised, and the Chair treats this subject in orderly fashion, and will submit his opinion to the

House, which, if not acquiesced in by the House, can be overruled by an appeal taken from the decision.

Mr. CRISP. By brute force.

Mr. COOPER. Mr. Speaker, I insist upon my appeal.

The SPEAKER. The gentleman must not mistake his situation. He is not to compel the Chair to do certain things. The Chair must proceed in regular order and the gentleman as a member of this body will undoubtedly permit the Chair to proceed.

Mr. ENLOE of Tennessee. If the gentleman is not in order, will the Chair state what rule is being violated?

Mr. COOPER. Do I understand that the Chair is about to answer my parliamentary inquiry?

The SPEAKER. There is no occasion for disorder.

Mr. COOPER. I understood the Chair . . .

The SPEAKER. The occupant of the Chair does not know what the gentleman understood, but if the House will be in order the Chair will proceed in an orderly way.

Mr. BLOUNT of Georgia. Mr. Speaker, may I make an inquiry?

The SPEAKER. Will the gentleman from Georgia permit the Chair to proceed?

Mr. BLOUNT. But the inquiry I wish to make was in view of the statement of the Chair. I understood the Chair to say that the Chair was stating a fact. I had understood that the Chair had directed the names to be put on the roll by the Clerk.

The SPEAKER. Put on the record by the Clerk. They will be recorded as present.

Mr. FLOWER of New York. I desire to be recorded as present and not voting.

The SPEAKER. The Chair will proceed in order if gentlemen will take their seats.

Mr. COWLES of North Carolina. Mr. Speaker . . .

The SPEAKER. Will the gentleman have the kindness to

take his seat. If he will do so, the Chair will be greatly obliged.

The Clerk announces the members voting in the affirmative as 161 and 2 who voted in the negative. The Chair thereupon, having seen the members present, having heard their names called in their presence, directed the call to be repeated, and, gentlemen not answering when thus called, the Chair directed a record of their names to be made showing the fact of their presence as bearing upon the question which has been raised, namely, whether there is a quorum of this House to do business or not, according to the Constitution of the United States.

It has always been the practice in parliamentary bodies of this character to determine the question whether there is or is not a quorum present by count. . . . There is a provision in the Constitution which declares that the House may establish rules for compelling the attendance of members. If members can be present and refuse to exercise their function, to wit, not to be counted as a quorum, that provision would seem to be entirely negatory. Inasmuch as the Constitution only provides for their attendance, that attendance is enough. If more were needed, the Constitution would have provided for more.

The Chair thereupon rules that there is a quorum present within the meaning of the Constitution.

* * *

"UNCLE JOE'S MAN"

It was 1910, and the revolt in the House against hard-boiled, likable Speaker Joe Cannon was mounting daily when the gentleman from Minnesota rose to toss a bouquet to the embattled czar.

Mr. FRANK NYE of Minnesota. I've got an opponent now up in my district. He is canvassing and making speeches and telling them that he is Uncle Sam's man and that Nye is Uncle Joe's man.

Now, he is a good fellow and I am willing to concede he will make a lot of people believe that probably, and perhaps enough so that he will have a chance to come down here and save the country. If he comes, I want you to use him as well as you have always used me. But what a difference there is in men's ideas and views of politics. As we are nearing the great natal day of the nation we are reminded that it is a noble thing to be an Uncle Sam's man. I hope in the chamber of my thoughts and aspirations that my heart beats somewhat at least in accord with Uncle Sam. I do not say that his does not, probably as much and maybe more than mine, I do not know; but he has got a vision of things, that he cannot be an Uncle Sam's man and be even a little bit of an Uncle Joe's man. I, according to my view, can be an Uncle Sam's man and enough of an Uncle Joe man to do him justice though the heavens should fall and the last spark of my political ambition be forever quenched.

Pardon me if I say a word about Uncle Joe. Where is the man who in his conscience and his life, if he is a student of his country's history, will say that Uncle Joe is not an Uncle Sam's man? Who is there that will read the history of the past fifty years and say that he should be denounced as an enemy to progress, to patriotism, to good legislation, and to good citizenship? Long after Uncle Joe is gone many of us will need defense more than he. Judge not that ye be not judged.

And while I speak at this time more particularly to men of my political faith, let me remind you that fifty years ago this summer this man, then in the morning of his majority, went fifty miles across the prairies of Illinois and sat as a delegate in the Decatur convention that sent a delegation to the national convention that nominated the immortal Abraham Lincoln. He sat there with plain, homely, humble Abraham

Lincoln, who was about to enter a path that would lead him to crucifixion and death. And for fifty years let it be said to Uncle Joe's credit he has been a Republican. He has seen us of the younger generation veer, wobble, and tack with every breeze, but he has moved in one course, toward one fixed star as he believed, of Republicanism and right, a star made luminous by the light of the immortal Abraham Lincoln himself.

Mr. JACK BEALL of Texas. Mr. Speaker, I listened with great interest to the funeral oration of the clerical looking gentleman from Minnesota, and, like most funeral orations, it proceeded upon the theory that concerning the dead it is not proper to say anything but good. Ever since I can remember, the Republicans have been hiding behind the tombstones of some of the founders of that party, and I am growing a little suspicious, because I have noticed that when they praise their ancestors most they have their hands deepest in the people's pockets. I can understand that they have much more ground to laud their ancestry than their ancestors would have if they were here to praise them.

If the Republican party was ever as good as the gentleman from Minnesota insists, he must now be harassed with the reflection that it has constantly grown worse. On this side we are comforted with the knowledge that if our party was ever bad, it is getting better. There may be some who will say it might be better than it is, but I dare say that there are very few who will say that the Republican party can ever be any worse than it is.

* * *

In one of the towns in this district the colored brethren, believing they belonged to the Republican party, organized a "conspiracy" against the South Carolina election laws. One of them who could read went in to inspect the two ballot boxes when he cast his vote. When he was in there, being able to read, he found that the right-hand box was the Presidential box, and on the left hand was the Congressional box, and when he came out he formed a line of the colored voters who could not read. Another one of them climbed a tree outside where he could look over the screen of boards the South Carolina election law required to be erected in front of the voting place.

The first colored man went in with his ticket, and he put his Presidential ticket in the right-hand box, and his Congressional ticket in the left-hand box, and so they went on in succession. Well, after a while, the judges of the election made the discovery that a "fraud" was being perpetrated and that the tickets were all going into the proper boxes, so they shifted the ballot boxes. Right then the man up the tree hollered out, "Change them tickets! De boxes is shifted!" So the colored voters changed the tickets and they went right along putting the right-hand ticket in the right-hand box and the left-hand ticket in the left-hand box, and the "fraud" against the grand old Palmetto State continued.

Representative John F. Lacey of Iowa

* * *

Mr. RANKIN of Mississippi. I have been trying to tell you Republicans for the last few weeks that if we do not take back the right of Congress to "coin money and regulate the value thereof," and stop the Federal Reserve System from inflating the currency, you will never be able to control the situation.

Mr. RICH of Pennsylvania. You have been coining and printing money. The Democratic administration started to print money when it came here fifteen years ago and you have been printing it until it is just like paper. It will be soon worth nothing. We must annul many of the laws this Democratic administration passed the past fifteen years, and the quicker we do it the better. It has been going on too long. Let the people elect a Republican President and I guarantee you we will do just that—repeal a lot of laws to undo the wrongs to America.

* * *

I want to refer the gentlemen on the other side to a book of rules that needs no amendment. I commend to them, not only as their guide in this House, but outside, that rule wherein the doctrine pertaining to stewardship is correctly given in the parable of the talents, wherein the Lord gave unto one of his agents, who was a Democrat, only one talent, and he gave to a Republican ten talents. (Laughter.) The Democrat, remembering his Democratic policy and notions, was afraid, and went and hid his talent in the earth. The Republican with his ten talents, went out and made another ten talents, and then they came back to report to the Lord. The man with the one talent said, "I know that thou art a hard man," which, in effect, is the position of the Democratic party, saying, "I know that you are narrow enough to be deceived by such so-called economic policies," and "I know that thou art a hard man and therefore I hid thy talent in the earth. Lo, there thou hast that which is thine." On the contrary the Republican, who had the ten talents, yielded up twenty talents to the Lord: and the Lord saith unto him, "Well done, good and faithful servant; thou has been faithful over a few things, I will make thee ruler over many things: enter thou into the joys of the Lord." And he said of the Democrat, with the little, measley, dried up, rusty one talent, "Take therefore the talent from him, and give it to him that hath ten talents; and cast ye the unprofitable servant into outer darkness: there shall be weeping and gnashing of teeth." (Laughter and cries of Amen!) Now the only Republican perplexity is what we shall do with the single, rusty Democratic talent.

Representative Joseph V. Graff
of Illinois, 1896

The Senators on the other side of the chamber are in the condition of the good old man up in New Hampshire who was formerly a Republican but left the Republican party. He had been a postal clerk as an ardent Republican for four years, and was very much delighted when he was informed that he could hold on for four years more. Eight years came around and under the operation of the civil service reform he was unexpectedly continued in office for twelve years. Twelve years came round. He had grown old and it was necessary to change him, but he insisted on being reappointed to hold on for sixteen years. When he found out he must go he immediately left the Republican party. He did not, however, join the Democratic party at once. He became a member of what was called the Labor party, and entered into an earnest campaign to elect a Labor ticket.

Some gentlemen were conversing with him about his party, and among other things he was asked, "What are the principles of this Labor party of yours?" "Principles?" he said. "Why, we haven't got into power yet. When we do get into power a few of us will get together and fix up some principles that will be about right."

Senator William E. Chandler of
New Hampshire

* * *

"THE LEFT WING OF THE NEW CONFEDERATE ARMY"

So charged Senator John Sherman of Ohio when, in 1887, President Cleveland issued an executive order returning the captured Confederate battle-flags to the South. Not a voice in the South had ever asked for the return of these flags. The idea originated with the Adjutant General of the army. President Cleveland approved it, but quickly revoked it—though not fast enough to squelch the furor that erupted in Congress and throughout the North. The Grand Army of the Republic threatened to march on Washington and head off the national "disgrace." In the House it brought on a small war between, not Southern Democrats, but Northern Democrats and the Republicans. Here is a set-to between a Northern Democrat, Luther F. McKinney of New Hampshire, and a Northern Republican, Byron M. Cutcheon of Michigan, both Civil War veterans. Worth noting is that in 1905, when President Theodore Roosevelt returned the battle-flags, the act was acclaimed as "graceful."

Mr. McKINNEY. Under this Administration not a single rebel flag has been returned or given up, but under the administration of Edwin M. Stanton twenty-one such flags were surrendered to the survivors of the organizations from which they were captured.

Mr. CUTCHEON. Surrendered to whom?

Mr. McKINNEY. To the survivors of the organizations from which they were captured. Those now in the hands of the government are in a room in the upper story of the building of the War Department where they can be easily visited and examined. Whatever of the captured Confederate flags were returned to those who bore them in the war were returned by the officials of the Republican party. I am glad, however, that they were not all returned, for there are many good men on this floor who were of age and in good physical condition when the war broke out, but whose patriotism never led them in sight of a rebel flag while the war was being prosecuted. I presume it was because it was not safe to investigate them at that time; but now as they read the history of that mighty struggle their patriotism is aroused, the blood boils in their veins, and the thought of returning these flags that were captured by their brave brothers is more than they can endure.

But luckily for their peace of mind, these flags are safe

from the hands of the enemy. They are stored in the attic of the War Department, where they may go at any time and under the guidance of a Democratic official they may feast their soul upon the tattered and moth-eaten emblems of the lost cause. Go, brethren, go, and look upon the trophies of brave and noble men, and remember while you look upon them that none of the glory that shall surround the history of those who bore them off the field in triumph will ever crown the history of your lives; and bear in mind, and enforce it upon your children and friends, that this Administration has returned no rebel flags. . . .

But there is one other charge that has been brought against the President. He has appointed rebel brigadiers to office, which is an offense to every ex-Union soldier who sacrificed for his country when these brigadiers were attempting to destroy it. . . . Now, as regards rebel brigadiers, I did not know we had any in this country. We did have them during the war; they were a part of that class of men who seceded from the Union, set up a government of their own, and declared their allegiance to it, and renounced the Union of which they had before been a part. But we of the North denied their right to go out of the Union. We declared they could not secede; and as an earnest of the faith that was in us we enlisted large armies, and at the point of the bayonet we enforced our idea. After four years of war, after the best blood of the nation, both North and South, had been shed, the Northern Army was victorious. The South laid down their arms, and General Grant commanded the armies of the South to go home and take their horses with them, to till their farms and raise bread for their wives and children. The Northern idea had been victorious; secession was a failure; the Union was as broad as ever, and reached from ocean to ocean, and from Canada to the Gulf. . . .

The South accepted the olive branch; they returned to their first love; they renounced the Confederacy; they proclaimed once more their allegiance to the Union; they sent their representatives to the halls of legislation, and were once more at peace with themselves and with the entire people. But when in the exercise of their right the voters of this country elected a majority of Democrats to this House this same Republican party that had invited them here set up the cry of rebel brigadier against them. And every Northern Democrat who voted with them was proclaimed an ally of the Confederacy. I have no apology to offer for those who rebelled against the government that nurtured them.

I have not a word to offer in palliation of their crime against the flag which had so long protected them; but I do say that it does not lie in the mouth of the Republican party, by whose own acts they are here, to raise the cry of rebel brigadier. They are here as a part of this nation, the mightiest on this earth. They have not refrained from joining the Representatives from the North in voting appropriations for the support of the government. They have not lifted their voice against the appropriation of the hundreds of millions of dollars that have been voted to the Union soldiers as a reward for their loyalty and sacrifice—the best possible evidence that they have accepted the result of the war, and are ready to join hands with us in bearing the flag of freedom to nobler heights than it has ever attained in the past.

The great sin, then, in the eyes of the Republican party, does not consist in the fact that a man has been a rebel brigadier. No matter how strong a fight he made against the Union, no matter though he disregarded every rule of civilized warfare, no matter though he was the last to lay down his arms and acknowledge the supremacy of the Constitution, all that was necessary was to proclaim allegiance to the Republican party, and though his sins were as scarlet he became as white as snow, and they gathered him to their bosom as one who was worthy of all honor, and the smile of love that wreathed their countenances was like the sweet smile of a young mother when she looks upon the face of her first-born. (Laughter.)

Mr. Chairman, the sin of having been a rebel is nothing in the eyes of the Republican party as compared with the sin of being a Democrat. That is the one sin they can not forgive. No matter how true they have been to the government, no matter how bravely they fought for the Union, to vote the Democratic ticket is the one unpardonable sin. . . .

Is it any wonder that the people in their indignation overthrew that party and proclaimed that henceforth they would follow the old Stars and Stripes rather than the Republican flag, the bloody shirt?

Mr. CUTCHEON. Mr. Chairman, there is one other matter on which I wish to speak for a moment, and then I shall yield the floor to other gentlemen. I want to make a brief allusion to what the gentleman from New Hampshire said about the order for the return of what are called the "rebel flags." The gentleman says that no flag was ever returned under the order of President Cleveland, and that therefore the President is to be held up as an example of patriotism and virtue. But, Mr. Chairman, I have this to say, that it is nothing to the credit of the President, who made the order, that the flags were not returned. It was the voice of the great loyal North and Northwest that came thundering down upon him like a cyclone that stopped the order and turned it back. (Applause.)

. . . . What would they do with them if they had them? Mr. Chairman, a flag means something. That flag over your head means something. It means something to me and to my comrades who followed it upon many a bloody field. It means country, it means Constitution, it means liberty, it means law, it means all the thronging future with its momentous possibilities. (Applause.)

It means homes and firesides; it means our children, and it means our kindred and our posterity that shall come after us down to the latest generations. That is what we fought for. (Applause.) That is what our comrades died for. It may be that the President did not realize this. It has never been burned into him in battle fires as it has been into some.

What did the other flag mean? You men who bore it bravely, you know what it meant. It meant the doctrine of the right of secession, and you yourselves now say that the doctrine of secession is dead. It meant the dissolution of this magnificent Union, and you yourselves say now that this is a grand, magnificent, indissoluble union of indestructible states. (Applause.) It meant war against the Constitution of your country. Does it mean that to you now? If you had received the flags, moth-eaten, tattered, torn, battle-rent as they are, what would you have done with them?

No, my friends; no, my brothers; I speak with malice to no one, with charity to all; it is better that they should rot and be moth-eaten in the attics of the War Department than that they should ever be returned to the hands that bravely bore them on the battlefield. Out of the tomb of the lost cause they will bring neither light nor glory nor honor. Let them rest. They no longer mean what they meant then; they can never mean it again, and God helping us we never intend that the symbols of disunion, secession, and war against the Constitution shall ever again go back into the hands that bore them on the battlefields of the rebellion. (Loud applause.)

GOLD, SILVER, AND GUSH

MIRACLES

Mr. Speaker, in thinking about this much discussed subject my mind reverts to the old Negro preacher who was addressing his flock with great earnestness on the subject of miracles. He said, "My beloved friends and brethren, the greatest of all miracles was 'bout de loaves and de fishes. There was five thousand loaves and two thousand fishes, and de twelve apostles had to eat 'em all. Now the miracle is that they didn't bust." Now the people, Mr. Speaker, have been stuffed on this subject for the last three weeks, or, I might say, for the last few years, with silver speeches, and the great wonder is that they haven't "busted."

Representative W. Jasper Talbert of South Carolina, 1895

* * *

During the campaign of 1896 a lank-haired silver orator was haranguing an audience in the backwoods of Pennsylvania. He got so much applause that he concluded there were no gold men in the audience. So he bellowed out, "If there is a gold bug in the house, please stand up and give me your name and where you live and how you feel." In the back of the house rose a tall gangling individual, who said, "Well, stranger, I'm a gold bug. My name is Jack Jones. I live down here by the crossroads, and I feel just like a thoroughbred horse in a field of jackasses."

* * *

To call names is no argument. It amounts to nothing. I am willing to admit that the gold men commenced calling names, and I am of the opinion that they followed the example set them by a young woman who heard her mother having a row with a neighboring woman. She thrust her head out of the window and shouted, "Hurry, mother, and call her thief before she calls you one!"

Representative James A. Johnson of California, 1870

* * *

Gentlemen say they are in favor of bimetallism, but they are opposed to free silver; that they are in favor of bimetallism, but they are opposed to the coining of silver. They remind me of a man who was a candidate for the legislature in the state of New York at a time when the question of the adoption of the Maine liquor law was before the people. He said:

"Fellow citizens: I am in favor of the Maine liquor law; I believe it is a good law. I believe it would promote temperance; but, fellow citizens, I am opposed to the enforcement of the Maine liquor law because it interferes with personal liberty."

Representative William W. Johnson of California

* * *

Those of us who are advocates of the free coinage of silver, straight and independent, by the United States, have offered you a system that for four thousand years has been demonstrated to be a safe one. It is true that the Populist party has a number of different remedies for the situation; and I am advised that they are about to add three additional planks to their platform. One of them is to make a cross between the lightning bug and the honeybee for the purpose of enabling the bee to work at night. Another that of breeding the centipede with the hog, for the purpose of having a hundred hams to each animal. And I am told that they have the further visionary scheme of budding strawberry plants into milkweeds, so that everybody can have strawberries and cream from the same plant.

Representative Charles S. Hartman of Montana, 1896

* * *

Mr. Speaker, I recollect to have heard one of the most distinguished editors and most eloquent orators in this country say when discussing the silver question that he had been for thirty years a writer and speaker upon economic and financial questions, and that it was his business as such a writer and speaker to be familiar with all matters regarding the finances of the country, and he said, "Now, at the end of that time, I am willing to make a confession that I know nothing whatever about the silver question, and never in my life knew but four men who did. Of those four men, two are dead and the other two never had a dollar in their lives."

Representative Asher G. Caruth of Kentucky

* * *

At the height of the Silver-Gold political crusade in 1896, Representative Grove L. Johnson of California offered this superior piece of wisdom in the House.

It is related in the chronicles of old that at one time a cunning artificer in metals hung over the road a most beautiful shield, one side of it embossed in gold and the other side embossed in silver, and both elaborately carved.

Two knights coming in opposite directions, one from the East and one from the West, stopped a short distance off to admire the shield. He of the East said, "What a glorious golden shield I see before me." The knight of the West responded, "Sir Knight, it is a beautiful shield, but it is silver." He of the East replied, "Do you mean to say I lie in reference to it? Surely it is golden." The knight of the West replied, "I know it to be silver." From words they came to blows; and they killed each other in defense of the opinions they had. While lying weltering in their blood and breathing their last, an honest peasant came along and, looking on both sides of the shield, said, "What a beautiful shield it is, with gold on one side and silver on the other." And the knights said, "God forgive us for killing ourselves: that we did not look on both sides of the shield before we fought, and thus save our valor and our blood for our common enemies."

And so today the American people are fighting among themselves because they do not look on both sides of this question of money of the country. The men from the East are for gold and the men from the West, like knights in legend, are for silver.

* * *

"GOOD OLD DEMOCRATIC DAYS"

This amusing give-and-take occurred during the 1870 debate on refunding the Civil War debts. Should the nation continue a double currency of metal and irredeemable paper or return to gold and silver? The vote and debate cut across party lines. Eastern Democrats lined up Eastern Republicans to defeat the proposed issuance of more greenbacks.

Mr. COX. [June 8, 1870] What is needed is resumption of gold and silver. On or before 1872 the Democracy will bear its old banner to success for gold and silver. This is our only hope. Gold and silver! The words trip pleasantly on my tongue. They are music to my ears. Gold and silver! They are the legal tender of commerce and the Constitution—I had almost said, what I once said, and I say it now reverently—the legal tender of God Almighty, who made it precious! Is there no one here to recur to the traditions of the party? Ah! I see that Pennsylvania has its ear open.

(Mr. Getz of Pennsylvania approached the seat of Mr. Cox and presented him two gold twenty-dollar pieces.)

Mr. GETZ. Here is the Democratic currency which Pennsylvania loves and longs for.

Mr. COX. I hear its chink. I see its beauty, I know it is precious. It reminds me of a better day of the Republic when the people knew what they had to deal with.

Mr. INGERSOLL of Illinois. [June 9, 1870] Yesterday, Mr. Speaker, we heard a solitary voice on the other side of this chamber ringing out clear and melodious for a return to specie payments. It was the voice of my elegant friend from New York. He spoke of the good old Democratic days when gold and silver chinked in the pockets of the people. That was a good while ago, but I remember them well. I was a Democrat then; and I remember, too, that more rags fluttered from the divine forms of the "happy" people than pieces of money "chinked" in their pockets. In those days we were called the "barefooted Democracy," the "great unwashed." I wondered at it then, but I do not now. It could hardly have been otherwise. We were not to blame for our appearance. The fact was we did not even possess enough of thin, jingling sixpences to buy shoes for our feet or soap for our ablutions. Good old Democratic days, indeed! How eloquently he spoke of the shining coin. Whose ears did he expect to tickle? Gewgaws and trinkets charm the red man and the half-civilized; hence the bright ringing coins have a peculiar charm over the ignorant. The gentleman does not seem to appreciate the fact that our people have taken a good many long steps in advance since the good old days to which he delights to refer. The people want no more of those days.

* * *

Mr. Speaker, I plead for the plowmen of the Republic. It is recorded in the wisdom of the ancients that in the reign of Henry VIII the question was presented to the minds of the best leaders of thought in the British Empire, "How can civil war be prevented? What remedy can be applied for that greatest national disorder, civil war?" The only remedy that then appeared satisfactory was this: Let the British Empire so govern the subjects that the greatest possible number of plowmen shall be the owners of their plows.

Let all the American products of silver be coined into legal-tender coins, and the plowmen of the land, the toiling masses, will have new lines of hope opened up to them.

Representive John S. Little of Arkansas

* * *

A colored boy working on the wharf in Savannah was paid off in silver. He put a half-dollar in his mouth to bite it and see whether it was silver or lead, and it slipped into his throat and stuck about half way down. In great alarm he ran to a surgeon and asked him to cut it out. "Can't cut that out," said the surgeon. "It's got to stay there. Say, boy, are you registered?" "No, sir, I isn't registered," the colored boy replied. "Well, you go and get registered right away," said the surgeon, "and vote for McKinley, because if Bryan is elected that half-dollar will be a dollar, and then you'll choke to death, sure."

A campaign story told on the floor of the House in 1897

* * *

Now, Mr. Speaker, we all know that there never has been enough either of gold or silver in the world to discharge the functions of money, and for that reason one third of the money of the world has been for centuries paper money uncovered by either silver or gold. Nature in her wisdom has guarded these two precious metals from man. Do you realize how limited they are? I made a calculation some years ago, verified by the Director of the Mint, which showed that all the silver coin in the world, the accumulation of the ages, that for which men have worked and fought for centuries, could be contained in a building one hundred feet long, one hundred feet wide, and thirty feet high, less space than that occupied by this chamber, and one sixteenth of that size.

Representative Francis G. Newlands of Nevada

* * *

Mr. President, there is no trouble to redistributing the wealth. The Lord God in heaven says it has to be done. Not only does He say it has to be done; He says a nation which does not distribute the wealth cannot survive. The Lord shows us in chapters and in paragraphs and in verses how He sent his apostles into countries where the wealth had become concentrated in the hands of a few people, and how they did redivide it, and how they did redistribute it. He says that the time will come, even in this generation.

Senator Huey P. Long of Louisiana, 1934

* * *

I have sat here and listened with a great deal of earnestness to speeches upon both sides of the question. I have listened seriously and patiently, and I must admit that sometimes I have been somewhat in the position of the little boy whose mother in making him his first pair of pants put the front in the rear.

The little fellow started for school the next morning and walked cheerfully along until he looked down and discovered the situation, when he burst out crying and said, "I don't know whether I am going to school or going back home."

W. Jasper Talbert of South Carolina on the bill to repeal the silver purchase act of 1890

COLD WAR, CIVIL WAR, AND AFTERMATH

"YOU HAVE KINDLED A FIRE!"

The American Civil War actually opened on the floor of the House on February 13, 1819, when Representative James Tallmadge, Jr., of New York offered an amendment to the bill admitting Missouri to the Union that would restrict slavery in the new state. Tallmadge's amendment was a time bomb that struck at the very root of slavery—and the Southern flame-throwers rose to denounce it. Tallmadge served a single term, just long enough to light the pyre of civil war. Bitter debate raged for days. Here you read a brief, burning passage from the melee of words that forty-two years later would erupt into gunfire.

Mr. COBB of Georgia. If you persist, the Union will be dissolved! You have kindled a fire which all the waters of the ocean cannot put out, which seas of blood only can extinguish!

Mr. TALLMADGE. Sir, if a dissolution of the Union must take place, let it be so! If civil war, which gentlemen so much threaten, must come, I can only say, let it come! My hold on life is probably as frail as that of any man who now hears me, but while that hold lasts it shall be devoted to the service of my country—to the freedom of man!

Mr. Speaker, the violence to which gentlemen have resorted on this subject will not move me from my purpose, nor drive me from my place. I have the fortune and honor to stand here as the representative of free men, who possess the intelligence to know their rights, who possess the spirit to maintain them.

Sir, the honorable gentleman from Missouri (Mr. Scott) has just told us to beware of the Ides of March, and has cautioned us to "beware of the fate of Caesar and of Rome." Another gentleman (Mr. Cobb) from Georgia has said that if we persist the Union will be dissolved and, with a look fixed on me, has told us we have kindled a fire which all the oceans cannot put out and which seas of blood only can extinguish.

Sir, language of this sort has no effect on me. My purpose is fixed, it is interwoven with my existence. I know the will of my constituents and regardless of consequences, I will avow it. As their representative, I will proclaim their hatred to slavery in every shape; as their representative, here will I hold my stand until this floor, with the Constitution of my country which supports it, shall sink beneath me. If I am doomed to fall, I shall at least have the painful consolation to believe that I fall as a fragment in the ruins of my country.

* * *

DELIGHTFUL INTERLUDE IN THE HOUSE IN 1840

Mr. BYNUM of North Carolina. I refer to the remark made by a certain abolitionist member of the House when the vote was being taken on laying Mr. Coles' resolution on the table, "Now come up, you Southern slaves, and show yourselves." Yes, sir, this was the language applied to these patriotic, high-minded men, who regard their Constitutional obligations to the South, who are for giving quiet to the

North on this exciting subject, and for preventing a servile and desolating war.

Mr. PECK of New York. Does the gentleman allude to me?

Mr. BYNUM. I allude to a gentleman by the name of Peck.

Mr. PECK. I can only say that if the gentleman alludes to me, and speaks of my language as coming from an abolitionist, he says what is not true.

Mr. BYNUM. If the gentleman is not an abolitionist, there is not one in existence; all his votes and all his speeches are given in support of the Abolition party. I believe he is one, and will venture to say that there are not ten members of the House who are not of the same opinion.

Mr. PECK. It is not true that I am an abolitionist.

Mr. BYNUM. Does the gentleman mean to say that I knowingly assert what is false?

Mr. PECK. I mean to say that the gentleman asserts what is not true.

Mr. BYNUM. Then I say the gentleman is a blackguard and a scoundrel. Mr. Speaker, it is now seen what course certain gentlemen take when their conduct is exposed—when their votes are brought to light in opposition to their assertions, they resort to bullying and browbeating for answer. The House will bear me witness that I never willingly insult anyone.

Mr. PECK. For the reason that he is incapable of doing so.

Mr. BYNUM. Mr. Speaker, I call upon you to call for order, and demand that that blackguard and scoundrel take his seat. (Here, amid loud cries of Order, Order, and while great confusion and disorder was prevailing, Mr. Bynum made some remarks which were not distinctly heard by the reporter.)

I admit that my language was harsh; that it was unparliamentary and unsuited to this body; but I was driven to it by the outrageous and wanton insult that was offered me.

Mr. PECK. If the House should determine that the language I have used was offensive, I will leave this place, I will leave the world before I will retract it. I am charged with being an Abolitionist. I deny the charge; and before I will retract that denial, I will cease to live.

* * *

In 1859 the Senate was considering a bill to purchase Cuba for thirty million dollars. Southerners wanted it. Northerners opposed it. In mid-debate Senator James R. Doolittle of Wisconsin moved that the Cuban measure be set aside to take up the Homestead Act. Senator Robert Toombs of Georgia saw red. Rising, he hotly denounced the Republican Senators as demagogues who stood in awe and fear of the "lacklanders" of the North. Roared back Senator Ben Wade of Ohio, "Are we afraid, sir? Do you mean to say, sir, that we are afraid? There is no man or thing on God's footstool that I am afraid of."

Toombs cooled quickly and said, "I except the Senator from my remarks." Cried Wade, "If you want to take it back you can! We gladly accept the issue which the Senator from Georgia presents and will go to the people with it: Land for the Landless and Niggers for the Niggerless!

* * *

AND THEN THE FIGHT STARTED

Into the House from South Carolina, in 1853, came lovable, highstrung Laurence M. Keitt, destined to die beating back Grant's mass attacks at Cold Harbor in 1864. Cut and thrust was the order of the day, North versus South, when Keitt took his seat. He was a hotspur from the start. In the wee hours of February 6, 1858, he provoked a fight with Galusha Grow of Pennsylvania, who, after tossing off a few slurs at slavery, strolled over to the Democratic side of the House to chat with a member. From there he objected to a Mississippian's remarks. Keitt went into action at once.

Mr. KEITT. If you want to object, go back to your own side of the hall.

Mr. GROW. This is a free hall and every man has a right to be where he pleases. I will object when and where I please.

Mr. KEITT. Sir, I will let you know that you are a black Republican puppy.

Mr. GROW. Never mind. This hall belongs to the American people. I shall stay in it where I please and no slave driver shall crack his whip over my head.

Mr. KEITT. What do you mean by such an answer?

Mr. GROW. I mean just what I said.

In seconds the House exploded. Grow punched Keitt in the jaw and knocked him unconscious. Knives and pistols flashed. Members dashed into the well of the House for a free-for-all. William Barksdale of Mississippi, fated to die at Gettysburg, had his wig snatched by a Wisconsin statesman. An earthenware spittoon went hurtling across the floor. Barksdale recovered his wig and stuck it on his head wrong-end foremost, a ludicrous move that restored order.

A year later, during the acrimonious eight weeks' crisis over the election of a Speaker, Keitt stormed up and down the aisles venting his wrath against the North. His challenging words were picked up by Thad Stevens of Pennsylvania.

Mr. KEITT. The South asks nothing here but its rights. As one of its representatives I would have no more; but as God is my judge, as one of its representatives I would shatter this Republic from turret to foundation stone before I would take one tittle less.

Let the government pass into the hands of the Abolition party of this country; let us know that, and it is all we wish to know. We of the South are on the defensive, and we shrink from meeting no act of aggression which may be committed against us from any field. We mean to defend ourselves.

Mr. STEVENS. I do not blame the gentlemen from the South for taking the course they do, although I deem it untimely and irregular. Nor do I blame them for the language of intimidation, for using the threat of rending God's creation from turret to foundation. All this is right in them, for they have tried it fifty times and fifty times have found weak and recreant tremblers in the North who have been affected by it and who have acted from those intimidations. They are right, therefore, and I give them credit for repeating with grave countenances that which they have so often found to be effective when operating upon timid men.

* * *

The time has come when I shall not only utter my opinions, but make them the basis of my political action here. I do not, then, hesitate to avow before this House and the country, and in the presence of the living God, that if, by your legislation, you seek to drive us from the Territories of California and New Mexico, and to abolish slavery in the District of Columbia, I am for disunion; and if my physical courage be equal to the maintenance of my convictions of right and duty, I will devote all I am and all I have on earth to its consummation.

Fiery Robert Toombs of Georgia during the violent Speakership contest in the House in 1849

* * *

"WHAT BECAME OF THE TEN TRIBES OF ISRAEL?"

Secession was the order of the day this February 4, 1861. The "more perfect Union" was splintering. South Carolina, Missis-

sippi, Alabama, Florida, Louisiana, and Texas had already seceded. Preening herself was North Carolina, whose senior Senator Thomas L. Clingman rose to brandish threats of North Carolina's coming secession at his fellows on the floor. To illustrate the fate of the Union after the Southern breakaway, he cited the Bible and the fate of the lost tribes of Israel. He was answered at once by Senator John P. Hale of New Hampshire, who also drew on the Bible and the fate of the lost tribes. Hale's riposte brought the galleries up standing.

Mr. CLINGMAN. When a Senator dies, his spirit goes from one state of existence to another; it may be a brighter and better one. When these Southern states no longer live for this government, they pass into a new Confederacy.

The Israelites, with wailing and lamentation, deplored the loss of one of their tribes. When recently the annunciation of the departure of a single state was made here it was met with strange levity on the other side of the chamber. How will it be, sir, when the ten tribes have gone, when fifteen states have departed?

Mr. HALE. The honorable Senator asks, in that overflowing rhetoric with which he has delighted the Senate so long, "What will you say when the ten tribes go out?" Sir, I was glad to hear that. Ten tribes did go out from the kingdom of Israel, but the ark of the covenant of the living God remained with the tribe of Judah. (Applause from the galleries.)

The PRESIDING OFFICER called for order.

Mr. HALE. I think the galleries ought to be excused for applauding a reference to the Scriptures. I say, there is where the ark of the covenant remained. What became of the ten tribes? They've gone God only knows where, and nobody else. It is a matter of speculation what became of them—whether they constitute the Pottawatomies or some other tribes of savages. But the suggestion of the Senator from North Carolina is full of meaning. There were ten tribes that went out, and, remember, they went out wandering. They left the ark and the empire behind them. They went, as I said before, God only knows where. But, sir, I do hope and pray that this comparison, so eloquent and instructive, suggested by the honorable Senator, may not be illustrated in the fate of these other tribes that are going out from the household of Israel.

* * *

OWEN LOVEJOY INTERPRETS GOD'S PROVIDENCE

A full-scale raking-over in the House followed the tragic Union defeat up the Potomac at Ball's Bluff in 1862, where Colonel (Senator) Ned Baker was killed. The whole pitiful truth was spread out for the statesmen to hear. Militant abolitionist Owen Lovejoy of Illinois would have his say. He charged that the disasters at Ball's Bluff, Bull Run, and elsewhere were a visitation of the Lord.

Mr. LOVEJOY of Illinois. I say, Mr. Speaker, the whole nation is standing impatient, trustful, hopeful, yet gradually losing confidence in the mode in which this war is conducted. They are standing just as the old hero, John Brown, stood on the scaffold—John Brown, whose soul, thank God, is marching on. I hope it will get through the whole army, and then we will not be quarreling about Ball's Bluff and other defeats. I call him an old hero, saint, and martyr. He stood there with the rope round his neck while General Wise was maneuvering his troops—parading them around the scaffold to look upon the old saint and hero. It was then that Brown said, "I am not impatient, sir; but I hope you will not detain me any longer than is absolutely necessary." That is the way the people feel who have to be taxed to pay the expenses of this war, and see their cherished ones fall by disease and the sword, in respect to the movement, or rather non-movement, of our troops.

But, Mr. Speaker, to return to that which I wanted chiefly to say, and that is this: I care very little about investigating these incidental facts. The great trouble is that this nation has failed, and is yet failing, rightly to interpret the providences of God. Although a reference to any higher law or providence may be received here with a smile and a jeer, yet the truth is that God is holding this nation, and refusing to allow us to achieve any victories because we are not just; because we are not true to the principles of justice and truth and human equality which we proclaimed in the original structure of our government. We are failing to proclaim "liberty throughout all the land to all the inhabitants thereof."

Mr. DUNN of Indiana. One word in reply to the gentleman from Illinois. He thinks the last day is come; that this is the day of judgment; that the tares must now be burned. Well, I believe in him neither as prophet, priest, nor king. If he be a true prophet, let him call down the fires of heaven to consume his sacrifice; and if the fires come, I will believe in him, but not until then. He undertakes to interpret God's providence, but I think he had better humiliate himself before his God, than undertake to be the interpreter of His providence.

* * *

HOW CONGRESSMEN WON THE BATTLE OF BULL RUN

Representative Sam "Sunset" Cox's rousing description of the precipitous Federal retreat from Bull Run in 1861 was a classic piece of humorous ridicule. It provided a much needed dash of levity for the grim Thirty-seventh Congress. A century later, in this Centennial Year of the first pitched battle of the Civil War, Cox's absurd rehearsal still brings a laugh. The day,

January 30, 1862, he offered this choice fare he laid the House in the aisles. Cox's target was his colleague, John A. Gurley of Cincinnati, a former preacher who, setting himself up as a military critic, had the day before flayed the Lincoln administration for incompetence and a lack of knowledge of how to make war.

Mr. COX. I do not know, sir, how much weight will be attributed to my colleague's military strictures. If his facts are no better than his conclusions—and I will demonstrate that neither are correct—his speech will only go for what it is worth: the scolding of an unmilitary Congressman.

But, sir, my colleague compels me to examine into his merits as a military critic particularly, and the propriety of military "movements" here in Congress and elsewhere by civilians. My colleague will admit that he is not a military man by education, nor a soldier, like Falstaff, on instinct. (Laughter.) His profession is that of a gospeler. (Laughter.) His studies do not fit him to discuss martial subjects. We do not go to a blacksmith to have our watch repaired, nor to a watchmaker to have our horse shod.

But, sir, criticism on the art of war, to be valuable now, must be backed by specific study and experience. What has been the study and experience of my colleague?

The country was thoroughly disgusted with the part Congressmen played at Bull Run. (Laughter in the galleries.) It may be remembered with what jocund levity the House adjourned to go over to see our army march upon Richmond. Not one of us ever got there, except my friend from New York (Mr. Ely), who was taken prisoner. The House may remember that I opposed the adjournment then on the ground that, by going over the river, we would only get in the way of the soldiers. It turned out that the soldiers got in the way of the Congressmen. (Laughter.)

The people, who have been under the impression that the

crowd never stopped till they got into Washington, will be now gratified to learn that the Congressmen won the Bull Run battle against our own soldiers. (Laughter.)

I refer to this precious bit of history to show how Congressmen fit themselves for military criticism.

There will be, Mr. Chairman, empyrics in medicine, pretenders in religion, pettifoggers in law, mushrooms in vegetation, secessionists in government, snobs in society, and we must not be surprised at military wiseacres in Congress! (Laughter.) Since my colleague has hurled the glove at McClellan, I have a right to examine his claims as a critic. He admits to being at Bull Run. His masterly activity on the retreat he admits. How that retreat was effected I only know from rumor. I have seen it reported—and perhaps it is as apocryphal as some of the facts upon which my colleague arraigns General McClellan—that my colleague after his fatiguing race to Centreville, and having passed that point with the speed of Gilpin—and not having the benefit of a carriage like the Congressmen who kicked out of it the "cowardly" and tired soldiers besmutched with their cartridges in battle—was careening along like the devil until luckily, he met—what think you, noble representatives?—a herd of stampeded cattle selected by their keeper for their stampeding propensity (laughter); when, seizing upon the extreme rear of a noble ox, he was borne from the field, holding on with vigorous prehension to the tail of the animal! (Great laughter.)

Mr. EDGERTON of Ohio. I rise to a question of order. It is out of order for members of the House to applaud, cheer, or laugh in the manner they have been doing (laughter), and I submit—

Mr. COX. Does the gentleman make that point on me? I have not applauded, cheered, or laughed.

Mr. EDGERTON. I submit that order should be preserved on the floor of the House.

The SPEAKER. The point of order is well taken.

Mr. EDGERTON. I hope the Chair will enforce the rules.

The SPEAKER. The Chair is satisfied that when gentlemen consider the impropriety of any disturbance, it will not occur again.

Mr. WICKLIFFE of Kentucky. I acknowledge a violation of order. I laughed; but for my life's sake I could not help it. (Laughter.)

Mr. COX. I will do justice to my colleague (Mr. Gurley), I put this as an apocryphal case, which I heard as a rumor. I am glad to do justice to him, and to that noble ox, my constituent, and to whom the gentleman should have apologized, if the story were true. Various as human ingenuity are the modes of human warfare, both in advance and retreat; but never, sir, in the accounts of Xenophon or Marshal Saxe; from the time of Joshua to General Taylor; in the contests of Achilles or Garibaldi, have we so unique a performance as this suppositious race of my constituent and my colleague on the fields from Bull Run. (Laughter.) Does he claim that this, if true, would make him a military expert?

My colleague is one of those whose politics and prayers have ever been to be delivered from the men of war. In times past he has thought more of Saint Peter than of saltpeter. I wish these masters of the art of war, who quote so inappositely and irreverently Joshua's writings, but forget how he won his battles, whose knowledge of Agamemnon and Achilles is purely poetic, would study some of the useful axioms of Hierocles, and would just go to sleep before a looking-glass to see how handsome they look with their eyes shut and their mouths closed.

* * *

"NO WEST POINT, NO REBELLION"

No man ever hated West Point more generously than hard-boiled Senator "Bluff Ben" Wade of Ohio, except possibly

General Ben Butler of Massachusetts. It was inevitable that civil war would summon West Point before the bar of the Senate, and the day was January 15, 1863 when the appropriation for the support of West Point was on the tapis. Wade pulled no punches in charging West Point with treason. Over the debate hung the shadow of victorious Confederate armies led by West Point graduates and resignees. But West Point had her defenders, chief among them Senator Henry Wilson of Massachusetts, Chairman of the Military Committee.

Mr. WADE. I have so often expressed my opposition to bills of this character, and to the policy of appropriating money for the establishment and support of this institution, that I do not propose to take up time now to argue against it. I know the institution has been of no use to the country. So far from it, sir, I believe, and I have so expressed myself before, that if there had been no West Point Military Academy, there would have been no rebellion. That was the hotbed in which rebellion was hatched, and from thence emanated your principal traitors and conspirators.

Mr. WILSON. I agree with the Senator from Ohio that there are some evils connected with West Point, but I think the Senator is mistaken in regard to its influence upon the loyalty of its graduates. In 1861, when the rebellion broke out, we had eight hundred and twenty West Point officers in the Army of the United States. Since that time one hundred and ninety-seven have resigned on account of the rebellion; nineteen of those were from the loyal states, and several of them are in the rebel army. One hundred and seventy-eight of these disloyal officers that resigned were from the slaveholding states. About two hundred out of eight hundred and twenty resigned, leaving about six hundred and twenty in the Army who have remained loyal to the flag of the country. About one fourth have resigned, because they were disloyal to the country. I think this fact goes to show that the men educated at West Point have been quite as loyal as the men of the country generally, no more, no less.

Mr. NESMITH of Oregon. Mr. President, I have heard it stated on this floor, and at the other end of the Capitol, over and over again, that slavery was the cause of the rebellion. It seems now that the Senator, in order to accomplish his purpose, to make an attack upon this institution, proposes to saddle the cause of the rebellion on a mere institution intended to educate young men, to make them serviceable for the interests of the country.

Why, sir, look at some of these men: I will merely refer to a few names of men graduated at West Point who have sacrificed their lives in defense of their country. I presume that their history, at least, is secure. I may name Greble, Winthrop, Lyon, Stevens, Mitchell, Mansfield, and Reno as a few of those who have not proved themselves traitors. Sir, we may say of them:

> How sleep the brave, who sink to rest
> By all their country's wishes bless'd!
> When Spring, with dewy fingers cold,
> Returns to deck their hallow'd mold,
> She there shall dress a sweeter sod
> Than Fancy's feet have ever trod.

Mr. WADE. It requires considerable poetry to make this go. (Laughter.) I am not very much acquainted with the tactics of Moses nor with the inspiration that ancient warriors had, but I feel that this institution has had no particular inspiration at all from any source. If Joshua had the art of blowing down walls with rams' horns, he did much better than the West Pointers are able to do at the present time. With all their improvements upon ancient inspiration, I have heard of but very few walls that have been battered down by them.

Abolish this institution, and I will go bail for it that the military science of the nation will not suffer a hair's breadth; but other institutions will spring up everywhere, divested of this objection of monopoly, of pride, of vanity, of superciliousness that overshadows your army, and has led almost to the destruction of the activity of your army. That is my judgment of it.

Mr. FOSTER of Connecticut. I am persuaded that the fact is not as the Senator from Ohio thinks. Why, sir, some of the leading spirits in this rebellion were educated in my own state, at Yale College, in New Haven. The honorable Senator does not believe that Yale College is a nursery of treason. He may not think it is a desirable college; I know nothing about his opinion as to that; but he does not believe it is a nursery of treason. Some of the leading spirits in this rebellion were educated at Williams College, in the hills of western Massachusetts; others at Harvard College, near Boston; others at other colleges in New England, none of whom the honorable Senator from Ohio, nor any other Senator, would think were places where traitors were educated. The charge would not be made by anyone. But if the fact that from these institutions traitors have come is any argument that the tendency, the influence of the institution, was to produce traitors, I see not why the argument is not just as conclusive in regard to these institutions as in regard to West Point.

Mr. WADE. I have not asserted that the institution made traitors. I have said and I say still that, from the time of the Saviour to the present day, the Senator can find no instance of an institution founded among men, whether favored by government or otherwise, where, of those that received an education, the same percentage of graduates proved themselves perjured traitors.

Mr. DAVIS. Mr. President, I have always been taught to believe that war was an art, and that, like any other art, it has to be learned.

I agree that the highest properties of a great military commander are a natural endowment. A Caesar, a Hannibal, a Bonaparte, a Cromwell, were given by their Creator the great faculties and qualities that constituted them great commanders; but Cromwell himself, with all his great genius and vigor, would have been in earlier life an accomplished commander if he had had the benefit of a military education. The other great captains had such an education. Well, sir, I say that this military art, so far as it is to be acquired, must be studied and learned just like any other art, and we must have schools and exercises in which to learn it.

Another proposition I make. We may learn by our enemies; and our enemies, the secessionists, we may learn something useful and valuable from them also. How does this matter of military commanders stand in the Confederate armies? Mr. President, let us take a view of the generals who have been educated at West Point, and who have rendered service, and brought glory even upon the Confederate arms by their skill in war and by their ability as captains; I will do them that honor. There is Robert E. Lee, Joseph E. Johnson, Albert S. Johnston, Stonewall Jackson, Stuart, Longstreet, Bragg, one of the Hills at least, and Magruder.

Mr. WADE. . . . This institution for more than thirty years has been under the absolute dominion of your Southern aristocrats. I say emphatically, that for the last twelve years it has been entirely and utterly under the dominion of Southern aristocrats, who have put their creatures in there, and have taught rebellion as a science more than they have any other military science.

Mr. GRIMES of Iowa. That is not the fault of the Academy.

Mr. WADE. It was the fault of the administration of the Academy; and I will show you how it worked, and everybody knows how it worked. We select an unsophisticated young man and put him in this institution, and before he is permitted to learn military science, he is taught to despise his own democratic section of the country, and is taught to despise labor, and the simplicity of our northern institutions; and he is taught there to admire above all things that two-penny, miserable slave aristocracy of the South. I ask the advocates of this system, has not that been the practice?

Mr. GRIMES. Does the Senator say it is so now?

Mr. WADE. I say it is so now. The evil of that pernicious poison is in the very heart of the institution, and how long it will continue God only knows. I judge it by its fruits.

* * *

DROWN THE REBELS!

The flags were furled, the last shot fired, but late 1865 brought further misery to the South. Rampaging waters of the Mississippi had spread over large sections of three states, gapping the levees for miles and miles. Before the House this January 1866 was a bill that would provide funds to repair the vast damages. Thad Stevens, South-hater, came roaring into the arena.

Mr. KASSON of Iowa. If gentlemen still indulging the war spirit want to hang the rebels, let them hang them by the rules of law and justice; if they want to starve rebels, let them enact it upon the statute-book that they shall be starved. But when we are legislating here for the great interests of the country, let us legislate like statesmen, not placing dependence upon newspaper articles which are dishonorable to the country from which they come, for they are in disregard of what every man knows to be the best interests of that country. I ask gentlemen not to disregard the fact that by the rebuilding of these levees we shall increase the production of cotton, thereby diminishing its cost to us who consume it, reducing largely the present high prices of cotton goods, as well as increasing largely our internal revenue.

Mr. STEVENS of Pennsylvania. If we all indulge in such

platitudes as my friend has, we will never get through this bill during this session.

Mr. KASSON. Did the gentleman say latitude or platitudes?

Mr. STEVENS. Platitudes. I hope nothing will come up again so near the heart of my friend in the interest of the rebels. This, in my judgment, is a most shameful attempt on the part of the enemies of the country. Of this General Claiborne who comes here I have nothing to say. I asked him whether he was a rebel and in the rebel army and he said that he was, but that he was now willing to submit. Not one of these states has yet made its peace with the Union. Not one of these states is represented here, not one of them has a Representative which can in its name rise on this floor and speak in behalf of its interests. They have to look abroad for men to act for them as attorneys. Shall we grant this when we refuse to pay our own honest debts? Shall we grant this when the respectable chairman of the Committee of Claims refuses to pay an old woman whose house was burned down, because we have no money? Let them build their own levees. Let them raise their own cotton. I would not be in favor of hanging them, but I do not think I should interfere if the Lord should choose to drown them out. (Laughter.)

Mr. SCOFIELD of Pennsylvania. I ask my colleague whether the difference is not while those who are opposed to him are for *damming* the Mississippi, he is for *damning* the rebels. (Renewed laughter.)

Mr. STEVENS. I am not for hanging them, but God forbid I should give them a reward for having cost us so many hundreds of millions of money and so many hundreds of thousands of lives!

* * *

"IT WAS NOT AN EAGLE, IT WAS A VULTURE!"

The historic collision between Senator George F. Hoar of Massachusetts and Senator Lucius Quintus Cincinnatus Lamar of Mississippi in 1879 served notice that the Southern bloc would oppose all assaults on the character of Jefferson Davis. Lamar, former Confederate soldier and later to adorn the Supreme bench, was one of the coolest, sharpest men in Senate history. Before the Senate, March 1, 1879 was a Resolution to extend to veterans of the Mexican War the same pension benefits as those enjoyed by the soldiers of the War of 1812. Without previous notice, Senator Hoar offered this amendment, "Provided further, *that no pension under this act shall ever be paid to Jefferson Davis, the late President of the so-called Confederacy." Davis had fought gallantly in the Mexican War.*

Mr. HOAR. Mr. President, the person named in my amendment has been selected by his own act as the representative and leader of an attack on the life of the country that had educated him and which had honored him. This gentleman has never given utterance to an expression of regret for his attack on the life of the Republic. And it is now proposed by the votes of this Senate to do to that person, his treason unrepented of, the signal honor of putting him on the pension rolls of our country, and to tax the widow and the orphan of the loyal soldier to pay to him that pension. I do not propose to do it.

Mr. GARLAND of Arkansas. Mr. President, so far as Mr. Davis is concerned, I do not suppose he wants a pension. He would scorn it if tendered grudgingly. He does not ask it, and would not receive it unless given freely and in the spirit it is bestowed on others. He was a gallant soldier in the Mexican War. His services are upon the record of this country, and while they may not surpass, yet they will equal in history all Grecian fame and all Roman glory. If there is anything of credit to the Senator for offering the amendment, he is welcome to it, but I do not envy him in this work.

Mr. SHIELDS of Missouri. Mr. President, my opinion is that it would be conferring a distinction upon Jefferson Davis that would elevate him much higher than I want to see him elevated. To make him the one soldier excepted is about the highest distinction that can be conferred on him in history. It was said of a distinguished Roman that his statue was not carried in a triumph because he was the most distinguished man of his time. So it went down to history. So it sounds to this day, and so will you send Jefferson Davis down by making him the one solitary, distinguished exception among ten million people.

Mr. HOAR. The Senator from Arkansas alluded to the courage which this gentleman had shown in battle, and I do not deny it. Two of the bravest officers of our Revolutionary Army were Aaron Burr and Benedict Arnold! It is related of Arnold that when in exile in England he met an American lady at the entrance to the House of Commons and asked her what the people of America would say if he returned to his native land. The lady's reply was, "They would burn with honor your leg that was wounded at Saratoga and hang the rest of you." No such spirit or temper has been displayed to Mr. Davis. He lives in peace. There is not a nation on earth which ever exhibited or would exhibit such clemency as the victorious American people exhibited toward the president of the late Confederate States. This is a little too bitter a cup to put to our lips and ask of us, which I say to his credit that he does not ask us.

Mr. GORDON of Georgia. And nobody else.

Mr. HOAR. And nobody else, to put him upon the roll of honor of the Republic and pension him at the cost of the widows and orphans of the soldiers of the late war.

Mr. LAMAR. It is with extreme reluctance that I rise to say a word upon this subject. I must confess my surprise and regret that the Senator from Massachusetts should have wantonly, without provocation, flung this insult . . .

The PRESIDING OFFICER (Mr. EDMUNDS in the chair). The Senator from Mississippi is out of order. He cannot impute to any Senator either wantonness or insult.

Mr. LAMAR. I stand corrected. I suppose it is in perfect order for certain Senators to insult other Senators, but they cannot be characterized by those who receive the blow.

The PRESIDING OFFICER. The observations of the Senator from Mississippi, in the opinion of the Chair, are not in order.

Mr. LAMAR. The observations of the Senator from Mississippi, in his own opinion, are not only in order, but perfectly and absolutely true.

The PRESIDING OFFICER. The Senator from Mississippi will take his seat until the question of order is decided.

Mr. LAMAR. Yes, sir.

The PRESIDING OFFICER. The judgment of the chair is reversed, and the Senate decides that the words uttered by the Senator from Mississippi are in order, and the Senator from Mississippi will proceed.

Mr. LAMAR. Now, Mr. President, having been decided by my associates to have been in order, in the language I used, I desire to say that, if it is at all offensive or unacceptable to any member of this Senate, the language is withdrawn; for it is not my purpose to offend or stab the sensibilities of any of my associates on this floor. But what I meant by that remark was this: Jefferson Davis stands in precisely the position that I stand in, that every Southern man who believed in the right of a state to secede stands.

Mr. HOAR. Will the Senator from Mississippi permit me to assure him and other Senators on this floor who stand like him that, in making the motion which I make, I did not conceive that any of them stood in the same position in which I supposed Mr. Davis to stand. I should not have moved to except the gentleman from Mississippi from the pension roll.

Mr. LAMAR. The only difference between myself and Jefferson Davis is that his exalted character, his preeminent talents, his well established reputation as a statesman, as a patriot, and as a soldier, enabled him to take the lead in the cause to which I consecrated myself and to which every fiber of my heart responded. There was no distinction between insult to him and the Southern people, except that he was their chosen leader, and they his enthusiastic followers; and there has been no difference since.

Jefferson Davis, since the war, has never counseled insurrection against the authority of this government. Not one word has he uttered inconsistent with the greatness and glory of this American Republic. The Senator from Massachusetts can point to no utterance of Jefferson Davis which bids the people of the South to cherish animosities and hostilities to this Union, nor does he cherish them himself.

The Senator—it pains me to say it—not only introduced this amendment, but he coupled that honored name with treason; for, sir, he is honored among the Southern people. He did only what they sought to do; he was simply chosen to lead them in a cause which we all cherished; and his name will continue to be honored for his participation in that great movement which inspired an entire people, the people who were animated by motives as sacred and noble as ever inspired the breast of a Hampden or a Washington. *I say this as a Union man today*. The people of the South drank their inspiration from the fountain of devotion to liberty and to constitutional government. We believed that we were fighting for it, and the Senator cannot put his finger upon one distinction between the people of the South and the man whom the Senator has today selected for dishonor as the representative of the South.

Now, sir, I do not wish to make any remarks here that will engender any excitement or discussion; but I say that the Senator from Massachusetts connected that name with treason. We all know that the results of this war have attached to the people of the South the technical crime of rebellion, and we submit to it; but that was not the sense in which the gentleman used that term as applied to Mr. Davis. He intended to affix (I will not say that he intended, but the inevitable effect of it was to affix) upon this aged man, this man broken in fortune, suffering from bereavement, an epithet of odium, an imputation of moral turpitude.

Sir, it required no courage to do that; it required no magnanimity to do it; it required no courtesy. It only required hate—bitter, malignant, sectional feeling—and a sense of personal impunity. The gentleman, I believe, takes rank among Christian statesmen. He might have learned a better lesson even from the pages of mythology. When Prometheus was bound to the rock, it was not an eagle, it was a vulture, that buried his beak in the tortured vitals of the victim.

* * *

Oh, but you say the South is solid. That is true. And you intimate to the North that we are solid against the Union. That is not true. There is not a word of truth in it. We are solid. Solid how? Solid against whom? Solid against the Republican party. Why should we not be? Do you wonder? The past is enough to make us solid.

Senator Ben Hill of Georgia replying to Senator John Logan, of Illinois, 1879

* * *

Mr. President, there is one thought I should like to state. A distinguished Southern writer has said that the Senate, in its organization and practices, is "the South's never ending revenge for Gettysburg." I do not want that to continue. Let me say that we in the North have no desire for revenge for Bull Run, although at Bull Run the Southerners gave us a terrific beating. We want to bury the bitterness of the Civil War, and do so that we can go forward as a united nation.

Senator Paul Douglas of Illinois, 1959

POTPOURRI

THEY'D BE GLAD TO BURY HIM AT THEIR OWN EXPENSE

The burial of Congressmen who die during their term in Washington has vexed many a legislator both before and after the event. Burial in the Congressional Cemetery was never too popular. "Private" John Allen of Mississippi once had his say, or rather his two says, on this subject during the Fiftieth Congress.

1.

You often hear the question asked here of a member if he is acquainted with another member, and he will say, "Oh, yes, I went with him on a funeral excursion and found him a real jolly fellow." I trust I may live out my official career, but, sir, if He who rules our destinies and does all things well should order otherwise, I only want such funeral or burial as my limited means will allow. I do not want the people taxed for a funeral pageant for me.

2.

I took occasion at the first session of the present Congress to submit some very pertinent and sensible remarks on the subject of Congressional funerals. Those remarks seem to have made a deep impression on the country, so much so that I was warmly endorsed and returned to the Fiftieth Congress without opposition. Just to illustrate how profoundly my constituents were impressed with my speech on that occasion, and how fully they appreciate their Representative, I will repeat what one of my old friends said to me on my return home last summer. He met me, and after congratulating me on the very brilliant record I had made in Congress, he said, "And John, old fellow, we read your speech about the Congressional funerals and the people all endorsed what you said. You are exactly right; and you tell them fellows up there in Congress that if you die while you are there, you do not ask them to bury you. You have plenty of friends down here who will take pleasure in doing that for you."

* * *

As I have sat here day after day and heard gentlemen give their refined definitions, always resting upon that condition precedent to their philosophies, "other things being equal," I have been reminded of the opening of an address I heard made many years ago.

> Ladies and gentlemen: Phrenology is an exact science. The proof of that is in the fact that, other things being equal, size is always the measure of strength. But since it has never pleased God Almighty to create two human beings in whom the other things were equal, our science is incapable of demonstration.

Representative John J. Gardner
of New Jersey, 1895

* * *

GREAT EXPOSTULATIONS

Mr. BARKLEY of Kentucky. I wish to say, in regard to the expostulation of the Senator from Missouri—

Mr. DONNELL of Missouri. Mr. President, I object to the

word "expostulation." I have a right to express myself on the floor.

Mr. BARKLEY. The Senator is talking–

Mr. DONNELL. I object to the word "expostulation."

Mr. BARKLEY. Well, go on and object.

Mr. DONNELL. I am objecting now.

Mr. BARKLEY. I am not yielding any further to the Senator from Missouri.

THE PRESIDING OFFICER. The Senator from Kentucky.

Mr. BARKLEY. If the Senator does not like the word "expostulation," which is a perfectly good English word, he has a right to object to it.

Mr. DONNELL. I object to any slighting language.

Mr. BARKLEY. The Senator is expostulating, and when anybody expostulates, he is indulging in expostulation.

* * *

When the able and distinguished majority leader and the able and distinguished minority leader and all the multitude of followers–I would not say in the manner specified in the twenty-third chapter of Exodus–voted to have all-night sessions, I thought they would be present to hear something about these bills. But I have decided that they are all like the old justice of the peace down in North Carolina who had the misfortune of having to try a lawsuit in which two lawyers appeared on opposite sides on the day he wanted to go fishing. When they got through taking the evidence, the justice of the peace asked the lawyers if they wanted to argue the case, and they said yes, they wanted to argue. Then he asked them how much time they wanted to argue, and they said an hour on each side. He told them they had that right. He said, "But I have to go fishing. You can proceed with the argument. I will go fishing. When you finish with the argument, look under this book on my desk. You will see I have the decision already written out."

I do not assume that Senators who are now locked in the embrace of Morpheus have actually written out their decisions, because I hope they will be willing to receive more light.

Senator Samuel J. Ervin, Jr., of North Carolina during the civil rights debate, 1960

* * *

There was a congregation in England once that wanted to procure new hymn books, but they were very poor and could not afford to pay for them at the ordinary prices. They understood, however, that a certain great advertising house, a business house that made patent medicines, was willing to furnish them hymn books at a penny each if they would allow some advertisements to be inserted in the books. They thought that would be no special harm, that they might have a few pages of advertisements bound up with Watts and Doddridge. Accordingly they agreed to the proposition. The books came, duly printed, and they got down to the church on the 24th of December. On Christmas morning the model Christians, who had no thought of anything but religion, got up to sing. Their pastor had given out by the first line a very familiar hymn, and in a few seconds they were aghast to find themselves singing:

Hark! The herald angels sing
Beecham's pills are just the thing.
Peace on earth and mercy mild;
Two for man and one for child.

Representative William Everett of Massachusetts, 1893

* * *

There is a class of people who find fault with widow pensioners and the old soldiers. They are in their way, and whenever a pensioner dies they rejoice. They are ready to sing a song like that suggested on one occasion by a lot of men who belonged to a society of undertakers. They had an undertakers' banquet in which it was agreed that the best act of man was to die. An undertaker does not have much use for a living man, but he has great respect for a dead one. Someone at this banquet got up and sang the Indian plague song, with a glass in his hand, and the others with glasses in theirs:

> So stand to your glasses steady;
> 'Tis here the revival lies;
> A cup to the dead already—
> Hurrah for the next that dies!

Representative Charles A. Boutelle of Maine, 1900

* * *

A friend of mine tells a story more suitable as an illustration in this connection than anything I can recall from history, fiction or fable. A wag carried about a queer looking box to scare people with. He pretended there was a terrible animal in it that would eat people alive. He had it in New York on one occasion. The beholders asked him what it was. "A kilabaroo," he replied. "Where did it come from?" "It came from Africa." "What is its color?" "Green as jealousy." "What does it live on?" "It lives on snakes." "Where do you get the snakes?" "I get them from my brother-in-law here in New York." "Where does he get them?" "Well, he gets them out of his imagination when he has delirium tremens." "Oh, then they are imaginary snakes." "Oh, yes, it's an imaginary kilabaroo, too. There's nothing in the box, but it scares a lot of people."

Representative Marriott Brosius of Pennsylvania, 1893

WHAT PRICE LEADERSHIP?

Time was running out for the eighty-sixth Congress when on June 17, 1961 Senator Lyndon B. Johnson of Texas rose to portray the woes of the majority leader of the Senate. And he topped it off with an amusing story.

Mr. JOHNSON of Texas. People question the leadership from time to time.

Mr. MANSFIELD of Oklahoma. Mr. President, I think there are times when the leadership takes undue and unusual punishment. I happen to know how difficult it is to get along with sixty-four prima donnas on the Democratic side.

Mr. JOHNSON. I have been in a position of leadership responsibility for ten years, and I have found it very easy and comforting to be able to work with members on both sides of the aisles. I have served with six or seven Republican leaders and with more than a hundred Senators.

The problems are always difficult. Last year we had the tax bill reported to the Senate too late; this year it was reported too early. Too early—too late.

It reminds me of the story of a train in our hill country which was brought to the foot of the hill and an old man said, "You'll never get it started up the hill." It went up the hill, and as it started down the hill he said, "You'll never get it stopped."

There are some people with whom we live in the world and with whom we do not get along too well. Likewise, we live in a world in which we do not get along too well with all nations. We see what is happening now.

* * *

Mr. RANKIN of Mississippi. The gentleman ought to know that the private power companies have the vast holding companies fastened upon them. I might say stacked upon them. They remind me of that little verse:

> Great fleas have little fleas upon their backs to bite 'em,
> Little fleas have lesser fleas, and so, ad infinitum.

They are sucking the lifeblood out of the power companies all over the country.

Mr. JENSEN of Iowa. Let me remind the gentleman that we will not only have fleas on this federal control, we will have bedbugs, rattlesnakes, and everything else eating up the American people.

During the debate on the Reclamation Act of 1948

* * *

"MY VERY BOWELS YEARN FOR HIM!"

Before the House on May 20, 1870 was a bill for paving Pennsylvania Avenue. In opposing the measure, J. Proctor Knott of Kentucky made one of the three speeches that established his name as one of the all-time great humorists in Congressional history.

I have heard one reason very frequently urged for the passage of this bill which candor compels me to admit almost convinced me that we ought not only to appropriate this sum of $180,000, but any other amount that might be necessary to repave Pennsylvania Avenue at the very earliest possible period of time; and that is, that it is so much used by the horde of office-holders that throng the thoroughfares of this city in numbers almost equal to the hosts which were hurled by Lucifer from the battlements of heaven. (Laughter and applause.) For, sir, if there is a being on this earth for whose comfort and convenience I entertain the profoundest solicitude, if there is one whose smallest want stirs my sympathetic soul to its serenest depths, it is your office-holder, your public functionary. (Laughter.)

When I see one of that "noble army of martyrs" bidding adieu to his home and all the sweets of private life, for which he is so eminently fitted by nature, to immolate himself upon the altar of his country's service for four long years, Homer's touching picture of the last sad scene between the noble Hector and his weeping family rises before my sympathetic imagination. (Great laughter.) When I see him plunging recklessly into an office of the duties of which he is profoundly and defiantly ignorant, I am reminded of the self-sacrificing heroism of Curtius when he leaped into the yawning gulf which opened in the Roman forum. When I behold him sadly contemplating his majestic features in one of those gorgeous and costly mirrors which is furnished him at the public expense, my heart goes out to him in sympathy. When I see him seated sorrowfully at a miserable repast of sea-terrapin and champagne, my very bowels yearn for him. (Laughter.) And when I see him performing perhaps the only duty to which he is fully competent—signing the receipt for his monthly pay—I am so overwhelmed with pity that I wish I were in his place. (Great laughter.)

When such considerations as these, sir, have come crowding upon my mind, appealing to every generous sentiment of my better nature; when I have thought how the official nerves of our poor neglected public servants are racked by "the car rattling o'er the stony street," I have felt, under the sudden impulse of the moment, that we ought to tear up the old cobblestone pavement on the avenue and supply its place with one of the new-fashioned patent wooden ones, over which the splendid carriages of our government officials, with their coats of arms and liveried outriders, might glide as smoothly and noiselessly as the aerial car of the fairy queen through the rose-tinted clouds of the upper ether. (Applause and laughter.)

But, alas, the House is estopped, Mr. Chairman, by its own action, to entertain any such considerations as these; for when my friend from Ohio (Mr. Mungen) some time ago offered a resolution inquiring how many carriages, horses, harness, and other trappings of nobility the government furnished its officials at its own expense, it was promptly rejected, on the ground, as I supposed, that it was a great state secret, and that it should not even be hinted to the plebeian taxpayers in the country that our government officials here ever rode in carriages at all, but that they should be left to indulge the innocent illusion that their self-sacrificing servants here at "the capital of the nation," bowed down by the cares of state or the painful burdens of their own ponderous intellects, plod slowly along, with eyes bent upon the ground, while their hearts are with the loved ones far away. (Laughter.)

Sir, I would like to meet one of your constituents (H. E. Paine, of Wisconsin, in the chair) in his suit of homespun butternut—pardon me, I believe some wear butternut in your state. (Laughter.) I say I would like to meet one of your honest-hearted, patriotic old constituents, who feels an honest pride in the fancied simplicity and purity of our republican form of government, down here at the junction of Pennsylvania Avenue and Seventh Street, where the one-legged veteran with his hand-organ grinds out his wailing appeal to the charity of his patriotic countrymen as they pass, when some gentleman high in authority sweeps by in his splendid phaeton behind a spanking span of thoroughbreds, driven by a flunky dressed in a drab overcoat and a stovepipe hat, with a silver buckle in front of it almost as big as a garden gate. (Laughter.) I would like to see him open his eyes and stare at the passing pageant. I think I can see him now watching the glittering equipage. As it fades away in the dim perspective the old man turns slowly away, muttering "Sic transit gloria mundi," and the maimed soldier strikes up, "That's the way the money goes; pop goes the weasel."

Yes, sir; I would like to accommodate our officeholders with a smooth and commodious pavement; but as I honestly think we cannot, the best advice I can give them is, if they cannot stand it, to resign. The whole country will approve their indignant resolution. (Laughter.)

* * *

In the sixteenth and seventeenth centuries wool was the great English industry, more important even in that country's economy than the dairy industry has ever been in the United States. It was feared that foreign hands might prove more skillful in the weaving of wool cloth than English hands, and that the finished product would then compete with English woolens. To increase wool's use a law was passed that funeral shrouds must be wool. Thus, for more than 120 years, it was illegal to bury a person in any other shroud or covering than pure English wool. Not everybody liked this kind of legislation. As was said at the time, "This law forces our dead to consume what the living were inadequate to purchase."

Representative William R. Poage
of Texas during the 1948 debate
on oleomargarine

* * *

In his "Old Horses and Military Coattails" speech, July 27, 1848, Representative Abraham Lincoln, Whig, from Illinois, turned his humor on the Democrats. At the moment the Whigs, though slightly divided, were zealously courting General Zachary Taylor, Mexican War hero, as their candidate for the Presidency. The Man from Illinois closed his remarks with his "Divided Gang of Hogs" story.

The Democrats are kind enough to frequently remind

us that we have some dissensions in our ranks. Our good friend from Baltimore, immediately before me (Robert M. McLane), expressed some doubt the other day as to which branch of our party General Taylor would ultimately fall into the hands of. That was a new idea to me. I knew we had dissenters, but I did not know they were trying to get our candidate away from us. I would like to say a word to our dissenters, but I have not the time. Some such we certainly have. Have you none, gentlemen Democrats? Is it all union and harmony in your ranks? No bickerings? No divisions?

If there be doubt as to which of our divisions will get our candidate, is there no doubt as to which of your candidates will get your party? I have heard some things from New York; and if they are true, we might well say of your party there, as a drunken fellow once said when he heard the reading of an indictment for hog-stealing. The clerk read on till he got to and through the words, "did steal, take and carry away, ten boars, ten sows, ten shoats, and ten pigs," at which he exclaimed, "Well, by golly, that is the most equally divided gang of hogs I ever did hear of." If there is any gang of hogs more equally divided than the Democrats of New York are about this time, I have not heard of it.

* * *

[Senator Henry] WILSON of Massachusetts. Sir, we have been but the poor, hesitating, halting, weak instruments in the hands of Almighty God to strike the fetters from a race and elevate it, and save the republican institutions of the United States.

[Senator Eugene] CASSERLY of California. If it be true that the Senator and those with him are the representatives or the instruments of that all-just, all-merciful, and all-wise Power, then, considering what things he and they have helped to do since the war ceased in the land, and the extraordinary spirit in which he and they have dealt with the great problems of the time, I should say that in the selection of such agents and instruments we have a new and most signal illustration of the truth that the judgments of Providence are inscrutable and His ways past finding out.

* * *

"FORTY ACRES AND A MULE IN FOAL"

The members of the House were debating the Revenue Act of 1950 and tossing billions of dollars about as if they were so much grass seed. An election was coming on. Politics, being what it is, crept in at every crack and crevice, as in the following sample.

Mr. CURTIS of Missouri. In 1931 the Democratic party captured this House where appropriations and tax bills must start. They continued to control the entire Congress, and the debt rose, and by the end of 1940 the national debt had more than doubled. The national debt increased by two and seven-tenths times in the prewar years of the New Deal.

In the last thirty years there has never been a bond paid off by surplus financing at any time when the Democrats have controlled Congress.

Mr. REED of New York. I thank the gentleman for his contribution. In order to verify his figures I shall ask unanimous consent just a little later to insert in the *Record* a table which will cover the question. Here it is:

Roosevelt's Peacetime Expenditures

1936	$9 billion
1937	8 billion
1938	7 billion
1939	9 billion

Truman's Peacetime Expenditures

1946	$64 billion
1947	43 billion
1948	38 billion
1949	40 billion

Mr. JENKINS of Ohio. Let us not forget that during the time when we were reducing the debt by a billion a year our national income was way down to probably not more than thirty-five billion dollars as compared with a national income of two hundred and nine billion.

Mr. REED. Yes, and you remember during that time, coupled with the sound fiscal policy we were pursuing, we were cutting expenditures to the bone. There was not this great New Deal propaganda agency that far surpasses anything Hitler ever dreamed of, pouring out its national boondoggling propaganda to spend, spend, spend. Nobody in the New Deal cares where in the world we spend it just so long as we spend.

Mr. LYNCH of New York. Will the gentleman recall that during the Hoover administration when we had this sound fiscal policy that we had the greatest unemployment we ever had in the history of the country.

Mr. KNUTSON of Minnesota. It was after the Democratic war you folks promised to keep us out of in 1916.

Mr. LYNCH. The gentleman from Minnesota ties the unemployment of the Hoover administration in 1930 with the war in 1917, World War I. If that is the best explanation it can give, I am sorry for the Republican party.

Mr. REED. The gentleman will remember that between 1931 and 1940 the gentleman's party had ten million unemployed.

Mr. LYNCH. There is no question about it.

Mr. REED. After having spent more than double the national debt that existed prior to that time.

Mr. KNUTSON. After having spent sixty-eight million dollars on relief they still have ten million unemployed. The gentleman from New York (Mr. Lynch) very conveniently forgot that the so-called Hoover depression started in Germany in 1926, swept all over Europe, came to Canada, and then came down here in the latter part of 1929. I suppose Mr. Hoover was responsible for the depression just like the Irish are responsible for all the good things they have here in the United States.

Mr. LYNCH. There is no question about the Irish being responsible for the good things and there is no doubt but what Mr. Hoover and the Republican party were responsible for the unemployment in 1930.

Mr. KNUTSON. The gentleman lets his blind partisanship overcome him. I find to my dismay there is no reference whatever to the President's plan to give everybody forty dollars, forty acres, and a mule. Why was that left out? Are you ashamed of your Commander-in-Chief? Have you repudiated your great leader, or what is the matter?

Mr. LYNCH. There has been no reference to forty acres and a mule. There has been reference to a forty dollar credit which the Republicans do not like just because it goes primarily to people with incomes under three thousand dollars.

Mr. REED. You know the bill which the President wanted you to sponsor was one which you felt you could not present to the House unless you brought it in with a disinfectant. The thing that worried you was the fact that President Truman entitled his proposal as a "cost of living credit," but he forgot about the nineteen million people who were so poor and so destitute they could not even pay an income tax. Of course, under the vote-getting formula of the New Deal the nineteen million destitute people did not get forty dollars each, but the other people had more votes, provided, of course, their votes could be bought for forty dollars each.

I want to say another thing, too, about this mule business.

You will remember you once tried to fake the people with forty acres and a mule in foal. You remember that?

* * *

HOW TO BE A CONGRESSMAN

Know-how is all important to the task of being a statesman, and there is no school for teaching this art. But no one has as yet come up with a better set of "Rules for a Congressman" than those devised and submitted to the House in 1940 by Representative Luther Patrick of Alabama. Apparently Mr. Patrick was well versed in this skill.

1. Entertain with a smile constituents, their wives, their sons, sons' wives, etc. Go with them to the White House; show good reason why you are unable to personally have them meet the President; take daughters to meet midshipmen at Annapolis.

2. Explain what bill is up for debate; point for discussion; how it will be passed; how you will vote and why.

3. Attend to balcony and point out Speaker Bankhead, leaders Rayburn and Martin, Ham Fish, Dewey Short, that man Martin Dies, and name each lady member of Congress.

4. Respond to worthy causes; make after-dinner speeches, before-dinner speeches; learn to eat anything, anywhere, any night—work all day, dictate all night, and be fresh as a rain-washed daisy for next day's duties.

5. Be a cultured gentleman, a teller of ribald stories, a profound philosopher, preserve a store of "Confucius say" gags; be a ladies' man, a man's man, a he-man, a diplomat, a Democrat with a Republican slant, a Republican with a Democrat viewpoint, an admirer of the Roosevelt way, a hater of the New Deal, a new dealer, an old dealer, and a quick dealer.

6. Learn how to attend six to eight major functions, rushing

home and back during each term on one round-trip travel pay.

7. Have the dope on hot spots in town, with choice telephone numbers for the gay boys from back home, and help to contact all local moral organizations and uplift societies in Washington.

8. Learn to be expert guide. Keep car in tip-top shape.

9. Know names and dates related to all points of interest, and be able to explain and supply information regarding public buildings and statuary about Washington.

10. Be an authority on history, travel, psychology, philosophy, education, economics, civics, finance, export trade, government printing, international relations, neckties, and fishing tackle.

* * *

A man said to me the other day, "What would you give, Mr. Cannon, for an insurance policy that you would live to be one hundred years old?" I said, "A real policy that would make me live—and would I have to die then?" "Yes," he said; "just a policy of that kind." I said, "Give? I would rather pay something not to have it." "Why?" he said. "Well, there is probably one man in half a million in the United States now living that will live to be one hundred years old, and I am going to take my chances." He said, "That is a slim chance." I said, "Yes; but I would not have the policy, anyway, because every day that would pass it would occur to me that it was one day less. The Great Father has arranged it properly; no man can foresee when he will die."

Representative Joseph G. Cannon of Illinois on his 80th birthday, May 7, 1916

* * *

Once a game of poker was played out West. There is a

chump in every game of poker, and the chump in this game got to the point where he held four aces. He got everyone into the pot and then showed four aces and reached for his money.

"Hold on," said one of his opponents. "I've got a whangdoodle."

"What's that?" asked the chump.

"Look at that sign behind you," said the other. The chump looked and saw a sign that read, "A whangdoodle beats anything."

He was cleaned out, but his companions suggested he look around and get some more money and recoup what he had lost. This he did. Pretty soon he found in his hand a whangdoodle. He bet the limit and everybody came in. Finally the chump announced he had a whangdoodle and reached for the money.

"Just a moment," interrupted the dealer. "Look at that sign over your shoulder." The chump looked. This time the sign read, "A whangdoodle can be played only once in a game."

Representative William W. Johnson of California

* * *

I confess myself some embarrassment in casting my vote without being more fully advised as to all the facts, for my information on this subject reminds me very much of how a magazine editor expressed himself to me some years ago in this city. I was introduced to him as an Indian and he said, "Are you a regular Indian?" I told him I tried to be fairly regular. "What I mean is," said the editor, "did you get your name put on one of these rolls and draw lands and money?" I replied, "I have my name on the tribal rolls of the Choctaw-Chickasaw tribes, and I hope some time in the dim, distant future, through the meshes of the red tape of our Indian Bureau, to draw my proportionate share of land and money belonging to our tribe." He then retorted, "Mr. Carter, I am doubly glad to meet you. I have written a great deal on the Indian question. I have just finished an article on 'The Habits and Characteristics of the American Indian as Viewed at Close Range' and you are the first dad-burned Indian I ever shook hands with in my life."

Representative Charles D. Carter
of Oklahoma

* * *

G-DAY 1959, AND THE FURRY GENTLEMAN WAS RIGHT

Each year on February 2, Representative Leon H. Gavin of Pennsylvania rises in the House to remind the members that the day belongs to the infallible soothsayer whose special weather prediction has given a legendary touch to his name.

Mr. Speaker, I want to call the attention of the members of the House—and, particularly, the new members, and it saddens me to find most of them on the wrong side of the aisle—that this is Groundhog Day.

And the one and only Punxsutawney Groundhog, that great prognosticator of the weather, who predicts with amazing accuracy weather conditions for the next six weeks, has spoken. He emerged from his den on Gobbler's Knob in the foothills of the Alleghenies in my district, the twenty-third of Pennsylvania, at 8:23 this morning.

He saw his shadow. This means, whether we like it or not, six more weeks of cold, severe wintry weather.

I was advised by the President of the Punxsutawney Groundhog Club, Mr. Sam R. Light, that this great prophet, the seer of seers, contrary to tradition, was for the first time in history sleeping soundly at dawn. To the consternation of those present, he did not appear until 8:23, after President

Light had repeatedly pounded on the top of his burrow with a heavy club.

Sure enough the burrow door slowly squeaked open and the sleepy-eyed prophet appeared, glanced about, saw his shadow and with chattering teeth intoned:

> Double, double, toil and trouble,
> Six more weeks of snow to shovel;
> Icy winds and zero nights ahead,
> This is one year I should have stayed in bed.

So there you have it. Six more weeks of wintry weather!

* * *

ONE WAY TO GET "PORK" OUT OF THE BARREL

The so-called "pork barrel" is as old as Congress. It means an appropriation of money for public projects that is cut up in chunks to be doled out across the nation. For years the annual River and Harbor Bill was the "gravy train." Seemingly every creek, inlet, ditch, millpond and hogwallow somehow got on board for a few thousand dollars to be "improved" by Uncle Sam. Representative Albert Brown of Mississippi perennially sought funds to remove snags and bars from the Pascagoula River. He finally, in 1852, after many futile tries, summed up his feelings in this charming ultimatum to the managers of the River and Harbor Bill who ladled out the "pork" to the favored districts.

I have offered that Pascagoula amendment for the last time. (Laughter.) I stand here pretty much in the attitude of the man who visited General Jackson when he was President. He came on to Washington asking for the mission to England. It was refused him. He then asked a Cabinet appointment.

That was refused him. He came down to a collectorship, and when that was refused him, he said he would put up with a clerkship. But that also was denied him. As a last dying hope he inquired of the old General if he could not give him a pair of old boots; and when they were refused he swore he would not be a Jackson man any longer. (Laughter.)

I have asked sixty thousand dollars to make improvements on the Pascagoula, and I have come down by little and little until now I ask only two thousand dollars for a survey. If you do not give it to me I shall certainly vote against this bill. (Laughter.) Gentlemen do not seem to understand the value of the Pascagoula River. Let me tell them it is a river of national importance and ought to be improved by the nation. Three rules have been prescribed by distinguished men for governing cases like this. One by General Jackson, another by Mr. Calhoun, and the third by someone else—I do not know who. This third party said a work to be national ought to be in salt water. But General Jackson thought you could improve up to the last port of entry on a river, whether it was on salt or fresh water; and Mr. Calhoun laid down the rule that a river flowing through three states could properly claim the jurisdiction and protection of the national Treasury.

Now, this improvement on the Pascagoula is in salt water, for it is in the Gulf of Mexico, and besides, I understand there was a salt barge sunk there about ten years ago. (Laughter.) Then it may be called a port of entry; for the river at this point enters directly into the County of Jackson, in my state. The Pascagoula River flows through three states. It rises in a state of prosperity—it flows through a state of affluence—but it empties into a state of embarrassment. If, however, you will only give me this two thousand dollars to make the survey, I have no doubt it will empty, ultimately, into a state of extraordinary wealth, and that will make four states. I will not take less than two thousand dollars for this survey. That is the last and lowest proposition. If you do not give me that

I shall vote against the bill most certainly. (Laughter.) I do believe you think I mean to do it anyhow.

* * *

THE STORY OF PETE AND GENERAL LEE

Senator Sam Ervin, Jr., of North Carolina has a way of larding his senatorial comments with amusing stories. He told this one after Majority Leader Lyndon Johnson announced, in March 1960, that the Senate would engage in round-the-clock sessions.

If we are to persist in these round-the-clock sessions I hope a way will be found to allow overtime to those of us who are trying to save the Confederacy as well as the Union.

Some persons remind me of the old Confederate soldier, Pete, who lived in Chatham County, N.C. Pete, in his old age, like some of the rest of us, liked to reminisce. He did not mind how long he talked about things. On one occasion one of his friends asked him, "Pete, did you know General Robert E. Lee?"

Pete said, "Yes, I certainly did know Marse Robert. As a matter of fact, he and I not only were comrades in the Confederate Army, but good personal friends, and I helped General Lee plan many of his battles."

Then he was asked, when was the last time he had seen General Lee. He said it was about six months after the surrender at Appomattox.

The more I see of this kind of bill, I think General Lee made a mistake in surrendering.

But I will go back to Pete. Pete said it was about six months after the surrender at Appomattox that he had last seen General Lee. He said he went to Lexington, Virginia, and stopped by to see his old friend, General Lee. He said that he and

General Lee spent a most pleasant afternoon discussing their common experiences. He said that finally General Lee, who had been in a somewhat jovial frame of mind, became very serious, and looked at him right hard and said, "Pete, were you at Appomattox?"

Pete said, "Yes, General, I was at Appomattox."

Then Pete said, "Well, General Lee said, 'Well, Pete, I certainly am sorry. If I had known you were there, I would never have surrendered.' " (Laughter.)

I trust that some people among the contingent who are trying to save both the Confederacy and the Union will be like Pete, or at least be like General Lee, and know that Pete or somebody like Pete is present on this occasion.

* * *

I wish indeed that my mother, whose memory I cherish across the vale of years, could have been here to see. By the way, I cannot help reflecting that if my father had been American and my mother British, instead of the other way around, I might have got here on my own. (Laughter and applause.) In that case, this would not have been the first time you would have heard my voice. In that case, I should not have needed any invitation; but, if I had, it is hardly likely that it would have been unanimous. (Laughter.) So perhaps things are better as they are.

Sir Winston Churchill to the Joint Congress during World War II

* * *

Mr. Speaker, I do not suppose it likely that the amendment offered by the gentleman from Arkansas will be agreed to. It leaves to local juries the fixing of the penalty, and I take it that they will also have something to do with the rule of evidence. When I heard the amendment read, it reminded me of that play, *A Temperance Town,* where the jury went out to decide the case of a liquor seller. It was up in Vermont, I believe. One of the items of evidence that had been offered at the trial was a bottle that had been rescued from the cellar of the liquor seller. The bottle was called "Exhibit A." After the jury had been out for a considerable time the bailiff came in with the empty bottle and said that the jury would like to have "Exhibit A" filled up again.

Representative Charles H. Grosvenor of Ohio

* * *

Patrick, an Irishman, was very sick and was visited by his priest. Said the priest, as he felt his pulse and the cold sweat stood upon his face: "Patrick, you are very sick!" "Yes, Father." "You are sick unto death, Patrick." "Yes, Father." "Are you afraid to meet your God, Patrick?" "No, Father; it is the ither fellow at the ither end that I am afraid of."

Senator John B. Gordon of Georgia, 1876

* * *

At the close of his speech on the admission of Oregon in 1859, Representative Alexander H. Stephens of Georgia (later Vice President of the Confederacy) spoke of the states as being "all bound together for general objects under a common head, as it were 'a wheel within a wheel.' " He then went into his magnificent peroration: "Then, indeed, may the nations of the earth look with wonder at our career, and when they hear the noise of the wheels of our progress in achievement, in development, in expansion, in glory and renown, it will appear to them not unlike the noise of great waters, the very voice of the Almighty—*Vox populi, vox Dei.*"

With applause ringing in his ears, he left the chamber immediately. As he passed along the corridor he overheard a gentleman enthusiastically declaring to a friend, "You should have been there and seen him, his slight form quivering, yet erect, his shrill voice ringing through the hushed hall in that grand climax—*Vox populi, vox Dei.*"

Said the other fellow, who had not heard the speech and seemed a little bored, "Yes, no doubt, but I'll bet you ten dollars you can't tell what *Vox populi, vox Dei* means."

"I'll bet I can. Put up your money," was the reply.

This little formality being quickly effected, the doubter said, "Well, what does it mean in English?"

"Why," said the enthusiast, "it means, 'My God, My God! Why hast thou forsaken me?' "

"That's right," agreed the other. "The money is yours. I didn't think you knew."

* * *

Men may think that by statute the Congress of the United States can change the nature of the rooster that crows at the stated time in the morning, but when the rooster crows and looks at the clock and sees that he is an hour ahead of time, he says the clock is a liar, and that the man who voted for that law was not quite so wise as the rooster himself.

Representative William E. Andrews of Nebraska, 1919

* * *

I could suggest something that might make the law more drastic. Just two hundred years ago this year Sultan Amurath of Turkey issued an edict which provided that the nose of any person who smoked tobacco could be cut off. If you want to enact these provisions, go ahead. There's a suggestion.

Representative John D. McCrate of Maine, 1919, during the debate on prohibition

* * *

NEW SEATS FOR THE MIGHTY AND COCKROACHES IN THE CAPITOL

Statesmen must have comfortable chairs to sit in while legislating for this great nation. Every so often the gentlemen of the House provide new "backbones" for themselves. But seldom have they been compelled to vote funds for war on the cockroach army that infiltrated the Capitol. Just such an emergency arose in 1953, and the Contingent Fund Bill boldly faced up to the situation with dollars for a single purpose: extermination of traitorous invaders of the sacred realms of the Capitol. Here is part of the debate.

Mr. SIKES of Florida. Mr. Speaker, this is a touchy item. This could become the hottest potato in this session of Congress. . . . We propose to vote for the Congress new chairs, which already are referred to by press and radio commentators as "fancy chairs" and "luxury seats."

Mr. BENDER of Ohio. This country wants Congressmen with backbone. My medical friends both inside and outside the AMA tell me that the best way to acquire a backbone if you do not have one or to retain it if you do is to stand up straight whenever you are sitting down. There is no sense in using the fine, comfortable 1953-model chairs we have in the House chamber a few hours daily if we must go back to offices equipped with 1854 horsehair torture chairs.

I think the country will receive a net gain in service with these good chairs instead of those a few dollars cheaper. Far more expensive legislation will be passed by back-weary Congressmen who cannot stand up to pressure groups because they can scarcely stand up at all than by the fine specimen of upstanding Congressmen whose backs are models of orthopedic virtue.

Mr. EBERHARTER of Pennsylvania. Does the gentleman

think this amendment would have been offered if some newspaper had not written about it?

Mr. BENDER. I do not think so. You hit the nail on the head.

While we are discussing corrective measures for the Capitol and House Office Buildings, I wish someone would offer an amendment to spend fifty thousand dollars, or whatever amount is required, to get the cockroaches out of the Capitol and the New and Old House Office Buildings. These pests become so numerous at times that we should take drastic steps to exterminate them. And while we are doing a clean-up job let us not overlook the restaurant downstairs.

Mr. ABERNETHY of Mississippi. If I understand the gentleman correctly, he feels that he needs one of these new chairs; is that right?

Mr. BENDER. I am satisfied with my chair.

Mr. MILLER of Kansas. There was one of the constituents of a certain Congressman who came up and looked over his office and the things up here, and he said: "Well, it's better than you're used to."

Mr. BENDER. It is possible that we have one or two members answering that description.

Mr. NICHOLSON of Massachusetts. May I say to the gentleman who just sat down that we are not used to cockroaches where I come from.

Mr. MAHON of Texas. In all seriousness, I think any member is entitled to any kind of a chair he wants within the bounds of reason. However, there are some of us who prefer those old chairs, and we do not want these new ones to be inflicted upon us.

Mr. BENDER. As far as I am concerned, if you want to sit on the floor that is perfectly all right with me.

Mr. LANHAM of Georgia. I heard it suggested by someone on a streetcar today that we ought to have beds over here instead of chairs. I do not approve of that suggestion, but I just pass it on to the gentleman.

Mr. BENDER. If there is any member of Congress who requires a bed instead of a chair, then his constituents should retire him, but I resent any implication on the part of anyone that we do not work here.

Mr. SHAFER of Michigan. Is there any truth in the report I hear that those boys who want these high-back chairs all have weak backs?

Mr. BENDER. Maybe the gentleman has something there.

* * *

SOME FROLICS! MURDER SONGS AND NEW WHISKEY

In 1840 the very air vibrated with references to log cabins and hard cider as the Whigs deluged the nation with the campaign hocus-pocus that elected William Henry Harrison to the Presidency. Here is a sample by Representative Alexander Duncan of Ohio of the verbiage poured out by the Whig orators in the House.

Mr. DUNCAN. Mr. Speaker, I delight in the very name of a log cabin. I was raised in a log cabin. All my youthful playmates were the tenants of log cabins; and all my youthful frolics were played off in log cabins.

There is no word in the English vocabulary that dwells upon my lips with so much delight as "log cabin." It brings fresh to my recollection scenes of youthful pleasure, which I have never since, nor ever will again enjoy. Many and oft is the time that I thought a day a month, in anxious watch for the setting sun which was the token for the rally to the frolic of the log cabin where I met the comrades of my youth. The frolic consisted in dancing, playing, singing love and murder songs, eating johnnycake and pumpkin pies, and drinking new whiskey and brown sugar out of a gourd. Our dancing in my youthful day, and in my neighborhood, was done to the performance of an old Irishman with one leg, with the heel of which he beat time, a fiddle with three strings, to the air of:

Barney let the girls alone,
And let them quiet be.
Judy put the kettle on,
And we'll all take tea.

For, if I recollect right, I think our fiddler played but one tune.

But let me tell you, sir, our girls were not to be sneezed at. They presented a form and beauty that marked the developments of nature, when unrestrained by corsets and the withering dissipation of fashionable and high life, and their guileless hearts looked through a countenance that demanded confidence in their innocence and unsullied virtue.

But, oh! their forms! When you plied your arm to their waist in the giddy waltz, with the twenty-five yards of warm linsey in which they were comfortably enwrapped, you had an armful of health and firmness. These constituted my pleasures in the days of log cabins.

* * *

My father was coming up the Mississippi River on a sternwheel steamboat when out there came from the bank two boys in a skiff, pulling for dear life and hallooing with all their might. Finally the steamboat was stopped. "What's the matter?" hollered the mate. With that the two little fellows turned round and rowed furiously back to the bank, exclaiming, "We stopped a steamboat, by golly!"

Representative Joseph G. Cannon of Illinois, 1896

When the great "Meat Axe" Ben Hardin, Representative from Kentucky, came to die, he sent for all the preachers. One of them said to him, "You have had a Catholic priest; you've had a Presbyterian minister; you've had a Methodist parson; I am a Campbellite. What do you mean by it?" "Well," replied Hardin, "Mr. Preacher, I am on my last legs and about to go, they tell me. I've heard that heaven is a very good place to go to, and I want to take all the chances of getting there."

* * *

Before the House was the 1885 River and Harbor Bill. It provided among other things for improvement of the Skagit, Steilaguamish, Nooksack, Snohomish and Snoqualmie Rivers, Washington Territory. It inspired Byron M. Cutcheon of Michigan to offer this amendment: "Mr. Speaker, I move an amendment in the nature of a proviso, that at least one thousand dollars of the money hereby appropriated shall be used in straightening out the names of said rivers."

* * *

It is related somewhere of a certain Christian gentleman that he contrived an easy and rapid method of saying his evening prayers. He wrote upon a placard a list of the petitions he wished to offer and tacked it to the ceiling over his bed. On retiring he would devoutly point to the placard and utter a long prayer in short meter by saying, "O Lord, them are my sentiments. Amen!" Why cannot our friends here initiate this device and carry on a placard their accustomed utterances about "loyalty" and "treason" and simply pointing to it, declare "Them's my sentiments. Amen!"

W. F. Switzler of Missouri in support of himself in an election contest before the House, 1870. He failed to make the grade.

Representative James A. Garfield once related to the House that in 1864 he made a war speech to a crowd at Ashtabula, Ohio. "Gentlemen," he said, "we have taken Atlanta, we have taken Savannah, we have taken Charleston, and we are about to capture Petersburg and take Richmond. What remains for us to take?" He got his answer from an Irishman in the crowd who shouted, "Let's take a drink!" It broke up the meeting.

* * *

"SLEEPY, TIRED, DRUNK!"

Brilliant though he was, Henry A. Wise of Virginia was given to wild, ranting harangue à la *John Randolph of Roanoke. On the opening day of the Twenty-fourth Congress, 1834, Wise unloosed in the House a stream of invective attempting to fasten responsibility for the failure of the Fortification Bill in the close of the previous Congress on Churchill C. Cambreleng of New York, Chairman of the Ways and Means Committee, and James K. Polk of Tennessee, now Speaker. Repeated calls to order brought only challenges from Wise of the Speaker's right to interrupt him.*

Mr. WISE. Such was the termination of the last Congress; and I so say, sir, it was one of the most disgraceful scenes I ever witnessed; it was unbecoming barbarians and savages much more the representatives of a civilized nation! Sleepy, tired, drunk!

Mr. BYNUM of North Carolina. Is the gentleman in order when speaking of the last Congress?

Mr. WISE. I do not pretend to say, Mr. Speaker, that all Congress was drunk, or one half, or one third, or one tenth of the members were drunk; but I know that some were; and so it was that, what with maneuvering, being tired, opposed to some measures, sleepy, and drunk, no quorum could be had unless it had suited certain individuals.

I have given the facts upon the *Journal;* but there are other important facts, facts unwritten. Sir, it is said the bill failed in the House. That is not true. It failed before it got to the House from the conference room. It dropped like a spent ball before it quite got here; it dropped near the door. Sir, there are two statements about the matter; they may be conjectural. I put it to the gentleman (Mr. Cambreleng), Did no "busybody" whisper aught in his ear as he was on his way to report to the House? Did no one tempt him to strangle the bantling in his care? Was there no "magician" near? No devil and his imps? Did no member of the committee receive a billet-doux after he resumed his seat? . . . What prevented the report being made? Sir, there were spirits haunting the Capitol that awfu' night; there were strange, whispering, chattering elfs—ghosts, as I am told—I did not see them—blue devils and imps! Is it true? Was there any dealing with the "infernals" that night? Tell us, I pray you; tell us, and let the curse fall on the necromancers—not on the victims of the horrid spell.

Mr. Wise proceeded in this strain, bringing charges against Mr. Cambreleng and Mr. Polk, and finally, having made a specific charge against the latter, exclaimed, in a bold, accusative tone.

Mr. WISE. Is it true? Yes or no? Guilty or not guilty? I call on the chairman of the committee of ways and means of the last Congress to answer.

* * *

He (the Postmaster General) reminds me of the pious Brahmin of the fable, who went forth to buy a sheep to sacrifice according to his vows. The first man he met, knowing his intention, accosted him, "Oh Brahmin! Wilt thou buy a sheep? I have a fit one for your sacrifice." "I came forth," said the pious man, "for that purpose." The man thereupon opened his bag and drew forth a miserable dog, lame and blind. "Wretch, callest thou that a sheep?" said the good man. "A sheep of the finest wool and sweetest flesh," said the impostor, "and O, good Brahmin, it will be an offering most acceptable to the gods." "Friend," said the good man, "either thou or I must be blind." Just at this juncture an accomplice of the trader came up. "Praised be the gods!" said the fresh rogue, "this is just such a sheep as I wanted; for how much wilt thou sell it?" The pious man begins to waver in his mind. "Sir," said he to the new fellow, "this is no sheep, but an unclean cur." "Oh, my good Brahmin," replied the rascal, "thou art drunk or mad." Here a third confederate approaches. "I will abide by the decision of this man," said the Brahmin. To this all agreed. "Oh, stranger," said the Brahman, "what beast is this?" "Surely it is a fine sheep," was the reply. "Praised be the gods!" said the pious one, and purchased the dog and offered it as a sacrifice to the gods, who, angry on account of the unclean offering, smote the good though misguided man with sore malady. Thus with our devoted chairman, who, following the voice of the insincere flatterers, in his choice of an offering has selected the improper one to sacrifice to the god of economy.

This fable was told by Senator Joseph S. Fowler of Tennessee, in 1870, in expressing his opposition to a proposal to abolish the franking privilege for members of Congress and others in the government.

* * *

When this mighty conflict was at its height and the roar of hostile cannon was heard from one end of the country to the other, eighteen million people stood like the youth in the streets of Paris when it was rumored that Mirabeau was dying. He had listened to the impassioned eloquence in the *Corps Legislatif*, and rushing to his physician he eagerly inquired, "What is the matter with Mirabeau?" and when told he was dying for want of blood, stripping bare his arm, he exclaimed, "Take blood from my veins and put it in his and let Mirabeau live." So eighteen million of the American people, when danger hung over the perpetuity of the Union bequeathed by our fathers, baring their bosoms, exclaimed, "Take our hearts' blood and let the Republic live."

Speaker Galusha A. Grow of Pennsylvania, 1865

* * *

A Congressman has become an expanded messenger boy, and employment agency; getter-out of the Navy, Army, Marines; ward heeler, wound healer, trouble-shooter, law explainer, bill finder, issue translator, resolution interpreter, controversary oil-pourer, glad-hand extender, business promoter, civic ills skirmisher, veterans' affairs adjuster, ex-serviceman's champion, watchdog for the underdog, sympathizer with the upperdog, namer of babies, recoverer of lost baggage, soberer of delegates; adjuster for traffic violators, voters straying into Washington and into the toils of the law, binder up of broken hearts, financial wet nurse, good Samaritan, contributor to good causes—there are so many good causes—cornerstone layer, public building and bridge dedicator, ship christener. To be sure, he does get in a little flag waving and a little constitutional hoisting and spread-eagle work, but it is getting harder every day to find time to properly study legislation—the very business we are primarily here to discharge and that must be done above all things.

Representative Luther Patrick of Alabama, 1940

Mr. Speaker, there is a certain class of men who, put them where you will, in any situation in life, will piddle—I mean old bachelors. I never will henceforth support any man for the Presidency who will appoint a bachelor to any office of honor or profit, and especially of responsibility. An old bachelor, sir, is a withered fig tree, he is a *vis inertiae*. Old bachelors are too near kin to old maids.

Representative Henry A. Wise
of Virginia shortly after he had
married for the third time, 1853

* * *

[Senator Simon] CAMERON of Pennsylvania. Every compromise of the Constitution in this country has been destructive of the interests of the country and destructive of the party which was flattered by the minority to make the compromise. That greatest of all our statesmen, Henry Clay, was destroyed by his first compromise on the Missouri question.

[Senator George F.] EDMUNDS of Vermont. How was he destroyed?

Mr. CAMERON. He was destroyed because he never received the support of the country for that office (the Presidency) which was the grand object of his ambition.

Mr. EDMUNDS. There are a good many destroyed people in this Senate chamber right now.

* * *

WASHING THE GREAT UNWASHED DEMOCRACY

1901 and the House was debating an appropriation for a bathing beach on the Potomac where residents of the District of Columbia could take their Saturday night baths—or such was the import of the bill. Much verbiage and considerable humor went into the Record. *Witness.*

Mr. TALBERT of South Carolina. The gentleman is taking the strange position that this bathing beach is being established for the purpose of washing the people of the District of Columbia. It is put there for pleasure, not for washing purposes. The gentleman says he quotes the Bible, which says that cleanliness is next to godliness. I would ask the gentleman to cite me to the portion of the Bible where that is found. He may do it. I do not believe he can find it in the Bible, but it may be a saying by some celebrated author. In my opinion the gentleman ought to establish a Sunday School for the people of his country to learn what is in the Bible and what is not in the Bible. By doing so he will do better than by establishing a bathing beach for the people of the District of Columbia to cleanse themselves in. It is sound Democratic doctrine to let the people take care of themselves without the assistance of the general government, to do their own washing in their own tubs. This is the doctrine, at least, of the unwashed Democracy.

Mr. FITZGERALD of Massachusetts. I will say that the city of Boston makes an annual appropriation of one hundred thousand dollars to maintain bathhouses where people can bathe the year round.

Mr. RICHARDSON of Tennessee. And that is a Democratic city, too.

Mr. FITZGERALD. A Democratic city, and the appropriations instituted by Democratic officials.

Mr. TALBERT. But you haven't got the unwashed Democracy up in Boston.

Mr. FITZGERALD. We are willing to have them, and we will guarantee them a good Democratic cleaning.

* * *

ON BUNCOMBE SPEECHES

Way back in 1852 a resolution was introduced in the House not to report in the Daily Globe *(now the* Congressional Record*) as a part of the proceedings speeches not made on the floor of the House. It met hard going. Here's an amusing flash from the debate on the subject.*

Mr. EWING of Kentucky. Speeches are made here, as we all know, not to enlighten the public. We are too modest servants of the public to pretend that we undertake to enlighten the public on any subject. Speeches are not made to enlighten this House. That is not the purpose. The object is simply—

Mr. GAYLORD of Ohio. Buncombe.

Mr. EWING. Yes, buncombe. That is the idea, a whole volume in a word. It is unjust, it is unfair that our laborious friends from the North to whom it is no trouble to write, who are in the habit of writing all their lives long, who love to write—I say it is unfair and unequal that those Northern friends of ours should have this advantage. The idea of a man publishing a speech as having been made on this floor and having it so stated in the *Globe*, when it was never made upon this floor is certainly an abuse because it is a fraud and it is false. I think one hour is long enough for any one man to speak and too long for any man to write, and it is unfair that those who love to write should have this advantage of sending buncombe speeches home and making the impression upon the minds of their people at home that they can speak (when they do not speak) and that they can speak better than the rest of us (which they might perhaps if they tried) but when they do not speak at all.

It is an imposition upon their constituents at home when, if they only knew it, they would complain, but, poor fellows, they don't know it yet.

WHAT MORE? ASKED SENATOR BAYARD

The 1870's saw castigation of the South in the Senate and House at flood tide. Senator John Sherman of Ohio was as fiery in his denunciation of the South as was his brother when sweeping across Georgia in 1864. But the South was not without her Northern defenders. One such was Senator Thomas F. Bayard of Delaware. In 1875, in answer to an anti-Southern tirade by Senator Sherman for "atrocities" against the Negro, Senator Bayard rose in his place to reply. In part he said:

The laws of the land have given all that human laws can give. They have given to the colored people–Equality of Opportunity. Now, that being given, how are you, upon the basis of equal rights, to undertake to supply the deficiencies and differences with which the Almighty has seen fit to mark his creatures, both as races and as individuals? We all know that men start in the race of life equipped perhaps with equal opportunities of information; it is so at the bar; it is so in every pursuit; but we start, how? We start with the natural gifts which are not created or bestowed by statute law. They did not come from man, and by him they are not to be controlled.

You might as well tell me that you could dwarf the intellect of a Webster to the stature of that of some half-idiot, and say that because these grand and almost Godlike gifts had raised the one to a position of weight where his counsel and thoughts swayed nations and senates, therefore the weak and the ignorant could, by some poor statute law or amendment to the Constitution, be raised to the level of the gifted and the strong. No, Mr. President, it can not be and it never will be. All that we can do is to give a fair chance, to give, as I said before, equality of opportunity to the people of this country, to the poor boy equally with the rich man's son, to the black man who comes from his hovel, or the rich man who emerges from his palace. They must take their chances in this battle of life, and, if they be deficient and defective, do not suppose that an act of Congress can undertake to remedy the fact. It will not be so.

* * *

ON SUBMARINES AND BATTLESHIPS, POLECATS AND LIONS

The House was going great guns on the 1919 Naval Appropriation but there arose a question of how to spend it. The submarine had revolutionized naval warfare, but some gentlemen were apparently not aware of the fact.

Mr. LITTLE of Kansas. Mr. Speaker, did the American people authorize us last November to spend $520,000,000 of their money before we have any information at all as to whether the big battleships have been junked by the submarine? When I asked the gentleman from Michigan yesterday about that, the gallant tar from the raging Ohio informed us that as long as a $20,000,000 ship could maintain a steady gait of fifteen knots an hour no submarine could harm it. Does our ability to dominate the seas depend upon our capacity for outrunning our foes?

Is this $520,000,000 navy they want us to furnish to seek safety in flight every time one of these little sea devils shows its periscope above old Neptune's kingdom? Oh, that does not answer the question as to which would be the victor. The eloquent gentleman from Michigan answered me yesterday that the submarine and the battleship were not comparable. Oh, that does not answer the question as to which would be the victor. Neither are the polecat and the lion comparable, but everybody knows which has the right of way when they meet.

The lion and the battleship depend upon their speed for their safety. Shall the next John Paul Jones, when called upon to surrender, cry gallantly back, "Oh, I haven't begun to run yet; just watch my smoke!" Should Lawrence have murmured as he fell, "Don't give up the ship as long as we can make fifteen knots an hour!" What would you think of the American Navy if history recorded that when the *Constitution* met the *Guerriere* Captain Isaac Hull had signaled to the Britisher, "We challenge you to a foot race! We can go fifteen knots an hour and fear you not"? The bumblebee stepped on the elephant's toe and hurt the poor thing so he could scarcely go; the elephant said with great tears in his eyes, "You coward, why don't you take on somebody your size?" Can anyone imagine old Farragut figuring on which ship should have the better pair of heels?

During nearly all of this war the greatest fleet the world ever saw was tied up in a Scotch harbor behind a blanket net for fear a little submarine would nose in and tie a can to the tail of a $20,000,000 ship and sink it to the bottom of the harbor.

Mr. GORDON of Ohio. Did the gentleman notice the dispatch from Paris yesterday to the effect that the peace conference has outlawed the submarine and was going to stop its use for all purposes?

Mr. LITTLE. Oh, yes. I saw that this was done by the advice of these naval experts who created the battleship. I know a submarine is no place for a well-dressed man. No place to hold a reception.

What are you getting out of it? If you put your money into submarines you would have $520,000,000 invested, and you would have five hundred submarines, and there would not be a warship in the world that would ever dare to go out to sea unless it had investigated thoroughly and knew that there was not a submarine in sight.

It's all nonsense, my friends, to talk about abolishing submarines. What is the argument in favor of this plan in the bill? Not a thing on earth except a mystic utterance here that nobody understands. Whenever a Greek politician got into hot water he appealed to the oracle at Delphi. Once informed as to the advice desired, the prophecy sought floated out in mystic profundity as readily as the limpid waters sprang from the desert rock that Moses smote. Mr. Daniels (Secretary of the Navy) was in trouble and he invoked the Delphic oracle of America and it gave forth an oracle utterance which he says means more battleships.

One man has as good a right as another to interpret the oracle. I interpret it to have intended submarines and mines. Gentlemen of the House, the taxpayers will demand of you why, at a time like this, you spend a billion dollars of our money on iron pots that submarines can sink as fast as they catch them.

* * *

I am a little surprised at the latitude taken by the chairman of the Committee on Banking and Currency, who came in here and openly and above board declared he was unwilling to stand on the platform on which he was elected and made a pretense that he was going to make the greatest speech of his life. My friend did spread himself tremendously. He reminded me of the little fellow who went out to set his mother's hen and when he came back was asked, "Did you set her?" He said, "Yes, I did." Then he was asked, "What did you put under her?" He replied, "Sixteen large goose eggs." His mother said, "What in the name of common sense did you do that for?" The boy said, "Because I wanted to see her spread herself." So the gentleman from Illinois did come in and "spread himself" all over the face of the earth and reminded me of the piney woods pond down in my country, scattered all over the face of the earth and not knee deep anywhere.

Representative Ephraim M. Woomer of Pennsylvania on the proposal to tax state bank notes ten percent, 1895

It was said in former times, by a great and eminent politician of Mississippi, in order to illustrate something about which he was speaking, that there were some things which were subject to the laws of science; that there were some things which could be controlled by man's ingenuity and man's devices; but that the Mississippi was not one of those things. He said that God Almighty, when he made the Mississippi River and bade its great floods flow from the mountains to the sea, said, "Let her rip; there is no law to govern it." (Laughter.) But I say that since his demonstration there has been established in our day the law that man's ingenuity and man's science can answer the question as to how that river can be best navigated, and as to whether the tributaries of that great stream can be made navigable.

Representative Charles E. Hooker
of Mississippi, 1890

* * *

Cast not away this only anchor of our safety. I have seen its progress. I know the difficulties through which it was obtained. I stand in the presence of Almighty God and of the world, and I declare to you that if you lose this charter, never, no, never will you get another. We are now, perhaps, arriving at the parting point. Here, even here, we stand on the brink of fate. Pause! Pause! For Heaven's sake, pause!

Senator Gouverneur Morris, in 1802, against the repeal of the act establishing the Supreme Court

* * *

INDEX

ABBREVIATIONS: *S*, Senate; *HR*, House of Representatives
Dem., Democrat; *Rep.*, Republican; *Fed.*, Federalist; *Pop.*, Populist;
Ind., Independent